Ten Notable Women of Colonial Latin America

Ten Notable Women of Colonial Latin America

James D. Henderson,
Linda R. Henderson,
and Suzanne M. Litrel

ROWMAN & LITTLEFIELD
Lanham • Boulder • New York • London

Published by Rowman & Littlefield
An imprint of The Rowman & Littlefield Publishing Group, Inc.
4501 Forbes Boulevard, Suite 200, Lanham, Maryland 20706
www.rowman.com

86-90 Paul Street, London EC2A 4NE

Copyright © 2023 by James D. Henderson, Linda R. Henderson, and Suzanne M. Litrel

All rights reserved. No part of this book may be reproduced in any form or by any electronic or mechanical means, including information storage and retrieval systems, without written permission from the publisher, except by a reviewer who may quote passages in a review.

British Library Cataloguing in Publication Information Available

Library of Congress Cataloging-in-Publication Data

Names: Henderson, James D., 1942– author. | Henderson, Linda Roddy, 1944– author. | Litrel, Suzanne, author. Title: Ten notable women of colonial Latin America / James D. Henderson, Linda R. Henderson, and Suzanne Marie Litrel. Description: Lanham : Rowman & Littlefield, [2023] | Includes bibliographical references and index. Identifiers: LCCN 2022019197 (print) | LCCN 2022019198 (ebook) | ISBN 9781538152997 (cloth) | ISBN 9781538153000 (paperback) | ISBN 9781538153017 (epub) Subjects: LCSH: Women—Latin America—Biography. | Latin America—History—To 1830—Biography. Classification: LCC CT3290 .H463 2023 (print) | LCC CT3290 (ebook) | DDC 920.72098—dc23/eng/20220722 LC record available at https://lccn.loc.gov/2022019197LC ebook record available at https://lccn.loc.gov/2022019198

∞™ The paper used in this publication meets the minimum requirements of American National Standard for Information Sciences—Permanence of Paper for Printed Library Materials, ANSI/NISO Z39.48-1992.

Contents

Introduction: Latin American Women, Old Perspectives and New   1

Chapter 1: Anacaona, 1464?–1503   13

Chapter 2: Malinche, 1504?–1528?   41

Chapter 3: Inés de Suárez, 1507–1572?   61

Chapter 4: Saint Rose of Lima, 1586–1617   83

Chapter 5: The Nun Ensign, 1585 or 1592–1650?   105

Chapter 6: Sor Juana Inés de la Cruz, 1651–1695   125

Chapter 7: Chica da Silva, 1733?–1796   147

Chapter 8: Micaela Bastidas, 1745–1781   171

Chapter 9: La Pola, 1795–1817   193

Chapter 10: Manuela Sáenz, 1797–1856   213

Glossary   237

Index   241

Spanish and Portuguese America 1780

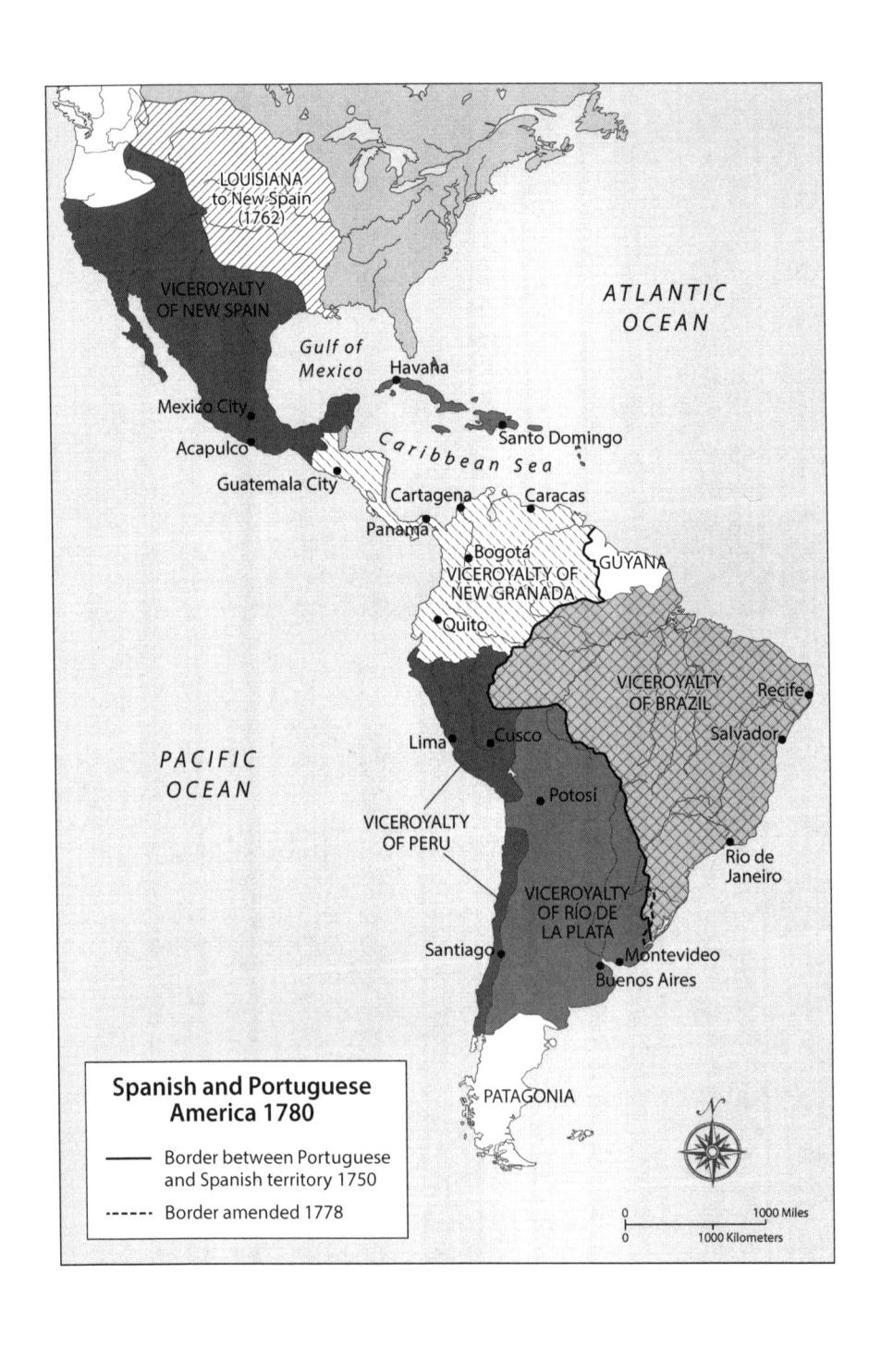

— Border between Portuguese and Spanish territory 1750

----- Border amended 1778

Introduction

Latin American Women, Old Perspectives and New

For more than six months, the little army piloted its brigantines down the ever-expanding river. As fabulous in its way as the Land of Cinnamon the Spaniards had set out to find over a year before, what would become known as the Amazon River had grown so wide that from midstream the huge trees on either shore were but narrow, dark bands sandwiched between river and sky. Along the way, the army fought pitched battles with indigenous peoples who succeeded in killing several of the Spaniards, often pursuing them for miles along the shore in their own canoes. Earlier they had met friendly natives who bolstered their spirits with stories of rich lands farther downstream and of a great queen called Coñorí whose empire was defended by armies of tall, powerful female warriors.

Captain Francisco de Orellana and his followers had no reason to doubt these tales. Many of them had seen the great ruined Aztec city of Tenochtitlán, destroyed just twenty years before, and they themselves had helped Pizarro humble the Incas and loot their empire. Women soldiers had not yet been seen by any modern man, but the ancients wrote extensively about warrior women who cauterized the right breast of female children so that they could better use the bow—Amazons they were called. And was it not true that just a few years ago the popular writer Garci Rodríguez de Montalvo recalled the same legend in his adventure novel about the young knight Esplandián and his adventures in a mythical land called California? Man-eating griffins fought there at the command of an Amazon queen, and Esplandián barely escaped with his life. Could it be that God had chosen them as the first to meet these formidable women?

The warrior queen and her soldiers remained mere phantoms until June 24, 1542, when the rude fleet rounded a bend in the river and, as Friar Gaspar de Carvajal recalled in his famous account, "here we came suddenly upon the excellent land and dominion of the Amazons."[1] Drawing close to shore the explorers saw houses that shone white in the distance, and at the water's edge warriors taunted the Spaniards, goading them into battle. After an hour the conflict still raged along the riverbank and in chest-deep water. "I want it to be known why these Indians defended themselves in this manner," wrote the chronicler of Orellana's expedition. "They are the subjects of, and tributaries to, the Amazons, and . . . we ourselves saw these women, who were there fighting in front of all the Indian men as women captains, and these latter fought so courageously that the Indian men did not dare to turn their backs, and anyone who did turn his back they killed with clubs right there before us."[2]

The good friar, who nearly lost his own life in the contest, described the women as tall and robust, almost naked, with long hair coiled about their heads. They did as much fighting as ten men and fired so many arrows that the brigantines soon "looked like porcupines." Carvajal marveled that one sent an arrow "a span deep" into one of the vessels.[3]

In his own day skeptics scoffed at Carvajal's description of Amazons along the great river, calling the incident either an outright fabrication or the product of a tropical fever. Francisco López de Gómara, author of the widely read *General and Natural History of the Indies,* wrote: "I do not believe either that any woman cuts off her right breast in order to be able to shoot with the bow, because with it they shoot very well."[4] Modern students are more tactful, reasoning that the Orellana party probably fought with indigenous Tapuya women who commonly accompanied their tribe into battle. Whether they were flesh-and-blood women or wondrous creatures that Carvajal perceived in his mind's eye, similar visions drove Spanish, Portuguese, and even English and French explorers to undertake the arduous voyages of discovery that unlocked the secrets of two vast continents. It was a case of quixotic adventurers whose flights of fancy lured them to strange new lands.

A short step takes us from the misty world of the Amazons into that of real women whose roles in the Latin American drama were as significant as those of their male contemporaries. If the warrior women of Orellana's riverside battle can be dismissed as rather commonplace Indian foot soldiers who happened to be women, the same cannot be said for the twenty-year-old Indian woman named María Candelaria. Some hundred years after the conquest of Central America and the forced conversion of the indigenous people to Christianity, Maria Candelaria led a general insurrection to restore the old gods and end foreign exploitation. That seventeenth-century Jeanne d'Arc was a genuine menace to Spanish rule in Central America, and though her revolt failed, she herself was never captured.

Another heroic and tragic incident of Latin American women's history was the defense of Paraguay by its women during the War of the Triple Alliance of 1864–1870. Over the course of the war, that landlocked South American country was so devastated that it would take a century to recover from the war's effects. When most Paraguayan regular soldiers fell before the relentless advance of largely Brazilian armies, teenage boys filled their places, fighting with outdated weapons, and ultimately sticks and stones. Six hundred Paraguayan women—mostly Indian and *mestiza*—died at the Battle of Piribebuy in mid-1868, but not before showering the enemy with sand and empty bottles in one of the most sublime yet futile acts of defiance recorded in military history. At the end of the contest even the women were gone, leaving preadolescents to maintain the resistance. A Brazilian officer surveying the dead after the Battle of Campo Grande said that there was no pleasure in fighting against so many children.

Not all heroic episodes of Latin American women's history are as somber and violent as those surrounding María Candelaria and the Paraguayan women. The story of ten wives of Spanish soldiers who accompanied the Narváez expedition to settle the Florida country has a much happier conclusion. On April 4, 1528, Pánfilo de Narváez landed three hundred men and forty-two horses at Tampa Bay, leaving one of his officers on board ship to protect the women and to find a harbor farther north where the expedition could reunite. The soldiers and their wives were to settle there, forming the nucleus of a new Spanish outpost. For more than a year the three supply ships sailed up and down the coast looking for Narváez and his luckless followers. Finally, assuming that all had perished, the search was called off and the ships made port in Mexico, then called New Spain. And the women? They married sailors from the ships and settled in New Spain, far from the wild north Florida frontier that was their original destination.

The Spanish and Portuguese in America did their best to re-create the Mediterranean culture they left behind. Except in the old centers of Aztec and Inca civilization where European and indigenous customs formed an uneasy amalgam, they were remarkably successful in bringing customs of late medieval times to their new home. An eight-hundred-year struggle to reconquer Spain and Portugal from the Muslims stamped on them a proud, warlike character tempered by a militant Catholicism that gave them the spiritual strength to carry the long struggle to success. Amazons had little place in such society.

Male-female relations were dominated by the concept of *machismo*, a form of radical individualism among men stressing all that is "manly" and virile. In everyday attitudes *machismo* translated into valor in battle, sensitivity to all insult, unwillingness to compromise, and an aggressive, domineering attitude toward women. The *macho* tried to impose his will on women around him, making love to as many as possible before marriage, fiercely jealous and protective of his own wife, yet willing and eager to continue his own outside love affairs. The institution of *machismo* tolerated the "double standard" and reveled in it. If the ideal male was aggressive and sexually promiscuous, the ideal woman was just the opposite. Custom and law demanded that she be chaste before marriage and a virtuous homebody afterward. Church teachings more than a thousand years old at the time of the Conquest instructed that she was the lesser vessel, obligated to respect her husband's judgment in all things.

Although the Latin American woman was often limited to the confines of her home, she played a pivotal role in Latin American culture and society. In an elite family, the home whose walls shut her away from the outside world was her bastion and source of strength. Mediterranean social theory singled out the family as society's fundamental building block, and the person around which the family centered was the mother. The father's presence was also important, but his principal field of action was the larger world. He was free to be a model of irresponsible parenthood if he so chose, but few such options were possible for his mate. She had to be a tower of strength through strict adherence to codes laid down by the church. The Catholic church provided the upper-class woman a supreme model for feminine conduct in the Virgin Mary. Mary, the greatest of all mothers, was to Latin American women the tearful saint of comfort and forgiveness whose example of divine forbearance gave them courage to persevere in adversity and to forgive and understand the manifold sins of husbands, sons, and brothers. Evelyn Stevens, a pioneering scholar in the field of Latin American gender study, coined the term "marianismo" to describe this cult of the Virgin. Marianismo was a necessary antidote to the willful individualism deeply rooted in Latin American culture. It gave the woman who exemplified its ideals a universally recognized moral superiority. Such a woman could be justifiably proud that more than anyone else she bore the burden of preserving and transmitting all the best in Latin Christian culture to her sons and daughters.[5]

The ideal of selflessness and abnegation did more than give some Latin American women, such as St. Rose of Lima (chapter 3), a sense of identity and self-worth. It also provided a delicate link of sympathy and understanding among women of all races and social conditions who bore the burden of machismo, motherhood, and certain of the homely tasks. Yet the shared experiences among the women of Latin America in no way made them a cohesive, self-conscious class within their culture. The powerful forces of economics, race, and family connections deeply divided Latin American women, as they did men.

At the top of Latin American feminine society stood the woman of pure European descent whose wealth came from her own family or that of her husband. Two complementary views of upper-class women have traditionally held. The first depicts them as living in the lap of luxury, surrounded by slaves or servants, having little to occupy their time except gossip and innocent flirtations; the second reveals them as hopelessly ignorant creatures barely able to read and write or to pursue conversation much beyond questions involving needlework and the care of children.

Contemporary male observers write of upper-class women as creatures of petty vices and possessed of unenlightened leisure. For many years the heavily veiled *tapadas* of colonial Lima upset society by wandering the streets at all hours peering furtively and seductively through their veils, secure in the knowledge that not even their husbands could recognize them. The count of Nieva, fourth viceroy of Peru, and many of his successors, considered the veils a threat to morality and tried unsuccessfully to prohibit their use. Mexican women of the mid-nineteenth century were described as grossly ignorant of events taking place outside their homes, never reading anything more controversial than a prayer-book. One of their great pleasures, according to a sympathetic but mildly scandalized foreign observer, was the smoking of small, pungent cigars. Well-to-do Brazilian women of the great sugar estates, or *engenhos*, were as poorly educated as those in Spanish America but tended to suffer more from fanatically protective husbands. Even physicians were usually refused permission to examine women. They were outsiders, after all, and had to content themselves with diagnosing from another room after hearing husbands describe the symptoms through an open doorway.

Easy generalizations like these never applied to all women of the elite. Research shows that wives of the wealthy had more freedom of action than was once thought possible and were not wholly slothful and ignorant. Wealthy women were part of an all-powerful Latin American ruling group. Consequently, they were always under pressure to marry men of good family so that the interlocking network of elite interests might remain unbroken. Thus, a new view emerges of the upper-class woman as one limited in her actions by group pressure, not indolence, by calculated economic self-interest, not stupidity.

Down the social scale from aristocratic European and creole women, or *criollas*, were those of the same racial stock but outside the monied class. They were a fortunate group in many ways, on one hand free from the stigma of "mixed blood" and on the other not shackled by the demands imposed on women of the upper class. Their relative poverty gave them leeway in choosing a mate (or not choosing one for that matter), engaging in economic activity outside of the home, and taking up other pursuits not deemed proper for women of status. Excluded from high society they may have been, but nonelite women enjoyed an independence that made their place an enviable one in the Latin American world.

The gap between white women and all others was wide. In Spanish- and Portuguese-speaking America, ancestry was a key factor which could unlock the portals of social ascent or could slam them shut. Indigenous, *mestizo*, and Blacks (the term is used here to include mixed-blood Blacks, or mulattos) formed the three largest groups. Indigenous people predominated in Andean America, *mestizos* in Mexico and mountainous parts of northern South America, and Blacks in the Caribbean and extensive portions of Brazil. In the fifteenth and sixteenth centuries, indigenous women occupied a unique place in Spanish American society. Taken as mistresses, and sometimes as wives by the first Spanish invaders, considerable numbers of them learned Spanish customs and soon began bearing the conquistadors' children. A few daughters of "Aztec" (Mexica) and Inca nobles married influential Spaniards, thus making their way into the upper echelons of colonial society. Others used concubinage status to gain socioeconomic entry into the Hispanic world. Their gender provided them mobility not possible for males, who were regarded as a potential source of revolt. The indigenous woman was also an important economic force in Latin America. She ordinarily ran the village and city markets supplying farm produce and household goods to the townspeople.

Offspring of indigenous women and European men made up a second element of nonwhite population—the mestizos. In some parts of Latin America a *mestizo* elite sprang up and after the Independence Period gained enough wealth and influence to challenge creole dominance. But they generally held an intermediate social position, excluded from white society and both unable and unwilling to take up indigenous ways. A few philosophers called the men and women of *mestizo* America a "cosmic race" uniting the best from their mixed ancestry; still others held that they were "half-breeds" possessing neither indigenous nor European heritage in appreciable measure. Whether the *mestiza* is considered one of the chosen or one of the excluded, she and her brothers were an ever-growing and significant population group in Latin America.

Stigmatized by the racial prejudice against all nonwhites, the third group, Black women, bore the hateful additional burden of slavery. Many were transported to Latin America with two, some would say three, strikes against them, which forced them into the lowest positions in society. Not until the abolition of slavery during the nineteenth century were the majority of Blacks able to seek an improved lifestyle. Like indigenous women, some Black females used their gender to gain social mobility for themselves and their mixed-blood offspring, and they were also likely to gain positions as domestics, and, if free, to engage in small businesses. Black males, whether slave or free, were mistrusted by the members of other groups who feared their potential to lead slave revolts.

The original edition of this work, *Ten Notable Women of Latin America* (1978) was inspired both by the women's movement and the historiographical turn to the study of gender in history. In the 1970s, few students of Latin American history had read the story of the Nun Ensign, the swashbuckling Basque cross-dresser from early seventeenth-century Spanish America. Today many have, thanks to the rise of gender studies. During the 1980s a new generation of Latin American specialists took up new approaches to the study of gender in Latin American history. They focused on intersectionality and the way it sheds light on how race and sexual orientation affect women's lives and lived experiences. They also began reading against the grain of source materials and, for instance, re-interpreting silences in archives. In this way, they pieced together fragmented archival evidence to employ agency-oriented approaches to their work.[6] In biographical writing, this has meant a gradual turn from portraying women as victims in male-dominated dramas to an examination of how they maneuvered through sociopolitical and economic challenges of their day.

A present-day problem for Latin American specialists involves the paucity of women's voices in documentary sources, particularly from the colonial period. Few women were literate in colonial Spanish and Portuguese America, and fewer still were in a position to wield the pen. Furthermore, while many of the women studied here were lauded during their lives and mourned greatly upon their passing, few from the early period were depicted as making significant contributions to their respective colonial-period histories.

Until recently two kinds of writing have dominated Latin American women's history within and beyond Portuguese and Spanish America. The first tends to praise heroines of national independence or notable women in the arts. A slightly less common but nonetheless popular biographical approach focuses on the unorthodox woman who flew in the face of social convention for romantic or other reasons. In recent years scholars have deemphasized this kind of "great woman history" in favor of studies dealing with women in groups, arguing that such analysis can give valid insights into the day-to-day problems of the people.[7] Biography, they argue, tends to glorify gifted or unique women while ignoring their ordinary sisters. Traditionalists counter with the charge that the sociological approach tends to economic and sexual determinism and squeezes the lifeblood from its subject matter. In postmodern scholarship, however, the movement of women—between and within borders, classes, and ethnicities—highlights how some created, developed, and utilized an intermediary status to great advantage.[8]

This biographical work offers another way of thinking about the Latin American past. We draw from eyewitness accounts, official records, personal correspondence, art, and prose, as well as recent secondary source work to represent major ethnic and economic groups from first encounter, in the fifteenth century, to the revolutionary era and beyond. The ten figures depicted here hail from African, indigenous, and mixed descent as well as women of the purest Spanish lineage. They include aristocrats, working women, and slaves. Their fields of action run from Mexico to Argentina, from Peru to Brazil and the Caribbean, and even to the Iberian Peninsula.

Examining this diverse group of notable women makes it possible to not only dispel myths regarding their agency—or lack thereof—but through the lens of their own experiences, to tell the early history of Latin America. For example, many people assume that in a male-dominated society, nonelite women were thoroughly oppressed, enjoying only brief moments of happiness during their lifetimes. In reality this was far from the case. Another groundless assumption is that noble lineage or special intellectual gifts were sufficient to free elite women hampered by role and custom; they did not, but still the elite women detailed here overcame stifling societal challenges and helped shape Latin American history. The biographical sketches also reveal that *machista* notions notwithstanding, unorthodox women helped push the boundaries in the Spanish American frontier and shaped a new society. The actions of the women described here provide vivid examples of race, class, and religion as motive forces in Latin American history. They also describe the fluidity of social roles and traditions as colonial and modern women navigated challenges an ocean away from Old World expectations and concerns.

This work surveys early, or colonial, Latin American history, told through the lives of ten extraordinary women. The experiences of the first three women represent early Iberian encounter and conquest in the Americas between the fifteenth and sixteenth centuries. Five of our figures lived through the mature colonial period, the seventeenth and eighteenth centuries. The life stories of the last two subjects reflect the tumult of the early nineteenth century, the time of the Spanish American struggle for independence.

Queen Anacaona of Xaraguá province, in western Hispaniola, gave material aid to Christopher and Diego Columbus, and to the first Spanish settlers on the Caribbean island as well. Despite that, she suffered a vile death at the hands of Hispaniola's third governor, Nicolás de Ovando. Priest Bartolomé de las Casas later described the massacre of Anacaona and her people in such a way as to place them at the center of the Black Legend of Spanish cruelty in the Indies.

La Malinche, born in the Valley of Mexico, was sold into slavery by her Aztec mother. At about age fifteen she was given to Spanish conquistador Hernán Cortés. Malinche gave invaluable help to Cortés in his conquest of the Aztec Empire. Afterward she bore him a son, Martín, one of the first mestizos (person of mixed indigenous-European ancestry) born on the mainland of America.

Inés de Suárez was the widow of a Spanish soldier who fought with Francisco Pizarro during his conquest of the Inca Empire. Not long after arriving in Peru in search of her husband, Inés de Suárez met Pedro de Valdivia and joined him in the conquest of Chile. Cofounder, with Valdivia, of Santiago de Chile, she went on to become a leading benefactor of the young Chilean capital.

Two notable women of early colonial Spanish America are Saint Rose of Lima (Isabel Flores) and the Nun Ensign (Catalina de Erauzo). Born in Lima, Peru, Isabel Flores became known as "Rose" Flores for her physical beauty. When, during adolescence, she read a biography of Saint Catherine of Siena (1347–1380), the young woman began emulating Saint Catherine in every aspect of her life. She became venerated by *limeños* for her piety and good works, and they promoted her canonization, something that occurred in 1670. Rose of Lima was both America's first saint and the patroness of America and the Philippines.

Born in Spain's Basque region, Catalina de Erauzo fled the convent at age fifteen, dressed herself in men's clothes, and made her way to Peru some three years later. There she soon became notorious for her quick temper and her skill in dueling—and later for her criminal acts. Captured and sentenced to death for her crimes, she confessed that she was a former nun and a virgin as well! Sent back to Spain, the king awarded her a pension for her military service. The Nun Ensign traveled on to Rome, where the Pope absolved her of her sins and granted her the right to live out her life dressed as a man.

Three figures representing Latin America's mature colonial period are Sor Juana Inés de la Cruz, Chica da Silva, and Manuela Bastidas. Born near Mexico City, Sor Juana [Juana Inés de Asbaje] was a child prodigy whose quick intelligence dazzled all who knew her. She was invited to join the viceregal court, where she became a favorite of the wife of the viceroy. In adulthood she became a cloistered nun, going on to earn fame both at home and in Europe as one of the great Baroque poets of the time. Today Sor Juana is remembered as America's first feminist critic of society's double standard in its treatment of women.

Chica da Silva was born a slave in Brazil. That fact notwithstanding, she became the lifetime partner of one of the wealthiest men in the Portuguese Empire, the crown's diamond contractor in Brazil's province of Minas Gerais. The happy couple ended up having thirteen children, all of whom were freed at birth and went on to become exemplary citizens of Brazil and of Portugal. Chica da Silva's life illustrates the social fluidity existing on Brazil's eighteenth-century mining frontier, a place where slaves greatly outnumbered non-slaves.

Micaela Bastidas is known as a precursor of Latin America's independence movement. The wife of social revolutionary Tupac Amaru II (José Gabriel Condorcanqui), she was an equal partner with him in a bloody late eighteenth-century revolt of oppressed indigenous peoples in Andean Peru. Alongside her husband, Micaela Bastidas suffered grisly execution at the hands of Spanish authorities. The Tupac Amaru rebellion thus stands as an opening salvo in Spanish America's fast-approaching revolutionary era.

Independence-era figures treated here are La Pola and Manuela Sáenz. La Pola was born in Guaduas, in present-day Colombia. She was an enthusiastic supporter of independence from Spain, rising to become a key member of the patriot underground in Bogotá, capital of the Viceroyalty of New Granada. When she was at last captured by Spanish authorities, she heaped abuse on both her captors and her own people, whom she accused of cowardice in the face of oppression. The young woman of Guaduas is remembered today as Colombia's preeminent female hero of its revolutionary era. Manuela Sáenz is remembered as "the liberator of the Liberator" (Simón Bolívar). She became Bolívar's consort mid-way through his campaigns to free northern South America from Spanish rule. Alongside him, she played a significant role in freeing both Peru and Bolivia from Spanish rule. She saved Bolívar from assassination in a celebrated episode from the year 1828. Born in Quito, Ecuador, Manuela Sáenz spent her final years in exile, in the port village Paita, in northwestern Peru.

All figures examined here illustrate the truth that biography extends to ideas, attitudes, and groups, and that social and intellectual history can be fruitfully explored through the unfolding of a human life. These lives underline the humanistic view that individuals have the power to rise above circumstance and impersonal forces of history through sheer force of intelligence, perseverance, and character. These facts, as well as the fascination inherent in the colorful personalities themselves, inspire this study of women who became makers of Latin American history.

NOTES

1. This and all subsequent translations from Spanish and Portuguese, both prose and poetry, are, unless otherwise noted, by the authors.

2. Gaspar de Carvajal, "Carvajal's Account," in José Toribio Medina, ed., *The Discovery of the Amazon*, translated by B. T. Lee (New York: American Geographical Society, 1934), 81.

3. G. de Carvajal, "Carvajal's Account," 83.

4. Francisco López de Gómara, *Historia general de las Indias* (General and Natural History of the Indies), Seville, 1540, 77.

5. Evelyn Stevens, "Marianismo, the Other Face of Machismo," in Ann Pescatello, ed., *Female and Male in Latin America* (Pittsburgh: University of Pittsburgh Press, 1973).

6. Merry Wiesner-Hanks, *Gender in History: Global Perspectives*, 2nd edition (Chicester: Wiley-Blackwell, 2011), 2-9.

7. One example is Susan Socolow's *The Women of Colonial Latin America* (New York: Cambridge University Press, 2000).

8. For instance, Camilla M. Townsend's *Malintzin's Choices: An Indian Woman in the Conquest of Mexico* (Albuquerque: University of New Mexico Press, 2006), "Introduction," especially pp. 2–3.

REFERENCES

Arciniegas, Germán. *América mágica,* vol. 2. "Las mujeres y las horas." Buenos Aires: Editorial Sudamericana, 1961.

Carvajal, Gaspar de. "Carvajal's Account." *The Discovery of the Amazon.* Ed. José T. Medina. Translated by B.T. Lee. New York: American Geographical Society, 1934.

Diner, Helen. *Mothers and Amazons: The First Feminine History of Culture.* Translated by J. P. Lundin. New York: The Julian Press, 1965.

López de Gómara, Francisco. *Historia general de las Indias* (General and Natural History of the Indies). Seville, 1540.:

Hahner, June E., ed. *Women in Latin American History.* Los Angeles: UCLA Film Center, 1976.

Lavrin, Asunción, ed. *Sexuality and Marriage in Colonial Latin America.* Lincoln: University of Nebraska Press, 1989.

Lavrin, Asunción. *Women, Feminism, and Social Change in Argentina, Chile, and Uruguay, 1890-1940.* Lincoln: University of Nebraska Press, 1995.

Powers, Karen Vieira. *Women in the Crucible of Conquest: The Gendered Genesis of Spanish American Society, 1500-1600.* Albuquerque: University of New Mexico Press, 2005.

Socolow, Susan M. *The Women of Colonial Latin America.* New York: Cambridge University Press, 2000.

Stevens, Evelyn. "Marianismo, the Other Face of Machismo." In Ann Pescatello, ed., *Female and Male in Latin America.* Pittsburgh: University of Pittsburgh Press, 1973.

Townsend, Camilla. *Malintzin's Choices: An Indian Woman in the Conquest of Mexico.* Albuquerque: University of New Mexico Press, 2006.

Wiesner-Hanks, Merry. *Gender in History: Global Perspectives*. 2nd edition. Chichester: Wiley-Blackwell, 2011.

Chapter 1

Anacaona, 1464?–1503

INTRODUCTION

Before there was Latin America there was indigenous America. The first humans traveled out of Africa to the Middle East 125,000 years ago, spreading from there through Eurasia over the ensuing 50,000 years. Next, they turned toward the Americas. The First Americans began crossing from Siberia into North America 40,000 years ago over a land bridge formed when ocean levels fell dramatically during the last Ice Age. In terms of earlier prehistoric human migrations, the Americas were populated relatively quickly. By 10,000 BCE there were settlements scattered over North, Middle, and South America. Monte Verde, in southern Chile, was occupied by paleo-indigenous peoples from at least 10,800 BCE.

Around the time Monte Verde was being settled, human migration from Asia ended. The planet warmed, sea levels rose, and the land bridge disappeared. Peoples of the Americas entered a time of isolation lasting ten thousand years. When that isolation ended and the First Americans came face-to-face with their fellow human beings from beyond the seas, the course of history changed fundamentally. At that moment, for good or bad, the world became irrevocably interconnected.

EARLY TRADITIONS AND A TRANSATLANTIC ENCOUNTER (TO 1492)

The epochal meeting of the New and Old Worlds came on the small Bahamian island of San Salvador, named by Genoese navigator Christopher Columbus, who first set foot there on the morning of October 12, 1492. Those welcoming him were an indigenous people who may have called out "nitaíno" as their canoes approached his vessel. Chroniclers, upon hearing this term in a language more recently known as Arawak, took the word "Taíno" to indicate this people.[1] The Taíno marveled at the Europeans, who they thought might be gods descended from the sky. The Europeans appraised the island-dwellers with detachment, wondering whether they possessed gold and would make good slaves. Those indigenous peoples were at a relatively early stage of technological development, while the Europeans benefited from thousands of years of technological advance in every field of endeavor. The immediate future of indigenous America was foretold in that fact. The Taíno Columbus discovered had no way of resisting the pale-skinned foreigners from beyond the seas.

The Taíno people emerged around 400 BCE in the Orinoco River delta in northeastern South America. Over two thousand years they moved northward through the Lesser Antilles, eventually occupying the four islands of the Greater Antilles: Puerto Rico, Hispaniola, Cuba, and Jamaica. By 1492 they numbered more than a million. On Hispaniola, the most politically unified of the four islands, they lived peacefully in well-ordered communities under the rule of five chiefs, called caciques in their language. Here in "Ayti," or Haiti, as they called it, the Taíno fully controlled the chiefdoms of Marién and Xaraguá, and they shared Maguana and Maguá with Caribs, a fierce Arawak people nominally enemies of the Taíno. Caribs predominated in the easternmost province of Higüey.

Prior to the arrival of the Europeans, the Taíno lived in what seemed to be a tropical paradise. They were a handsome people who wore no clothing save for a small apron used by married women. All others, men, unmarried girls, and children, were naked save for adornments such as necklaces and bracelets. The adults harvested and smoked a fragrant weed called tobacco; they also cultivated cassava, from which they made a delicious bread. They spent much of every day relaxing in suspended swinging beds they called hammocks, rousing themselves from time to time to watch or play a spirited game of *batay*, involving two teams and a bouncing rubber ball. They lived in round, timbered, and thatched-roof houses called *canay*. The only thing troubling the Taíno of the Greater Antilles were the great storms called hurricanes that ravaged their islands from time to time and raids by Caribs living on neighboring islands. Like the Taíno, the Caribs had emigrated northward through the Lesser Antilles, occupying them as they progressed. It was from bases on the smaller islands that the Caribs staged incessant raids on coastal villages of the Taíno.

When Christopher Columbus approached the northern coast of what Europeans would call Hispaniola, the island possessed five chiefdoms, as seen in figure 1.1, one of which would be ruled by Anacaona. In ten years' time, Anacaona would be the last remaining ruler of an independent

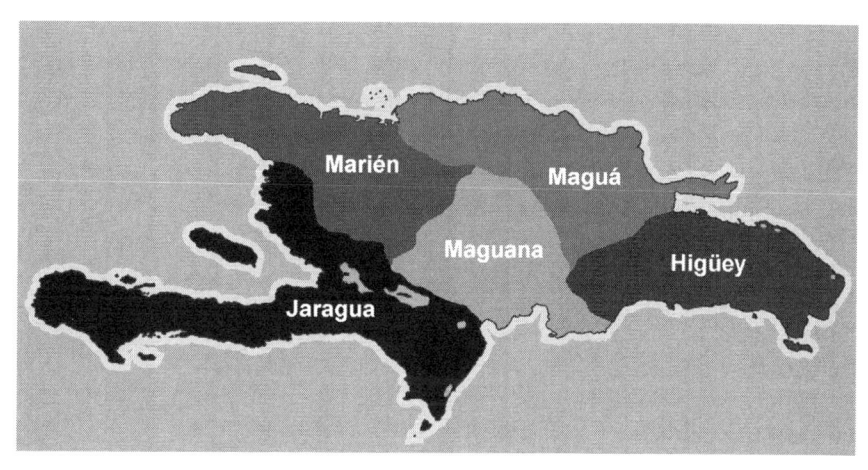

Figure 1.1 Map of Taíno chiefdoms (cacicazgos) at the time of Columbus's arrival

chiefdom. The smallest chiefdom, Marién, was located in present-day northern Haiti. South of Marién was Maguana, extending down through mountains known as the cordillera of the Cibao. Maguana was ruled by Carib chief Caonabó, respected by the Taíno of Hispaniola for his wisdom and his skill in fighting Carib raiders. West of his chiefdom lay Xaraguá (Jaraguá) province, ruled by Chief Bohechio, brother of Caonabó's wife Anacaona. The richest and most populous chiefdom in Hispaniola was Maguá, ruled by Chief Guarionex. That province occupied the fertile valley lying east of the island's central mountain range. Dotted with scores of towns and villages, its fertile soil was watered by dozens of rivers flowing down from the mountains. A third of Hispaniola's 300,000 Taíno lived in the broad valley constituting Maguá province. Spaniards who first viewed it likened Hispaniola's central valley to the biblical Garden of Eden. The Spanish named it the Vega Real. At the eastern end of the island Guayacona ruled the province of Higüey, whose soils yielded the island's finest and most important staple, cassava.

Despite their trouble with Carib raiders, there were signs by 1492 that these two groups might be on the verge of reconciling their differences. Despite long-standing tribal conflict, an equally enduring tradition offered the chance for a more peaceful future. In Taíno political culture, a woman could become a chief when there was no brother or son available to preside over the chiefdom. More than a decade before the voyage of Christopher Columbus, a royal wedding took place uniting Anacaona, the sister of Taíno chief Bohechio of Xaraguá province in western Hispaniola, and Carib chief Caonabó of neighboring Maguana province. The Carib chief and his Taíno princess produced a daughter, named Higuamota. As half Carib and half Taíno, when she became an adult, she was in a position to preside over the rich chiefdoms of Xaraguá and Maguana provinces, occupying most of western Hispaniola. Had that occurred there would have been significant political implications for the island and for the entire Caribbean. When Columbus arrived on San Salvador, Higuamota was about eleven years old, and her mother Anacaona was about twenty-eight. Caonabó was in his fifties.

During October and November of 1492, Caonabó and the other caciques of Hispaniola compiled information about their unexpected visitors. Word of their movements came via oceangoing dugouts that the Taíno called pirogues. As soon as a pirogue reached Hispaniola, teams of couriers relayed news by both land and sea, along the island's well-worn trails and along the coast in small, fast dugouts called canoes. According to the dispatches reaching the island's leaders, the visitors traveled in three large vessels not rowed but seemingly powered by the wind. They had pale skin, facial hair, and wore clothing. While they appeared to be friendly, they carried fearsome weapons of unknown manufacture. As these reports poured into Hispaniola, excitement grew that the mysterious newcomers were in fact supernatural.

Thoughtful Taíno, perhaps Caonabó and Anacaona among them, worried that the foreigners might not be as benign as reported. They had, after all, traveled across the waters where hurricanes were born. As for their possible divinity, all Taíno knew that the great god of creation had two sons, one good and the other evil. God's good son made the plants and the animals. The other, Guacar, grew jealous of his brother and changed his name to Juracán and inflicted misery on the world. Was it possible, some Taíno leaders might have wondered, that the strangers who had come from the east were sent to them by Juracán, the evil god of destruction?

Chief Guacanagarí of Marién was not concerned when the foreign lords at last appeared off the coast of his province in late December 1492. For several days signal fires in the west had alerted him to the approach of three wondrous vessels, seemingly propelled across the water by magic and immensely larger than the longest pirogues. The oceangoing dugouts had been bringing word about the strangers for more than two months. The strangers had been friendly during the days they spent wandering among the Bahama Islands to the north, trading with the people who lived there. It had been the same in Cuba, where they had spent more than a month. Guacanagarí hoped the strangers would befriend his people. Perhaps they would help defend them from the troublesome Caribs who lived on islands to the south and west. Despite the union of Anacaona and Caonabó, Carib warriors from other islands killed many Taíno during their raids. They took women and boys away with them. The latter were said to be killed and eaten in cannibalistic rituals.

Christopher Columbus reached Hispaniola in December 1492, traveling east after his month exploring Cuba. On December 21 he reached Marién province. There Chief Guacanagarí and his people greeted him enthusiastically, with what the Genoese explorer described later as singularly loving behavior. Like other indigenous people of the Americas, the Taíno had the custom of flattening the foreheads of swaddled newborn infants, but this did not stop Columbus from describing their physical appeal. On December 21, Guacanagarí and thousands of his followers celebrated the strangers' arrival with a banquet at their main village. The foreigners then invited the chief and his top leaders aboard ship, where the two groups exchanged gifts and the Taíno were entertained with musical performances and even dramatic presentations by members of the admiral's crew. Meanwhile hundreds of Taíno in dugouts bobbed alongside while trading tropical fruit, cassava bread, and other foodstuffs for the small bells and other trinkets exchanged by the Europeans. Similar visitations and celebrations took place during the following two days, after which Columbus continued sailing eastward along the coast. Near midnight, December 24, disaster struck. The flagship *Santa María* struck a reef and had to be abandoned. Columbus used wood from the ship to construct a beachside settlement that he named Navidad. After provisioning it as best he could and leaving thirty-nine members of his crew to man it, he returned to Spain.

SETTLEMENT AND SUBJUGATION (1492–1494)

When Columbus set out on his first voyage to the New World, the king and queen of Spain named him Admiral of the Ocean Sea. His new Taíno friends would have been appalled had they understood that by his repeated ceremonies with flag and crucifix the visitor claimed their islands and themselves for Spain. During the weeks he spent returning to the Spanish port of Palos, his original point of departure, Columbus noted in his ship's diary that he had discovered islands that he was certain lay close to Japan and China, and therefore were not too distant from India. For this reason, he wrote that the islands were populated by countless "Indians." Columbus noted laconically in his diary that none of them objected to his actions. Columbus returned across the Atlantic to report his findings to Queen Isabella of Castile and her husband, Ferdinand of Aragon. It was they who had financed his expedition. Across the Atlantic, Hispaniola's original residents would not have been pleased to learn that the admiral and his fellow foreigners intended to continue the crown's imperializing policy, colonizing their island. They would have been horrified by the foreign chieftain's plan to haul the most robust among them away to be sold in the slave market of Sevilla.

It did not take long for the Taíno to understand that the crew members Columbus left behind did not mean them well. The native inhabitants had the three things the Spanish needed: land; human labor to work it; and, most importantly, gold. Chief Guacanagarí of Marién had given Columbus gold ornaments and had spoken of rich gold mines in Hispaniola's cordillera of Cibao. The foreigners' abuse of the indigenous people began with their search for gold. As they roamed the countryside, the Spaniards took their hosts' food at will, subjugated Taíno men, and seized their wives and daughters for service as concubines and maids. Taíno husbands, fathers, and brothers had little hope of resisting. Their flimsy wooden weapons were ineffectual against the steel swords, lances, and daggers of the Spanish. The men left behind by Columbus were quick to use their weapons against any Taíno who raised a hand against them.

On November 28, 1493, eleven months after he had departed, Columbus returned to Navidad to find that all of the men he had left behind were dead. Visiting the town had been his top priority when he set out on his second expedition to the New World. Greeted once again by Chief Guacanagarí, Columbus learned that over the intervening months his men had died of disease, in fights with one another, and at the hands of Taíno led by Carib chief Caonabó of Maguana province. Guacanagarí explained that the foreigners' abuse of his subjects had led a delegation of them to seek the help of Caonabó, famous for his fighting ability. Guacanagarí told Columbus that the eleven Spaniards found unburied on the beach near Navidad were victims of Caonabó's attack. The admiral concluded philosophically that his men had brought about their own destruction through their indiscipline and bad behavior.

The admiral's plan for Hispaniola and its people became apparent soon after his departure from the ruins of Navidad. His ships continued eastward along the coast searching for the spot where they could build a permanent settlement, one providing easy access to the gold-producing areas of central Hispaniola. Columbus found the spot he was searching for at a sheltered inlet some twenty miles east of the mouth of the Yaque River, which drained Hispaniola's central valley. The Spanish renamed it the River of Gold. On January 6, 1494, Columbus christened his new town La Isabela.

The gold objects that Columbus had presented to Ferdinand and Isabella upon his return to Spain at the end of his first voyage to the New World in early 1493 generated great excitement at court and throughout Spain. As a result, the monarchs had lavishly outfitted his second expedition, which consisted of seventeen ships and more than a thousand men, many of them soldiers tasked with putting the Taíno to work in the goldfields. Alonso de Ojeda was the commanding officer of that military force, and in April 1494 he was sent to discover the location of Hispaniola's gold. Ojeda's expedition, accompanied by one hundred soldiers, set off as soon as a prison was constructed at La Isabela. Shortly before Ojeda departed, Columbus instructed him to deal sternly with the Taíno to accustom them to subjugation. Ojeda accomplished the task brutally, first through mutilations and killings and then by capturing several sub-chiefs of Maguá province. He sent them back to La Isabela to be executed for disobeying his demands. Meanwhile Ojeda's men moved into the mountains west of the valley searching for the source of the alluvial gold they found in rivers flowing down from the cordillera.

Hispaniola's chiefs were aghast as they followed those events. They routinely stayed in contact with each other as a means of countering the effect of Carib raids. But suddenly the danger they faced lay at the center of their island and was personified by fearful foreign lords obsessed with the bright metal found in streambeds. Chief Caonabó and his principal wife, Anacaona, closely monitored the Spanish rampage through the neighboring province to the east. Their alarm mounted when Ojeda's men began searching for gold in the mountains of Caonabó's own province. By that time both knew that Caonabó's capture was a priority of the foreigners, ever since Chief Guacanagarí, now an ally of Columbus, had blamed him for the death of Spaniards left behind in Navidad. Now, in early 1494, rumors circulated that Caonabó planned to lead an attack on Fort Santo Tomás, established by Columbus during the month of April at the headwaters of the River of Gold. It was a spot the admiral had decided would be the center of Hispaniola's gold mining. Anacaona's husband was thus doubly sought after by the foreign lords. As a precaution he sent Anacaona and Higuamota to Xaraguá province, where they would be protected by Anacaona's brother Bohechio.

FORCING TRIBUTE: RESISTANCE AND REBELLION ON HISPANIOLA (1494–1496)

On April 24, 1494, Christopher Columbus sailed away from La Isabela to continue his exploration of Cuba. During his absence of nearly five months, conditions deteriorated there and throughout Hispaniola's central valley, now called the Vega Real, where Ojeda's soldiers continued the search for gold and committed outrages against the Taíno. The anger of the Taíno's leaders mounted. Not long after the admiral's departure, a Taíno sub-chief named Guatiguaná led an attack on the hospital of La Isabela, killing the ten Spaniards who guarded it and burning it along with the forty patients it housed. Columbus was unpleasantly surprised by these events when he at last returned to La Isabela on September 29, 1494. The Taíno of the Vega Real were in open revolt. Food deliveries to La Isabela had ceased, threatening the town's residents with starvation. Further complicating things was the ill-health of many of Columbus's men. One of the most serious diseases afflicting them was syphilis. Unknown previously in Europe and seemingly dormant among indigenous Americans, syphilis became virulent when Spanish men began having sex with Taíno women. Just one thing cheered Christopher Columbus when he returned to La Isabela. That was the presence there of his brother Bartolomé. The admiral had sent word to Spain requesting his brother's help in governing the island, proclaiming him Adelantado of Hispaniola. It was the task of the Adelantado, a word meaning "advance agent," to defend the crown's interests in trouble spots.

Columbus compounded his and the island's problems in early 1495. As he readied four caravels to return to Spain for medicine and food, he and his men enslaved fifteen hundred Taíno men, women, and children living in villages around La Isabela. He selected five hundred of them to be sold in Sevilla, sending them away on one of the caravels that departed on February 24, 1495. As soon as the remaining thousand Taíno saw what was taking place, they rioted and four hundred of them managed to escape. The six hundred who were not so lucky were distributed as slaves among residents of La Isabela. Columbus next ordered his chief lieutenant, Alonso de Ojeda, to organize a military campaign aimed at crushing Taíno resistance to Spanish occupation of the Vega Real. On March 25 the admiral and the Adelantado led a force of two hundred men, twenty of them mounted, along with several hundred Taíno allies under the direction of Chief Guacanagarí, against the Taíno of Maguá province. Twenty mastiffs also formed part of the military force. On March 27 Columbus and his force confronted several thousand Taíno under the command of District Chief Guatiguaná. The Battle of Vega Real was over quickly. Taíno warriors, without armor and using wooden weapons, were slaughtered by the Spanish. When panicked warriors fled into a dense tropical thicket, the Spanish unleashed their mastiffs, which set upon and quickly killed a hundred more of the terrified warriors. Those who survived were marched back to La Isabela and sold as slaves. Under terms of the "just war doctrine" in effect at the time, anyone defeated in legitimate warfare was subject to enslavement. The fate of Taíno survivors of the Battle of Vega Real was the same as that of the residents of Málaga, on the southeastern Iberian Peninsula. Because the town's residents refused to surrender to Castilian forces besieging it, when the city fell all its residents were sold into slavery. That had occurred in 1487, just eight years before Columbus defeated the Taíno of Hispaniola's central valley.

Following the Battle of Vega Real, Alonso de Ojeda moved through the Cibao range, crushing any remaining indigenous resistance. While so doing he had a stroke of good luck. On April 12 Ojeda arrived at Chief Caonabó's village in mountainous Maguana province. By that time Ojeda knew enough of indigenous battle tactics to capture the Carib chief and husband of Princess Anacaona through trickery. He marched Caonabó back to La Isabela and locked him away in the town's prison.

In mid-1495 Christopher Columbus could write to his royal patrons that "the entire island is completely subjugated."[2] By his view he had accomplished one of the main tasks expected of him and could begin preparing for his return to Spain early the following year. The Admiral of the Ocean Sea was anxious to return to defend himself against those who charged that he was a poor, even incompetent, administrator of the crown's first major possession in the New World. Many on the island supported that view. Hunger and disease stalked La Isabela during 1495, and famine and death afflicted the Vega Real. Columbus had demanded tribute in gold of every Taíno male above the age of thirteen, payable on a quarterly basis. That requirement, impossible to fulfill in the face of the island's rapidly dwindling supply of alluvial gold, drove the Taíno to despair. Food production was disrupted throughout the central valley, driving many of its residents into the mountains in search of nonexistent food. So great was the despair of the Maguá Taíno that many of them, starving and unable to present the gold Columbus demanded, committed suicide. Columbus was philosophical about the chaos he had wrought throughout the Vega Real. In early 1496 he noted in his journal, "If they survive . . . I hope I can earn a little profit."[3]

Anacaona and her daughter were forced to flee their home when the foreign lords menaced it. Still, as sister of Chief Bohechio of Xaraguá province and wife of the chief of Maguana province, she assumed rule as needed. Not long after Alonso de Ojeda had captured her husband, the Spaniard fought and easily defeated a force commanded by Bohechio and captured him as well. Bohechio soon escaped and limped home to Xaraguá. During the time Bohechio was held captive, Anacaona served as acting chief of her home province of Xaraguá. This was in accordance with Taíno customs, which made no gender distinction when it came to power and rule.

In the latter part of 1495, intriguing reports began reaching Anacaona of a friendship that had developed between her husband and Christopher Columbus. According to those reports the admiral had taken to spending hours in conversation with Caonabó, during which Columbus questioned the Carib chief about the customs, traditions, and beliefs of both Carib and Taíno. By early 1496, as the admiral readied his return to Spain, Anacaona was at once frightened and pleased to learn that the foreign lord intended to take Caonabó with him to meet and speak with his king and queen, Ferdinand and Isabella. She understood that the personal bond with Columbus was one of Caonabó's making. It was clear that once the initial anguish of his captivity passed, her husband had made a successful effort to win the admiral's friendship. Her informants had told her that the only time the admiral smiled and laughed was during his long conversations with Caonabó. Anacaona may well have hoped that when he met the great chiefs of Spain her husband might convince them to lighten the burdens that were crushing the Taíno of the Vega Real. As she meditated on these things, Columbus was noting in his diary: "He is a man well up in years, courageous and intelligent, and of a most piercing wit and much knowledge. . . . There is no subject he does not know about."[4] Columbus assured the king and queen that his captive/friend would speak both knowledgeably and entertainingly with them and they would relish the experience. Sadly, that never came to pass, as Caonabó died during the voyage to Spain.

Trouble continued to brew between Taíno and Spaniards. When Columbus and his party departed for Spain in two caravels on March 26, 1496, the admiral left behind a host of problems. La Isabela was no longer a viable settlement. Its residents were hungry, ill, and rebellious. The scarcity of food was in large part the admiral's fault, because he had desolated the surrounding countryside through his slave raiding and military campaign. Meanwhile the Taíno were dying in great numbers. Columbus had left his brother in charge during his absence. That was foreordained not to work out well. Bartolomé Columbus was an honorable but unimaginative man entirely lacking in charisma. Furthermore, many of the Spaniards under his command saw him as a foreign interloper. A final and definitive complication had been imposed on the Adelantado by his brother. Bartolomé Columbus was tasked with establishing a new capital for the island, at a location far from La Isabela, on Hispaniola's southeastern coast. He departed the island's first capital in mid-1496 to supervise construction of a new one to be called Santo Domingo. The man he left in charge of La Isabela was a Spaniard named Francisco Roldán, appointed by Christopher Columbus alcalde, or chief administrator, of the settlement.

ANACAONA, "GOLDEN FLOWER" OF XARAGUÁ: COOPERATION, CRISIS, AND CHALLENGE FOR (1496–1500)

By 1496 it was clear to Anacaona and her brother that the foreign lords could not be resisted by military means, and therefore that if they and their people were to survive, it would be through means suggested by Caonabó through his relations with Christopher Columbus—that is, by being helpful to the foreigners, lending them their support, making them laugh, and pledging allegiance to their sovereigns who lived across the seas. During the middle months of 1496, Bohechio and Anacaona received a steady flow of news about construction of the foreigners' new settlement on the southeast coast, in Higüey province. They knew that although the chief of Higüey, Cotubanamá, sent tribute to the new town, especially in the form of cassava bread, it was never enough to feed Santo Domingo's growing population. Spaniards continued moving there from the dying settlement of La Isabela. That meant it would not be long before the foreign lords visited Xaraguá. That province was as yet untouched by the Spanish because it possessed no gold. Also, it was an exemplary place, full of handsome people and replete with the earth's bounty. So it was that in late 1496 word reached Bohechio and Anacaona that Bartolomé Columbus was preparing his visit to Xaraguá province. Soon they could test their strategy of helping and befriending the foreigners.

Chief Bohechio and hundreds of Xaraguá Taíno greeted Bartolomé Columbus in late December 1496 on the banks of the Río Nieba, which flowed down from the mountains of Cibao and formed the boundary between Maguana and Xaraguá provinces. The Adelantado had marched westward from Santo Domingo with a hundred men. Bohechio escorted Columbus from the river more than ninety miles westward, to the main village of Xaraguá and to the chief's residence, dominating the clearing lying at its center. The procession had all the pomp of a monarch's visit to one of his dependencies. When the Adelantado reached Xaraguá's capital, he was greeted by a breathtaking sight. Several thousand smiling Taíno stood arrayed before him, among whom were all of Bohechio's sub-chiefs, family members, retainers, and servants. Also present were many members of the province's aristocratic class, their retainers, and slaves. All were naked save for adornments and the small aprons worn by married women. Unmarried women wore little more than ribbons tied around their foreheads. The Spaniards noted all this, and that the Xaraguá Taíno were the most physically attractive of all the indigenous residents of Hispaniola.

Under Anacaona's close supervision, Bohechio's provincial capital had been turned into an enchanting place. Garlands of flowers adorned every building as well as the woven framework erected behind the polished mahogany stool upon which the honored guest would be invited to sit. When the Adelantado was seated, Bohechio's sub-chiefs filed by and bowed to him. Then each of Bohechio's thirty wives approached him, bowing and placing palm fronds at his feet. Finally, all stepped back as the chief's sister, Anacaona, clad in garlands of flowers, made her appearance on a palanquin born by her attendants, as in figure 1.2. The flowers were an allusion to her name, which meant "Golden Flower." At that moment Anacaona was about thirty-three years old. Despite her mature age she was still acclaimed as the most beautiful woman in all Hispaniola.

A day of celebration followed, featuring a banquet replete with all the delicacies that the tropics offered. There were fruits and fruit juices, roast meats, featuring the hutía, similar to rabbit, and iguana. The meats were seasoned with peppers and sauces made from nuts such as peanuts, all unknown in the Old World. There was baked squash of several varieties, fried and steamed cassava, sweet plantain, banana, and several varieties of potato, another staple

Figure 1.2 Anacaona's likeness on a Cuban stamp, part of the postage series "History of Latin America," circa 1987. (rook76/Shutterstock.com)

unknown to Europeans. Oysters, clams, crabs, and lobsters were served, along with all varieties of fish, broiled, baked, and fried. The food was heaped on platters and served to the visitors in endless procession. Every course was accompanied by baskets filled with hot cassava bread.

The festivities accompanying the Adelantado's visit featured an ongoing cycle of the ball game called *batey*, played on courts located throughout the provincial capital of Xaraguá. Similar courts existed in every Taíno town on the island of Hispaniola. Taíno men, women, and children played *batey*, which featured teams competing to drive a rubber ball through a goal using only hips, knees, and elbows. The Spanish were intrigued by the game and never tired of watching it. The highlight of the reception given for Bartolomé Columbus was the singing of *areytos*. The *areyto* was a song-poem lauding an honored guest, normally a Taíno chief or some other venerable figure within the tribe or outside of it. *Areytos* were accompanied by music and dance, and they were listened to critically, with audience members judging the linguistic skill and quality of voice of its singer. The *areyto* was considered the highest form of gift-giving among the Taíno. Across the Hispaniola of that day Anacaona, Golden Flower of the Xaraguá Taíno, was acclaimed as the most accomplished singer of the *areyto*. Her presentation that day of an *areyto* to the Adelantado of Hispaniola, Bartolomé Columbus, marked the culmination of the day's celebration.

Bohechio's and Anacaona's display of friendship and cooperation served exactly as they hoped it would. At the end of Bartolomé Columbus's visit, an agreement was struck by which the Xaraguá Taíno would supply foodstuffs, especially cassava bread, as well as raw and woven cotton, to the Spanish. Additional land would be devoted to cassava cultivation as well. At the end of the visit Columbus departed, telling Bohechio and Anacaona that he would return to collect the tribute as soon as it was ready. Accordingly, the residents of Xaraguá set about gathering the foods and nonfood items stipulated in the agreement of early January 1497. At the end of two months, Bohechio sent word to the Adelantado that the first shipment of tribute was ready for delivery. By that time food had become scarce in eastern Hispaniola, especially along the island's central valley, where the native inhabitants continued to die in large numbers. In contrast, Xaraguá province not only had yet to experience the impact of the Spanish, but its agricultural production was expanding at the request of the Adelantado.

In April 1497 Bartolomé Columbus returned to the capital of Xaraguá province and was again received with feasting and celebration. Bohechio, Anacaona, and thirty-two of their sub-chiefs awaited him with a large quantity of cassava bread and other foodstuffs. They presented all of it to him and introduced a new kind of bread not known previously to the Europeans. His hosts explained that it was derived from a plant called "maize." A variety of meats, dried and salted and ready for transportation, were also delivered. Columbus sent word overland to La Isabela to send a caravel that had recently been repaired following a storm to the harbor of Xaraguá province, which was located some ten miles west of Bohechio's capital. As the consignment of food and raw and woven cotton made its way to the coast, Anacaona invited the Adelantado and other members of his party to spend the night at her estate, located halfway between the capital and the port. When the Spaniards reached Anacaona's palatial round-timbered, thatched-roofed *canay*, a breathtaking display of crafts and manufactures awaited them. Historian Bartolomé de las Casas, who later interviewed eyewitnesses of the event, described them as "a thousand things made of cotton, and stools and many vessels and things of service in the house, made of wood, and marvelously worked."[5] Anacaona encouraged Columbus to take whichever among the items he thought might be useful to him. Also presented to the Adelantado were four balls of spun cotton so large that each was difficult for a man to lift. Columbus was given to understand that Lady Anacaona owned the large island of Ganabara, just off the coast of western Hispaniola, where women under her direction manufactured the carved mahogany stools prized by members of the Taíno elite.

There they also wove the cotton aprons worn by married women throughout the island. Through her display of courtly generosity to Bartolomé Columbus, Anacaona demonstrated her status as the highest-ranking woman on the island of Hispaniola. As sister of Bohechio, widow of Caonabó, and mother of Higuamota, probable heir of both Maguana and Xaraguá provinces, her status rivaled if not surpassed both those of her brother and of Cotubanamá, chief of Higüey province.

Before the tribute was loaded onboard the caravel, Bartolomé Columbus invited Xaraguá's chief and his sister to inspect the vessel. At that moment Anacaona's high status was revealed yet again. As Las Casas put it, "the king and queen, his sister, each had canoes, very large and well-painted and prepared, but the lady being so regal, did not want to go in the canoe, but only with Don Bartolomé in the boat." Once aboard ship the Adelantado ordered that it sail around the bay so Xaraguá's rulers could observe the workings of the sails. In the words of Las Casas, "They stood without fear in quiet admiration, that without oars and paddles the caravel, so huge, would go where they wanted and with a wind only coming from one direction that they could turn against it."[6] The demonstration of sailing was yet another way the Spanish revealed they were vastly superior to the Taíno at the level of technology. The Spanish, and Europeans generally, began developing their nautical technology thousands of years before ancestors of Bohechio and Anacaona first reached the islands of the Caribbean, paddling dugout canoes from the mainland of South America. The foreigners demonstrated their technological superiority a second time when sailors on the caravel fired a small ship's cannon without warning and not far from where their guests stood. According to Las Casas the noise so frightened the Taíno rulers that they "threw themselves into the water" to the amusement of the foreigners.

The Adelantado's visit coincided with the outbreak of strife among Spaniards living on Hispaniola. Between mid-1497 and late 1499, Spaniard Francisco Roldán, alcalde of La Isabela, rebelled against Bartolomé Columbus. Roldán and his followers resented being commanded by the Genoese brothers and resolved to remove them from power. Roldán's revolt took shape during late 1496, while the Adelantado was away supervising the construction of Santo Domingo and at a time when hunger, illness, and hurricanes made life miserable for those left behind in La Isabela. In mid-1497 Roldán and eighty of his followers launched their rebellion, marching up the Vega Real to the fortress-town Concepción de la Vega, where they fought Bartolomé Columbus and troops loyal to him. Unable to dislodge the Adelantado, Roldán and his followers withdrew westward, over the cordillera of Cibao, to Xaraguá province, where they established themselves in early 1498.

The arrival of Francisco Roldán and his rebel force would have fateful consequences for Anacaona and Bohechio. After settling in Xaraguá, rebel captain Roldán took Anacaona's daughter Higuamota, then about eighteen, as his mistress. This was a calculated decision: Higuamota not only had inherited her mother's beauty, but she also was second in line to rule the Xaraguá Taíno. Chief Bohechio was in his forties, old by standards of the day. Also, he had suffered during his brief captivity by Alonso de Ojeda, in June 1495, an event that damaged his health. Anacaona was not unduly distressed when the foreign lord took her daughter to his bed, as chiefs took multiple wives in Taíno culture. As in the case of Anacaona's own marriage, relationships across tribal lines were also accepted. Higuamota's father was, after all, a Carib, and his match with Anacaona had pointed the way toward improved relations between the Carib and Taíno peoples. The foreign invaders, with their pale skin, impressive physical size, and frightening weapons, were a far greater danger than the Caribs. It was known, too, that their queen Isabella smiled on the marriage of Spanish men and indigenous women, and that her priests had solemnized the marriages of Spaniards and Taíno women in other parts of Hispaniola. The Taíno did not prize virginity nor chastity, and Anacaona may also have viewed the relationship between Higuamota and her lover as a step toward harmonizing interests of Spaniard and Taíno. All this is explained by the fact that Taíno culture was matrilineal. Even though Taíno chiefs were usually male, they could never be sure they were the biological fathers of their sons and daughters. For this reason, inheritance among the Taíno passed through the female line.

Roldán and his followers had stumbled into a lovely place full of inhabitants able, if reluctant, to do their bidding. Unfortunately for the Taíno, however, when Christopher Columbus at last returned to Hispaniola in August 1498, at the end of his third voyage to the New World, he was scandalized to learn of Roldán's revolt and of the way his brother's sworn enemy had taken over Xaraguá province. The carnal side of Roldán's enterprise was underlined for the prudish Columbus by a syphilis epidemic that raged among Roldanistas in Xaraguá at the moment of his return to the island. That only heightened the admiral's fury against the treasonous Francisco Roldán.

Christopher Columbus had indeed been a poor administrator of Hispaniola, no surprise in that as a navigator and explorer, proclaimed Admiral of the Ocean Sea, he had no previous experience in governing. He and his brother developed goldfields that yielded little. He never built a viable base in the West Indies from which to launch Spanish colonization efforts. In fact, every time the admiral departed Hispaniola to continue his exploration of what he stubbornly insisted was East Asia, the island fell into anarchy. That had happened in 1494, when marauding Spaniards tyrannized residents of the Vega Real, causing an uprising that Columbus and his brother were required to crush. Hispaniola's decline into anarchy was repeated in 1496, after Columbus returned to Spain while leaving his brother in charge of governing

Hispaniola. Roldán's rebellion burst into flames no sooner than the admiral was out of sight. Columbus's persistence in enslaving Taíno peoples, something Queen Isabella had repeatedly ordered him not to do, may have contributed to his own men's defiance in his absence. In 1498, Columbus allowed Roldán to seize Xaraguá Taíno and use them as forced laborers—a practice that later became known as *repartimiento*. When Columbus finally came to terms with Roldán in late 1499, he had lost the support of the crown.

In 1499 the king and queen of Spain replaced Christopher Columbus as governor of Hispaniola with the nobleman Francisco de Bobadilla, a court favorite and a man of proven administrative ability. In commissioning Bobadilla, the monarchs charged him with conducting a *residencia*, or a judicial inquiry, into the admiral's performance as governor. They were anxious to receive firsthand testimony that either proved or disproved charges leveled against Hispaniola's first governor by his enemies in Spain. They accused Columbus of having been an arbitrary, incompetent, and cruel administrator of the island. The monarchs granted Bobadilla the power to send Columbus and his brother back to Spain to face judgment in the event they were found to have violated the monarchs' trust. When Bobadilla reached Hispaniola in August 1500, he found the island in an uproar. Another uprising had taken place against Columbus and Francisco Roldán as well. Roldán had made peace with an exhausted and discouraged Columbus ten months earlier, and now he was working with the admiral as his ally. At the same time, and perhaps curiously to Bobadilla, it was Roldán, and not Columbus, who was the chief target of rebellious Spanish colonists.

As troubles deepened for Christopher and Bartolomé Columbus, Anacaona suddenly found herself elevated to chief of Xaraguá. Her ailing brother, Bohechio, had died early in 1499, and the months of January and February were filled with traditional rituals marking the burial of a chief and the installation of his successor. At one tragic moment reported by Bartolomé de las Casas, thirty of Bohechio's widows entered his crypt and were sealed in it with him. After that came ceremonies installing Anacaona as chief of the Xaraguá Taíno. Anacaona's subjects honored her with banquets and athletic competitions involving the game of *batey*, and they celebrated both their new chieftain and her brother with *areytos*. Chief Anacaona the "Golden Flower" sang an *areyto* celebrating the life of her brother.

Anacaona had served as chief of Xaraguá for just a few months when an unwelcome group of foreign visitors arrived there, in mid-1499. It was led by none other than Alonso de Ojeda, who had returned following his exploration of South America's northeastern coast. A Florentine resident of Sevilla named Amerigo Vespucci accompanied him. Anacaona had not previously met Ojeda but was aware of his reputation as an ill-tempered man quick to pursue conflict and punishment. In April 1494, Ojeda had mutilated a Taíno man, thus ending good relations between indigenous people and invaders; he had captured Anacaona's husband, Caonabó, who was never seen again by his family; he defeated a force led by Anacaona's brother, Chief Bohechio, subsequently imprisoning him and sending his health into a decline. Anacaona had every reason to hate Alonso de Ojeda. But she could do nothing more than smile and offer him hospitality when he appeared at her doorstep. To do otherwise would have been dangerous, especially in the case of Ojeda, who never hesitated to maim or kill any Taíno who angered him. At least during the odious Spaniard's stay in Xaraguá, Anacaona could enjoy the company of Ojeda's courtly companion, the Florentine Vespucci.

As soon as Ojeda reached Hispaniola and learned of Roldán's revolt against Columbus, he attempted to profit from the upset. When Ojeda learned that Roldán and Columbus had made peace with each other, he enlisted the help of disaffected Roldanistas in an attempt to overthrow and kill Roldán. Francisco Roldán's followers felt abandoned by their erstwhile leader and therefore knew they were in a tenuous position on the island. Within that setting Alonso de Ojeda recruited a force of several dozen Roldanistas and led them in an attempt to assassinate their former leader. The attempt failed and Ojeda and his men found themselves outnumbered by the combined forces of the new allies Columbus and Roldán. After two additional months of troublemaking, Ojeda agreed to continue on his way to Spain. His ships departed Hispaniola in February 1500. The island was at last at peace.

Anacaona watched the fighting among the Spaniards with dismay. What, she must have wondered, is coming next? The answer was more trouble—for her family and herself. A few days after Ojeda's departure, a young Spaniard named Hernando de Guevara arrived at the main village of Xaraguá. He had been sent there by Columbus for unknown reasons, on orders to return to Spain with Alonso de Ojeda. Guevara was a member of a well-known family in Castile and cousin to Adrián Mújica, a lieutenant of Francisco Roldán. At the time Mújica lived on an estate not far from the port of Xaraguá province. Pending further orders from the admiral, however, Roldán ordered him to stay at Anacaona's nearby estate in Cahay.

The moment Hernando de Guevara arrived at Anacaona's home he threw it into turmoil. Guevara was instantly captivated by Higuamotas, her beauty and poise, and by her command of Spanish as well. From the couple's first meeting everything moved at breakneck speed. Within a day Hernando de Guevara had declared his love for Higuamota and asked her to marry him. When Higuamota, with her mother's permission, agreed to marry Guevara, he sent for a priest who then baptized her. The priest departed Anacaona's estate announcing the marriage, scheduled to take place one day later.

This affair of the heart had tragic consequences for all concerned: Christopher Columbus, Anacaona and her family, Hernando de Guevara and his cousin, and the Taíno of Xaraguá province. Guevara's engagement to the Taíno heiress of Xaraguá touched off the last major outburst of violence seen among Spanish settlers living in Hispaniola. Guevara likely had some idea that as the only child of Anacaona and Caonabó, Higuamota stood to inherit the chiefdoms of both Xaraguá and Maguana. He had angered the admiral, who ordered him back to Spain, but he likely understood that marriage to an indigenous princess would enhance his status. Royalty was royalty, after all, whether in Europe or in a distant land. These considerations may—or may not—have flashed through Hernando de Guevara's mind as he was introduced to Higuamota, daughter of Anacaona.

Hernando de Guevara ignored the fact that Higuamota had already been claimed as the mistress of Francisco Roldán. Although Roldán had not gone to the trouble of marrying her, or even having Higuamota baptized, Roldán understood it was wise to link his personal fortunes to the island's indigenous leadership class. That likely explains his anger when he learned that the young Spaniard sent to live in Anacaona's home was on the verge of marrying the chief's daughter. Francisco Roldán burst on the scene during the third day of Hernando de Guevara's romantic interlude. The older man ordered the younger one to depart forthwith and to abandon all hope of wedding Higuamota. In words whose meaning could not have been lost on Guevara, Roldán informed him that he, Francisco Roldán, "had always defended the young lady."[7] For good measure Roldán added that the admiral, too, would be angry when he learned what had taken place in the home of Anacaona. Guevara begged Roldán to relent but the former rebel chief of Xaraguá refused to yield.

A furious Hernando de Guevara rode to his cousin's estate and explained what had just happened to him at the hands of Francisco Roldán. He was able to convince Adrián de Mújica that Roldán must be overthrown. Then they rode through Xaraguá province recruiting disaffected Roldanistas to their cause, something easy to do because of the prevailing climate of anger over the Roldán-Columbus peace accord. As soon as Columbus learned of the uprising, he was beyond angry. As the admiral saw it, he had no sooner completed the arduous task of bringing peace to Hispaniola when two Spaniards barely known to him, one a Roldanista and the other a callow youth, raised the specter of rebellion yet again. And over an indigenous woman! The admiral acted decisively. He sentenced Guevara, Mújica, and the other leading troublemakers to death and ordered Francisco Roldán to have them arrested and sent to prisons located in La Concepción and Santo Domingo. Roldán did this easily. Meanwhile Columbus began executing the rebels. Adrián de Mújica was the first to die, hanged from the battlements of La Concepción. Others were hanged in the plaza of Santo Domingo. Columbus traveled to

Xaraguá with a priest in tow, hanging more than a dozen rebels after the priest had heard their confessions.

Columbus was in Xaraguá hanging rebels when his replacement, Francisco de Bobadilla, arrived in Santo Domingo. Columbus was unaware that his royal patrons had lost faith in his ability to govern and had sent Bobadilla, an officer in the crusading order of Calatrava, to replace him. The first thing Bobadilla saw when coming ashore at Santo Domingo on August 24, 1500, was two bodies dangling from gibbets in the town plaza. When he made out that they were Christians whose bodies had been left rotting in the tropical sun for four days, it confirmed what he had heard from the admiral's enemies in Spain: Columbus was a cruel foreigner bent on ruining the crown's imperial project in the New World. When the admiral returned to Santo Domingo ten days later, Bobadilla had him arrested, clapped in irons, and sent back to Spain along with his brother.

Chief Anacaona viewed these events with renewed alarm. Why did the foreign lords continually fight one another? Why had their sovereigns suddenly turned against their governor of Ayti? Within that setting the chief of the Xaraguá Taíno doubtless wondered too what her own future held at the hands of the unpredictable foreigners. One thing surely comforted her: the birth of a grandchild in late 1500. Higuamota had given birth to a daughter, who was given the name Guarocuya, whose father was either Francisco Roldán or Hernando de Guevara.

Francisco de Bobadilla's own tenure as governor of Hispaniola was brutish, unsuccessful, and brief. After jailing Columbus and his brother and remanding both of them to Spain in chains, he seized the admiral's possessions and set about pandering to the Spanish settlers. He ended the requirement of Columbus that settlers pay their taxes in gold, a measure that had plagued the island's Spanish settlers. As Bobadilla's early measures were taking place, Christopher Columbus landed at Cadiz and, affecting the dress and manner of a penitent Franciscan monk, made his way to Granada, where Ferdinand and Isabella were holding court. When the discoverer of the New World appeared before them, his health broken and displaying scars inflicted by Bobadilla's shackles, the monarchs were scandalized. The king and queen immediately pardoned Columbus and set about finding another governor for Hispaniola. The man they settled on was Nicolás de Ovando, a long-standing favorite at court who had a high reputation both for valor and administrative ability. Ovando was appointed governor of Hispaniola in September 1501 and ordered to assemble a colonizing force capable of making the island a viable outpost of Spain's empire beyond the Ocean Sea.

FATAL DECEPTIONS

Fray Nicolás de Ovando was an Extremaduran and administrator of the military Order of Alcántara, the crusading arm of the Cistercian order. Hence, he adhered to strict monastic discipline and required it of other knights of the order. Ovando had been fervently committed to the reunification of Spain from the time he entered royal service as a young man in the 1470s. Rising to become a principal official in the Order of Alcántara, he took part in the last stages of the Reconquista, which featured the fall of Málaga in 1487 and that of Granada in 1492. Austere and loyal to a fault, there was no doubt that Nicolás de Ovando would unswervingly carry out the queen's orders.

During late 1501 Ovando set about assembling the largest colonizing expedition ever sent to the New World. His flotilla, consisting of thirty ships and twenty-five hundred colonists, departed Spain in mid-February 1502 and reached Santo Domingo in mid-April of that year. Two members of the flotilla's company were colonist Bartolomé de las Casas, then age twenty-six, and soldier Francisco Pizarro, age twenty-four. One of the new governor's first tasks was to end forced labor by the island's indigenous population, as the queen had instructed. Ovando also informed the island's Spanish settlers that the queen commanded them to treat the Taíno humanely and to pay them wages for their work in agriculture and mining. Meanwhile Ovando readied a flotilla to transport former governor Bobadilla back to Spain, along with the considerable quantity of gold that had been extracted from the streams and mountains of Hispaniola. Among the flotilla's passengers were Francisco Roldán and former chief Guarionex of Maguá province.

Just as the homeward-bound fleet was ready to depart in June 1502, four ships commanded by none other than Christopher Columbus appeared in the harbor of Santo Domingo. The admiral was beginning his fourth and final expedition to the New World. Not a supporter of Columbus, Governor Ovando denied him access to the harbor. When Columbus advised Ovando not to allow his flotilla to set sail, as a great storm was approaching, Ovando ignored the advice. As a result, his fleet hoisted anchor on June 29, 1502, and sailed into the teeth of a fierce hurricane. The storm sent most of the ships to the bottom of the Atlantic Ocean just as they exited Mona Passage, off the east coast of the island. Lost were Francisco de Bobadilla, Francisco Roldán, and Chief Guarionex, along with a fortune in gold bullion and records chronicling Hispaniola's earliest years under Spanish rule. Master mariner Christopher Columbus saved all his vessels and was able to continue his voyage westward to explore the coast of Central America.

The latter half of 1502 found Nicolás de Ovando supervising the reconstruction of Santo Domingo, which had been leveled by the hurricane. He ordered the new capital laid out on the same grid plan that had so impressed him ten years earlier at the military encampment before the besieged city of Granada. With its principal avenues running north and south, and its streets running east and west, the city plan of Santo Domingo became the model for all subsequent towns built in Spanish America. While Santo Domingo was being reconstructed, Ovando confronted a dilemma threatening the entire colonizing project for Hispaniola. Upon his arrival he found that the indigenous people living in the eastern part of the island were close to rebellion. That resulted from the strain imposed on Higüey province of having to feed and maintain eight hundred Spanish colonists who constantly humiliated and abused them. Following the queen's orders, the new governor released them from forced servitude. They then returned to their homes in the mountains above Santo Domingo. In his search for indigenous labor to replace the absent Higüey Taíno, Ovando first traveled to the island's central valley. But the Vega Real had been depopulated by warfare, famine, and disease and by labor demands rising from a gold rush. Ovando returned to Santo Domingo with few new indigenous workers. Upon reaching the island's capital, he was greeted by a poorly provisioned town full of angry colonists who had traveled to the New World expecting to find wealth and easy living—not hunger, natural disaster, and disease.

Within a week of his return to Santo Domingo, in October 1502, Governor Ovando was presented with the excuse he needed to temporarily meet his labor needs. While he was on his trip to the Vega Real, a Spanish-bred mastiff disemboweled a sub-chief who at the time was supervising the loading of cassava bread onto a Spanish ship. The incident took place on Hispaniola's northeastern coast in the agricultural zone of Higüey province called Saona. Enraged Taíno set upon the eight-man food-gathering squad and killed all save one, who made his way back to the capital to report the deaths of his colleagues. That killing of Spaniards gave Ovando leave to conduct a "just war" against the native population. He dispatched Juan de Esquivel and a force of four hundred men to punish those living in northeastern Hispaniola. What followed was a slaughter: Captives were burned alive and infants were hurled into lakes and streams. Esquivel rounded up six or seven hundred villagers and ordered their throats slit. Then he had their bodies gathered and counted at the village ball court. Eyewitness Bartolomé de las Casas later recalled that "infinite was the number that I saw burned alive."[8] Nevertheless, Esquivel's brutality had the desired effect. Chief Cotubanamá of Higüey came to Esquivel and begged him to call off his soldiers. What resulted was a treaty under which Spaniards would not be harmed in Higüey province and food grown there would continue to be sent to Santo Domingo. Juan de Esquivel marched back to the capital with hundreds of slaves. He turned them over to the governor, who in turn sold them to colonists. But Ovando knew that enslaving indigenous peoples via "just war" was not a long-term solution to his ongoing problem of scarce indigenous labor. Furthermore, the residents of Higüey continued to resist working for the Spaniards, preferring to live in their own villages. These serious drawbacks notwithstanding, in his December 1502 report, Ovando assured Queen Isabella that the native population of eastern Hispaniola was pacified and Hispaniola entirely under Spanish control.

In May 1503 Nicolás de Ovando received an extraordinary royal *cédula* (decree) from Spain. Drawn up during March 20 to March 29 of that year by the Council of Castile, it constituted the most explicit set of instructions he or any other administrator in the New World had ever received regarding how to deal with the island's indigenous population. The provisions reflected Queen Isabella's satisfaction that the people of Hispaniola had accepted the authority of their new overlords and stood ready to become cooperative subjects of Spain. The *cédula* stipulated that the natives were to work under the supervision of colonists. They were also to be paid for their work, something that would permit them to become taxpaying citizens and permit them to tithe to the church. All Taíno and Caribs were to be baptized and, when possible, made to live in the new towns that were to be founded throughout the island. They were to be given houses in these new towns, where Spanish colonists would be required to dwell as well. Each of the towns was to have a central plaza, with a church, government buildings, commercial establishments, and a school, positioned around its four sides. Indigenous children were to be taught to read and write. Adults were to renounce their pagan beliefs, to be baptized Christian, to refrain from cursing, to wear clothing, and to bathe infrequently. At such times that they did bathe they should do so while clothed.[9]

The governor studied his new instructions. He may have smiled at the regulation of indigenous bathing. It was well known that the queen believed bathing to be harmful to one's health. Ovando, however, most assuredly agreed that the Taíno should wear clothing and cease bathing in the nude. As a man sworn to celibacy, he well understood the impact of indigenous nudity on male colonists living in a setting where there were few European women. Other parts of his new instructions troubled Nicolás de Ovando. The queen had an overly rosy view of Spanish-Taíno relations in Hispaniola, in part owing to the governor's own misleading report on the positive outcome of his unjust and blood-drenched campaign against the people of Higüey province. Nicolás de Ovando knew well that it would be impossible to treat indigenous peoples humanely while forcing them to leave their villages and become workers under Spanish supervision. Yet if he failed to secure a supply of dependable Taíno labor, Spain's colonizing venture in Hispaniola would fail.

As Hispaniola's governor studied his instructions, he pondered how to act on them. To the east, Higüey was not a good place to put the crown's comprehensive colonization plan into effect. It was still reeling from Juan de Esquivel's rampage through the province months earlier. The island's central valley was not appropriate either. Few of the Taíno who had lived in the once densely populated province remained alive in 1503. That left only Xaraguá, at the western end of the island. Xaraguá province was as yet untouched by war and famine, something having a great deal to do with the wise leadership of its sibling chiefs, Bohechio and Anacaona. In Ovando's view, however, the success of its leaders had come at considerable expense to Spain. For almost a decade Xaraguá had been a place where lapsed Christians lived with native women and defied royal authority. This in mind, Fray Nicolás de Ovando, Knight Commander of Lares, member of the crusading Order of Alcántara, and governor of Hispaniola, planned the manner in which he would put his sovereign's orders into effect in Xaraguá province.

When Anacaona learned in late July 1503 that the new governor was coming to visit, she prepared much as she had for the visits of all the other foreign lords. She ordered the principal town of the province to be cleaned from top to bottom and its ball courts readied for the *batey* matches that so pleased the foreigners. Her subjects gathered special foods and readied for feasts extending over several days, leading to the critical moment when she knew the governor would make known his demands. During the talks she would apply her negotiating skills to the crafting of the best agreement possible. Anacaona knew that all previous foreign lords had been charmed by the lavish receptions, and she also knew that her people's survival hinged on making a good impression on the Spaniards. It had been amply proved that when given cause, the foreigners killed suddenly and without remorse.

For the past seven years, ever since the visit of Adelantado Bartolomé Columbus in 1496, Anacaona had seen that cooperation with the Spaniards had spared Xaraguá the destruction occurring elsewhere on the island. That had been the case when Christopher Columbus traveled to Xaraguá to put down the Guevara-Mújica rebellion. Even the troublesome Alonso de Ojeda had spent happy months in Xaraguá, as had Rodrigo de Bastides and Vásquez Núñez de Balboa. The two provisioned their ships in Xaraguá during June 1500. Anacaona knew all this and therefore resolved to greet the new governor of Hispaniola with the same show of cooperation and friendship that she had shown all other foreign visitors.

What Anacaona did not know was that Nicolás de Ovando would arrive with a plan to radically reshape Xaraguá province. She did not know that Ovando intended to turn the province into something resembling the landed estates of Spain, granted to Spanish nobles by the crown and known as *encomiendas*. She certainly did not suspect that Ovando viewed Taíno governance of Xaraguá as an obstacle to be overcome. Finally, Anacaona did not know that to achieve these goals Ovando was determined to kill her and all other Taíno leaders in Xaraguá province.

In August 1503, Nicolás de Ovando entered Xaraguá with a heavily armed force of four hundred soldiers, seventy of them mounted, and three hundred native allies and slaves. He proceeded slowly, surveying the low-lying terrain spread before him from a mountaintop in the cordillera of Cibao. He sent a small force south to occupy the brazilwood port of Jacmel and then continued on westward. When he reached the province's main town the governor received an extraordinary welcome. Anacaona and her family and the other members of the provincial nobility greeted the governor with great celebration. More than sixty sub-chiefs had been summoned to join the meetings that would be held following the festivities. Nervous Roldanistas, with their Taíno wives and mixed-blood children, were also present. They fervently wanted to pledge their allegiance to the crown in hopes Ovando would pardon their disloyalty to the island's first governor, the Genoan Christopher Columbus.

Days of feasting and celebration took place, featuring spirited *batey* matches and the singing of *areytos*. All the while Nicolás de Ovando looked on impassively. Ever true to his monastic vows, he hid his distaste for the naked throng that surrounded him at the endless round of formal events. At last the moment all had waited for arrived. For Anacaona, her sub-chiefs, and her other political advisers, it was now time for the new Spanish lord to explain what he wanted of them. At the appointed hour hundreds of Spaniards and Taíno leaders filed into the great domed residence of the chief, by far the most dominant *canay* in the city. Built of stout timbers, round, and covered with overarching thatch, it comfortably seated a thousand people. At night hundreds normally slept in the great dwelling: the chief, her family and servants, and members of the Taíno nobility, and their own extended families and retainers.

Sunday featured a full Mass, a lunchtime feast, the playing of a championship *batey* match, and an exhibition of Spanish weaponry and horsemanship. But the day would end in horror. At the conclusion of all social niceties, Taíno and Spanish leaders alike entered the *canay* to begin negotiations. Once all were inside, Nicolás de Ovando touched the jeweled cross of the Order of Alcántara hanging at his breast. This was his signal to slaughter: Spanish soldiers subdued and bound the sub-chiefs, killing any who resisted, and then set the building and all inside afire. Anacaona, her hands tied behind her, was dragged outside, where Ovando's troops cut down her family members and sub-chiefs. Taíno bystanders too slow to flee the scene were hacked to death; many who fled were pursued by mounted soldiers. One young boy had both legs severed with a mighty sword stroke. Some Roldanistas snatched up their children and attempted to flee. But they too were ridden down and killed by mounted soldiers. One man, his child behind him, died when both were run through from behind with a single lance thrust.

That was how Nicolás de Ovando began his pacification of Xaraguá province. His men took Anacaona to Santo Domingo, where she was charged for rebellion against the crown and summarily hanged in the town's plaza. Her hanging was a concession of sorts, a sign of recognition that she was of the indigenous nobility. Ovando and his force spent the next seven months crushing Taíno resistance throughout Xaraguá. Anacaona's execution produced a brief uprising in eastern Hispaniola, giving Ovando the excuse to hang Cotubanamá, chief of the Higüey Carib. That completed his task of destroying Hispaniola's indigenous leadership.

Nicolás de Ovando went on to implement a program of distributing indigenous labor to Spanish colonists through the *encomienda* system. The recipients of such workers were known as *encomenderos*, and they were assigned lands that they were charged with putting into agricultural production. During his months in Xaraguá Ovando founded numerous towns, all on the grid plan by then familiar to residents of the island. The new capital of Xaraguá was built on the ruins of the old provincial capital, where Bohechio and Anacaona had once held court. In a final macabre touch, Ovando named it Vera Paz—True Peace.

EPILOGUE

A few days after Ovando's slaughter in Xaraguá, an indigenous woman walked out of the mountains and down into the Vega Real. Carrying a small female child in her arms, she made her way to the cassava plantation of Bartolomé de las Casas, a Spaniard known to be sympathetic to the Taíno. She had saved herself and the child from Ovando's slaughter, hoping to find safety in Hispaniola's central valley. Over several days the traumatized woman recounted what she had seen to Las Casas. Like most other Spaniards living on the island, Las Casas was horrified at Ovando's gratuitous brutality. Many in Spain shared that same sentiment. When she learned of the massacre, Queen Isabella was said to have muttered "I'll see to it that Ovando pays for this."[10]

The Taíno woman and child were quietly integrated into the indigenous workforce on Las Casas's plantation. Some later said the child was Guarocuya, daughter of Higuamota and granddaughter of Anacaona. That was indeed possible. Higuamota may well have thrust the infant into the woman's arms as she was being cut down by Ovando's soldiers. Regardless of her parentage, the child received by Bartolomé de las Casas likely had children of her own, possibly fathered by a Spanish settler. If true, Anacaona lives on in the DNA of many residents of present-day Haiti, the western half of the island known as Hispaniola.

Aghast at his countrymen's brutality, Bartolomé de las Casas joined the priesthood and spent the remainder of his long life lobbying the crown for legislation protecting the indigenous peoples of Spanish America. His graphic account of Spanish cruelty against First Americans, related in his 1522 exposé, *The Destruction of the Indies*, described in detail Ovando's actions in Xaraguá province and the hanging of Anacaona. This work played a role in the passage of Spain's New Laws of 1542, regulating *encomiendas* and the treatment of indigenous labor. The Spanish crown awarded Bartolomé de las Casas the honorific title "Protector of the Indians."

And what of Anacaona, "golden flower" of the Xaraguá Taíno? Within such a setting, she and her cruel fate lift her to the center of what became known as the "Black Legend" of Spanish cruelty toward indigenous Americans. She emerges from history as a heroine, an extraordinary woman more skillful than her male counterparts in holding the Spanish at bay until that fateful day in August 1503. Today her memory is celebrated throughout the Caribbean through story, song, and theater.[11] It has implications that transcend Latin America. In recent decades international law has evolved a principle known as "the responsibility to protect" doctrine, which holds that human beings have a moral obligation to intervene when the strong tyrannize the weak. Philosophers have argued this from earliest times through what is known as natural rights doctrine. In modern times the argument has been restated in the Universal Declaration of Human Rights. Human history has ever witnessed the struggle between those like Nicolás de Ovando, for whom the end justifies the means, and others like Bartolomé de las Casas, who insist that nothing justifies the criminal violation of human rights. This age-old debate stands at the center of the story of Taíno chief Anacaona.

NOTES

1. Scholars, including Leslie-Gail Atkinson, describe the inhabitants encountered by Columbus as Taíno, rather than Arawak, the ethnic name for the peoples who once populated northern Guyana. We follow suit. Leslie-Gail Atkinson, *The Earliest Inhabitants: The Dynamics of the Jamaican Taíno* (Kingston: University of the West Indies Press, 2006), 1–3.

2. Samuel Eliot Morison, *Admiral of the Ocean Sea: A Life of Christopher Columbus*, 2 vols. (Boston: Little, Brown, 1942), vol. 1, 490.

3. Laurence Bergreen, *Columbus: The Four Voyages, 1492–1504* (New York: Penguin, 2011), 212.

4. L. Bergreen, *Columbus*, 213.

5. Bartolomé de las Casas, *Historia de las Indias* (Mexico City: Fondo de Cultura Económica, 1951), 1, 379-80.

6. Las Casas, *Historia*, 379-80.

7. Las Casas, *Historia*, 2, 273.

8. Franklin W. Knight, ed., *Bartolomé de las Casas: An Account, Much Abbreviated, of the Destruction of the Indies, with Related Texts* (Indianapolis, IN: Hackett, 2013), 15.

9. Details of the royal *cédula* are found in Ursula Lamb, *Fray Nicolás de Ovando, Governador de Indias (1501-1509)* (Madrid: Consejo Superior de Investigaciones Científicas, 1956), 54-58, 71.

10. Lamb, *Fray Nicolás*, 141.

11. For example, Edwidge Danticat's young adult historical fiction *Anacaona: Golden Flower, Haiti, 1490* (New York: Scholastic, 2005).

REFERENCES

Atkinson, Leslie-Gail. *The Earliest Inhabitants: The Dynamics of the Jamaican Taíno*. Kingston: University of the West Indies Press, 2006.

Bergreen, Laurence. *Columbus: The Four Voyages, 1492-1504*. New York: Penguin, 2011.

Casas, Bartolomé de las. *The Devastation of the Indies. A Brief Account*. Translated by Herma Briffault. Baltimore: Johns Hopkins University Press, 1992.

———. *Historia de las Indias*. 3 vols. Mexico City: Fondo de Cultura Económica, 1951.

Danticat, Edwidge. *Anacaona: Golden Flower, Haiti, 1490*. New York: Scholastic, 2005.

Floyd, Troy S. *The Columbus Dynasty in the Caribbean, 1492-1526*. Albuquerque: University of New Mexico Press, 1973.

Knight, Franklin W., ed. *Bartolomé de las Casas: An Account, Much Abbreviated, of the Destruction of the Indies, with Related Texts*. Indianapolis, IN: Hackett, 2013.

Lamb, Ursula. *Fray Nicolás de Ovando, Governador de Indias (1501-1509)*. Madrid: Consejo Superior de Investigaciones Científicas, 1956.

Morison, Samuel Eliot. *Admiral of the Ocean Sea: A Life of Christopher Columbus*. 2 vols. Boston: Little, Brown, 1942.

Rouse, Irving. *The Taínos: Rise and Decline of the People Who Greeted Columbus*. New Haven, CT: Yale University Press, 1992.

Tracy, Olivia. "Rise Up through the Words." *Journal of Haitian Studies*. 24.1 (Spring 2018). 101-26.

Wilson, Samuel M. *Hispaniola. Caribbean Chiefdoms in the Age of Columbus*. Tuscaloosa: University of Alabama Press, 1990.

Chapter 2

Malinche, 1504?–1528?

INTRODUCTION

To the far right of an image in the *Codex Azcatitlan*, an indigenous woman stands next to a pale European man with fair hair and a curly beard. Rosy-cheeked, she appears at the head of a retinue of European soldiers, one of whom carries a bright red banner symbolizing Christianity. Indigenous porters, bowed under the weight of their goods, take up the rear. The woman's eyes are bright and knowing. The gaze of Spanish conquistador Hernán Cortés, by contrast, seems unfocused; he appears unable to take in the scene.[1]

This pictographic history of the Aztecs, who were also known as the Mexica, describes their empire from its mythical origins to its sixteenth-century conquest by the Spaniards. Page twenty-two verso (reverse side) of this Mesoamerican work, painted on European paper, depicts the woman facing another man—likely Montezuma. That page, however, has been lost. What remains is this twenty-five-folio work, as well as other *lienzos*, or indigenous histories, and contemporary descriptions both Aztec and Spanish describing the fall of the Aztec empire to the Spanish.

Common to all such records of Spanish-Mexica encounter and conquest is the presence of the woman who has alternately been known as Malinche, La Malinche, Malinalli, Malintzin, and Doña Marina. She is best known as a translator whose linguistic ability aided the Spanish in their conquest of the Aztecs. In one of his letters to Carlos V (Charles V, King of Spain), Hernán Cortés referred to her as "my tongue." Lost in translation, however, is her own voice, as she never recorded any of her thoughts or doings.

History has played a cruel trick on the consort of Cortés. It has largely overlooked her as a striking personality in her own right—an intermediary figure without whose help Cortés might well have failed to defeat Montezuma and his people by 1521. Rather than being remembered for her human qualities of intelligence, loyalty, and courage, or even for her strength and beauty, the slave girl who helped conquer an empire has been despised by her own descendants. Her name has become synonymous with traitor, as the Mexican Eve who led her people into enslavement by foreigners. Recently, however, Chicana writers have held La Malinche up as a point of feminist pride. Here was a woman, mother of mestizos, who brought down one empire and helped forge another.[2] Thus, the historical Malinche remains open to interpretations that contextualize turning points in history.

One such pivotal moment came long before dawn on an October morning in 1492. A lookout on Columbus's ship *Pinta* sighted white cliffs shining in the moonlight and cried out that land had been discovered. That event and the later explorations of Columbus marked the first effective European penetration of America.

Columbus and the men and women who soon followed him into the Spanish Americas did so as agents of the Spanish Queen Isabella of Castile. With the notable exception of Columbus himself, the great majority of them were Spanish. They brought with them the customs and language of Spain, and within a generation they firmly fixed their Iberian culture upon the society that developed in Hispaniola, other Caribbean islands, and beyond.

Those Europeans who spoke wonderingly of America as a "New World" were not the first humans to set foot on the land. For many thousands of years people of Asian descent had made the Americas their home and had developed their own unique civilizations. When the Europeans arrived late in the 1400s, several of those "Indian" cultures rivaled anything that Europe could offer at the time. One of them was the Aztec empire, lying west of the small Spanish island settlements.

In the early 1500s the Spaniards launched a series of probing expeditions along the seemingly endless coast to the west, each time bringing back rumors of fabulous wealth somewhere on the mysterious land mass. Early in 1519 the fateful expedition of Hernán Cortés departed Cuba, and in a matter of months the dazzling Aztec civilization was revealed to European eyes.

The story of the conquest is one of the most incredible in American history. Cortés the conquistador and Montezuma the emperor soon confronted each other at the gates of the Aztec capital. The date was November 8, 1519. Their encounter was the first act of a drama that would soon destroy one of them and immortalize them both. And standing at the side of the Spaniard was a third figure—that of the woman known by many names. Controversial even today, Malinche the person can best be judged by history.

TRIALS OF A CACIQUE'S DAUGHTER

La Malinche may have already been sold as a child-slave when inauspicious signs indicated a frightful future for the Aztec empire. Montezuma was hardly a decade into his reign as ninth *tlatoani* (emperor) when the lake around his island city of Tenochtitlán rose in sudden waves without apparent reason. Comets appeared in the sky and could be seen even by day. A temple burned to the ground, struck by lightning, and mournful voices were heard everywhere yet seemed to come from no living person. In 1515 Montezuma, the proud warrior-prince, consulted his great ally Nezahuapilli, chief of the Texcocans and famed reader of astrological signs. His verdict: The powerful Aztec empire would soon fall. Montezuma, always aloof and stern, became increasingly withdrawn as he pondered the disturbing signs from the gods.

Some two hundred miles to the east of Montezuma's gleaming city, in a hot lowland *altepetl* (local political entity) near the Gulf of Mexico, lived a young Nahua girl. Malinalli, as she was known then, would soon play a vital role in fulfilling those omens. Her life began auspiciously enough. She was born a princess, daughter of the cacique of a town of Coatzacoalcos province. As a cacique's daughter she enjoyed a degree of education not available to daughters of less-powerful parents and looked forward to a life of comfort and power. This pleasant future was never to be. While she was still a child, Malinalli's father died and her mother remarried, soon bearing a son. According to Bernal Díaz del Castillo, a soldier of Cortés, Malinalli's mother plotted to rid herself of the little girl. Diaz devoted an entire chapter of his chronicles to the woman he called Doña Marina. Sixty years after the conquest of the Aztec empire, he wrote that in order to clear the boy's path to power, Malinalli's mother sold her under the cover of darkness to another tribe, the Xicalangos. Later she was sold to yet another tribe, the Tabascans, who lived farther to the south.[3]

Malinalli's life as a slave of the Tabascans was one of daily toil and drudgery. She likely ground corn, made bread, and engaged in other such domestic tasks. The Tabascans' many religious festivals called for the cooking of special dishes and the sewing of elaborate clothing decorated with feathers and embroidery. In addition to these chores, she helped care for children, itself a never-ending task. While she lived with the Tabascans, however, Malinalli faced a further hardship. Her native language, Nahuatl, spoken by the Aztecs and other subject peoples, was not the language of the Tabascans. Nevertheless, she soon learned to speak their Mayan dialect as fluently as her own.[4]

During 1517 and 1518, the Tabascans and other Mexican tribes were troubled by rumors and stories that spread from town to town, even reaching the shining palaces of Montezuma. Scouts reported that strange canoes of immense size had appeared and moved ominously up and down Mexico's coast. The men who traveled in those ships were bearded and fair-skinned, clothed in steel. They carried arms far different from the familiar arrows, darts, and two-bladed clubs, and their language could not be understood even by those who knew several tribal tongues.

Stories linking these intruders to the Aztec god Quetzalcoatl sprang up among the Mexica people. According to legend, the tall, fair-skinned, and bearded Quetzalcoatl was the civilizing god who had led his followers to a period of abundance many years before. This god was eventually forced to leave the Valley of Mexico. He sailed away into the rising sun, promising to return someday to reestablish his rule. When Montezuma heard reports of strange, fair-skinned men, he pondered the similarities between Quetzalcoatl's legend and the sudden appearance of strangers along Mexico's coast.

Despite the troubling omens and news of the strange visitors from the east, Montezuma's reign had never seemed more secure. His empire stretched in all directions from the mountain-locked Valley of Mexico—over high passes and down into the hot, tropical lands to the south and east, and westward to the Pacific Ocean. From all the towns and cities in this vast region came caravans of slaves loaded with goods produced throughout the empire. They bore richly embroidered cotton textiles, feathers and gems, gold and silver ornaments of every size and design, jadeite and precious stones. Traveling with them were people of all ages who were to be sold in the huge marketplace of Tenochtitlán. This flood of riches was the tribute Montezuma exacted from subject towns.

To guarantee his continued good fortune, Montezuma dedicated much of his time and wealth to satisfying the Aztec gods. Large pyramid-shaped temples towered over the one- and two-story houses of Tenochtitlán, and drums beat to the rhythm of the gods' demands for ever more human lives. Once rare in Aztec religion, the sacrifice of slaves and captive warriors had become part of almost every ceremony in order to appease the Nahua gods. The pious Montezuma had recently sacrificed ten thousand people during the dedication of Tenochtitlán's principal temple.

That great structure, a monument to the Aztec architectural genius, functioned as a working symbol of Montezuma's power. At the entryway, black-robed priests, whose lives were governed by penance and self-denial, swept clean the temple's immaculate courtyards. At the top were dark, blood-spattered rooms where sacrifices were performed. There the person to be sacrificed was bent backward over a stone altar and his chest laid open with a sharp flint knife. A priest then twisted out his still-beating heart, raising it high as a dripping tribute to his god. After sacrifice, the victim's body was cut up and disposed of according to strictly regulated religious practice.

Novice priests displayed the head outside the temple, mounted with many others on long poles; the torso was fed to wild animals that Montezuma kept on his palace grounds; and the arms and thighs were sometimes cooked and eaten by worshippers. Only the most important priests were permitted to perform this rite, and their long, black hair, tangled and matted with dried human blood, easily set them apart from others.

The Nahua-speaking Mexicas believed that great numbers of sacrifices were needed to ensure the favor of the many Aztec gods. Hence, Montezuma ordered his warriors to capture rather than kill enemies during battle, and he often demanded tribute in the form of slaves from the towns within his empire. In order to appease the Fire God, one selected warrior per year, chosen for his skill, would enjoy his last months alive enjoying the best food, drink, and companionship before his sacrificial death atop the temple. Almost no one, even the greatest warrior, was safe from the possibility of sacrifice. And a simple slave girl like Malinalli was quite at risk.

INTERPRETING OPPORTUNITY

Malinalli was about fifteen years old in March 1519 when word came that strange men in canoes had been sighted again along the coast to the south. The Tabascans braced to confront them and assembled twelve thousand warriors to defend their towns from the strangers. But they soon discovered that the intruders, Castilians as they called themselves, were unlike any enemy force they had ever before faced. Armed with powerful arrows, swords, and long metal rods that shot fire from one end, the new enemy was able to beat back the Tabascans even though they were outnumbered by three hundred to one. Their most awesome weapon was the horse. Even the bravest warrior turned and ran from the animal that seemed half man and half monster and stood far taller than the strongest fighter.

Faced with defeat, the Tabascans decided that the Castilians were not ordinary men but *teotl* (plural *teteo'*). This the Spanish heard as "teules" and which they translated to mean "gods." They instructed the Tabascans to address them as such. Hoping to placate them and regain peace, Tabascan caciques assembled gifts to offer their conquerors. A large party of chieftains from Tabasco and neighboring towns arrived at the Castilian camp with slaves carrying maize cakes and every kind of fish and fruit known to that region. Among the gifts they brought were rolls of quilted cotton material used as armor by indigenous warriors, presents of gold ornaments shaped like lizards, little dogs and ducks, several masks, and gold-soled sandals. And last among the gifts were twenty slave women to do the backbreaking work of grinding corn and making bread for the Spanish. Among them was Malinalli, the only one of the twenty who is remembered by history.

The prospect of being given to these fearsome, godlike men must have been frightening for Malinalli. Yet in spite of her fears, the chance to see them and their weapons, dogs, and horses excited her interest, and she was able to keep her poise when brought before them. In spite of her years of subjugation, Malinalli was gifted with grace and a quick intelligence that set her apart from the other slave women. Her long, black hair and regular features gave her a sweet but dignified look that attracted attention wherever she went. Bernal Díaz noted that she was "good-looking, intelligent, and self-assured."[5]

Through Jerónimo Aguilar, a Spaniard who learned the Mayan language when shipwrecked earlier on the Mexican coast, the slave women learned that their new master was named Cortés and that he had given one of them to each of his most important captains. Malinalli was given to Cortés's friend captain Alonso Hernández de Puertocarrero, and she was told to do as he commanded.

The next day Cortés called the enslaved women together and, through Aguilar the interpreter, introduced them to Father Olmedo. This man, he said, was a priest of the Catholic faith who would teach them about the religion of their Castilian masters. Malinalli was amazed to see a man so unlike the indigenous priests she knew. Gone were the black robe, the blood-matted hair, the ears disfigured by self-inflicted cuts and cheeks pierced by cactus thorns. Instead, Malinalli saw a barefoot man, simply dressed, whose words told of a kindly father-god, his baby son, and the virgin mother. Instead of human sacrifice, this god asked only that believers be baptized, and on that day, shortly before Palm Sunday 1519, Malinalli was herself baptized. From that time forth she was known as Doña Marina to the Castilian soldiers, who never failed to call her doña, a title of respect given to the Christian daughters and wives of caciques.

Six days later, on the Monday after Palm Sunday, the Castilians boarded their eleven ships and sailed northward along the coast. Marina was impressed by the size and swiftness of these "canoes" and more than astonished that in a short time they passed the Coatzacoalcos River, the same river that flowed through her native province.

On the Thursday before Easter, the ships had hardly dropped anchor at San Juan de Ulúa when two large canoes bearing Aztec officials approached Cortés's flagship. As soon as they spoke, Doña Marina recognized their language, for it was her own, Nahuatl. She pointed this out to Cortés and suddenly found herself interpreting for the mighty Cortés himself, translating from Nahuatl to Mayan so that Aguilar could then translate their words into Castilian. Immediately after an exchange of formalities, Cortés called Marina aside. If she would serve him faithfully, he said, and translate as honestly as she could, he would protect her and treat her well. Marina pledged that she would indeed serve him as interpreter, and from that time on she found herself always at Cortés's side.

Montezuma knew about Cortés's victory at Tabasco the day after it happened. In less than twenty-four hours a system of runners carried the news from the coast to Tenochtitlán, a distance of two hundred miles. The events of the previous day gave Montezuma ample cause for worry. Unlike the members of the short Spanish expeditions of 1517 and 1518, Cortés and his soldiers were successful in battle and had won the allegiance of a whole province formerly counted among the Aztec prince's subjects. Montezuma suspected that these foreigners might indeed be representatives of the god Quetzalcoatl, and, concerned about the proper course of action, he called together his allies and priests. Some of his counselors urged him to assemble a great army of warriors that could capture all the Castilians for sacrifice. Others advised that the strangers might be teules and should be treated carefully, like gods. Montezuma, himself afraid of angering the gods, decided to send messengers to Cortés with word that the Spanish should accept gifts from the Mexican prince but should not try to come to Tenochtitlán to see him. Hoping to intimidate the Spanish with his wealth and power, he sent his best diplomat, Tendile, to San Juan de Ulúa to meet with Cortés.

Tendile and his caravan arrived at the Spanish settlement on Easter 1519. Marina and Aguilar were called to Cortés and between them translated words of welcome from Castilian to Mayan to Nahuatl and back again. Both sides exchanged gifts and Cortés ordered his cavalry to demonstrate their horsemanship on the firm sand of the beach. Aztec artists carefully painted everything they saw—ships, horses, cannon, the Castilians' bearded faces and clothing, even Marina and Aguilar—so that Montezuma could see these things as if with his own eyes.

Sometime after this meeting, Tendile returned to the Castilian camp with a caravan of one hundred slaves carrying gifts of immense value from Montezuma. Many of the ornaments were taken from the temple of Quetzalcoatl: a large, wheel-sized disk of gold, a larger one made of burnished silver, many ornaments of precious metals, and enough gold dust to convince the Spanish that a visit to Montezuma would be well worth the effort. Tendile, however, cautioned them against traveling to Tenochtitlán and urged them instead to be content with their gifts and to stay on the coast.

During the long conversations between Tendile and the Castilians, Cortés told of his allegiance to Carlos V of Spain, the great king in whose name he had come to Mexico, and of the Catholic religion that he hoped all Mexico would embrace. Father Olmedo and Cortés's four hundred soldiers paraded with great reverence before the large wooden cross they had raised in their camp. Tendile asked many questions about the new religion and after a great show of friendship withdrew and raced to carry news of all these things to his prince.

One morning several days later the Spaniards awoke to find themselves alone. Tabascan allies no longer came to their camp bringing food or seeking to trade. Soon supplies ran low and the Castilians, cut off from local sources of food, were reduced to a scant diet of fish. From his distant palace Montezuma had received news of the Spanish religion with alarm. If these intruders were messengers from Quetzalcoatl, how could they not worship Mexico's traditional gods? Beset by doubt, Montezuma ordered the Spanish cut off from local towns, hoping that starvation would force them out of his empire.

It had been days since any Tabascans had come to Cortés's camp when sentries reported the approach of five brightly dressed chieftains, caciques of the Totonac tribe. Cortés called Marina and Aguilar and through them learned that the Totonacs were dissatisfied with Montezuma's taxes and constant demands for more tribute and ever-more slaves. In this way Cortés learned that Montezuma's rule was not absolute, and, much encouraged, he decided to move his camp inland to Cempoala, the largest Totonac city. Along the way, the Castilians passed many towns that were deserted as they approached. Everywhere they reacted with dismay to the bloodstained temples that offered clear evidence of the Mexica's practice of human sacrifice. Marina explained the use of sacrifice to Cortés and told him that slaves, captive warriors, and even infants were used. She was surprised that the Spanish, so brave in battle, were horrified by what had seemed an ordinary religious ritual to her.

The Cempoalans, led by a wise chieftain called the "fat cacique," met Cortés and his soldiers in the broad central plaza of their city. Marina was by now accustomed to translating from her permanent spot at Cortés's side. She talked easily with the Cempoalans and translated their long list of complaints against Montezuma in a tone that let Cortés understand their bitterness. At that moment, as if to underscore their complaints, five men strode into the plaza. They were clad in brilliantly colored cloaks; their long, black hair was tied at the crown of their heads; and each carried scarlet flowers in one hand, a crooked staff in the other. The Totonacs fell back from them trembling with fear as the men, Montezuma's tax collectors, scolded them for aiding the Spaniards. As punishment they demanded twenty Totonac men and women for sacrifice.

Cortés was amazed at this spectacle and asked Marina what had happened. She explained that Montezuma wished to enslave the Castilians and had forbidden his subject tribes to aid them. Cortés rose to his feet and in the name of Carlos V of Spain ordered the Totonacs to seize the tax collectors and imprison them. No longer, he said, would his friends the Totonacs pay tribute to Montezuma. His great emperor Carlos V prohibited his people from seizing and sacrificing human beings to Montezuma's false gods. The Totonacs did as Cortés commanded and, frightened by their own act of rebellion, allied themselves more closely with the Castilians, hoping for protection from Montezuma's certain anger.

That same night Cortés secretly freed two of the five tax collectors and with a great show of regret and friendliness claimed that the Totonacs alone were responsible for their imprisonment. He then urged them to go quickly to Montezuma with the warmest expressions of friendship from Cortés. By the time the two escapees reached Tenochtitlán, however, Montezuma had learned of the Totonac rebellion. Preparations were already underway to wage war on the Totonacs and their Castilian allies, but the soothing messages from Cortés aborted these plans. Instead of war, Montezuma sent greetings to Cortés and maintained an attitude of watchfulness. The Totonacs were astonished at this mild response, and Cortés's reputation improved rapidly, attracting many more allies among the towns and cities of both the Totonacs and neighboring tribes.

The Aztec messengers had given the Spanish forces so many gifts of gold and silver, precious gems, and embroidered cloth that Cortés decided to send a ship to Spain laden with an impressive array of gifts for Carlos V. Cortés chose Alonso Hernández de Puertocarrero to be his representative on this mission, and Hernández embarked for Spain during the summer of 1519. However, Cortés refused to send Marina on the voyage. She had become far too valuable to him in her role as interpreter. By this time, too, she had learned Castilian so well that she could talk easily with the Spanish in their own tongue. No one among Cortés's troops understood the indigenous as well as she; no one else could grasp the subtleties of their speech and make them instantly clear. Without her he would have been like a deaf-mute, unable to communicate or understand anything but the grossest gestures and expressions.

LA LENGUA AND THE SPANISH ADVANCE

So Marina remained with the Spanish in Mexico, where her own special position did not go unnoticed by her countrymen. Did not the Spanish, and Cortés himself, call her *la lengua*, as she acted as his own tongue? Did she not act as such and speak for the great Cortés himself? Her prestige was so great that the two of them—Cortés and Marina—came to be called by the same name, "Malinche." As there is no "r" sound in Nahuatl, she was known as "Malina," a corruption of her own Christian name, to which was added the respectful title *-tzin*. Thus given her actions and clear status in the Cortés camp, her fellow Nahua also referred to her as Malintzin. But they also called both the man Cortés and the woman who spoke for him Malinche. In their eyes, they functioned as one person.

Yet Cortés must have had some doubts about Marina. He knew from experience that a disloyal interpreter could cause disaster and even death. Would the allegiance Marina once felt for Montezuma be stronger than her seeming obedience to the Castilians? Would she be able to resist a call to return to her own people? As yet he had no cause to doubt her loyalty, but he still could not trust her totally. Marina herself probably never wondered about these things. Life with her people had been hard and disillusioning. She had been denied her inheritance and passed from one tribe to another, finally to be given to these strange invaders. If anything, she felt fortunate that the Castilians treated her so well. Had they not promoted her from slave girl to Cortés's own translator? Was she not a vital part of this quest for wealth and power, always there when decisions were made and when great caciques came to confer with Cortés? Indeed, there was nothing in her past that could compete with the excitement of life with the Castilians. Very soon, any question Cortés might have had about her loyalty vanished.

The Castilians left Cempoala in August 1519 and began the tortuous journey over the mountains to Tenochtitlán. In battle after battle they subdued each town along the way. Montezuma watched with mounting anxiety as Cortés's few soldiers defeated huge armies of defenders, using tactics undreamed of by even the best Aztec warriors. First Cingapacinga, then Zocotlán, finally Tlaxcala fell under Cortés's rule. How could these teules be stopped and by whom?

Montezuma decided that Cholula would be the place to defeat the Castilians. To that end he sent twenty thousand warriors to the rocky ravines west of the city where an ambush could most effectively be executed. At the same time the caciques of Cholula were ordered to receive the Castilians with every sign of friendship. Within three days of Cortés's arrival, however, signs of the plot began to surface. Two high priests secretly told Marina of the barricades and trenches dug in the city streets in preparation for battle. The Cholulans, at first lavish with food and supplies, soon relaxed their deceptive efforts and mockingly carried only water to the Spanish soldiers. Then one evening an old woman, the wife of a Cholulan chieftain, came clandestinely to Marina to warn her of the danger she was in as long as she stayed with the Spanish. She had taken pity on Marina, so young and pretty, and offered her a safe place in her own home as her son's wife. Marina thanked her warmly and, pretending to accept the offer, arranged to meet her later that night after packing her clothes and gold jewels. But instead of escaping, Marina told Cortés the details of Montezuma's plot just as she had learned them from the old woman.

The next day Cortés summoned all the Cholulan caciques, chieftains, and several thousand of their warriors to the courtyard where the Spanish were camped. Mounted on horseback, with Marina at his side, he told them of the bad treatment he had received from them and described the plot against his life and the lives of his men. Marina translated his words in a loud, clear voice, adding color to his anger by the force of her own. Malinche knew, she said, that priests were already prepared to sacrifice the Castilians, that pots with peppers and tomatoes stood ready to cook them for the post-battle feast. But such treason against Carlos V, King of Spain and Holy Roman Emperor, could not go unpunished. At that moment a musket was fired as a signal to Cortés's soldiers, who, armed with broadswords and some mounted, fell on the men trapped in the courtyard. The slaughter of their best warriors was a blow the Cholulans could not withstand. Soon caciques from towns throughout the province came to pledge their allegiance to Cortés and his Spanish king, and Montezuma's warriors hastily withdrew to Tenochtitlán with word of the disastrous defeat suffered at Cholula.

If Cortés had ever doubted Marina's loyalty, such suspicions never again crossed his mind. Given the chance to escape from the Castilians and to marry the son of a wealthy cacique, she chose instead to remain with Cortés. No further proof of her trustworthiness was required. Cortés and Marina, firmest collaborators in public, soon extended that partnership to their private lives as well. Their union was informal, sanctioned neither by law nor religion, yet common enough in an age when a woman, slave or princess, could be given away as a mere gift to a wealthy or powerful man. From that time until the end of the conquest three years later, Cortés and Marina were inseparable companions, in war as well as peace, in triumph as well as defeat.

After the massacre of his Cholulan subjects, Montezuma realized to his dismay that he could no longer avoid meeting Cortés at his own gates. For two anguished days he consulted with his priestly advisers and finally decided to welcome the Spanish to Tenochtitlán. There, enclosed and surrounded, they could at last be defeated in one giant bloodletting. Confident that this desperate plot would succeed, he ordered all the caciques of the cities of Mexico to prepare for Cortés's arrival.

On the evening of November 7, 1519, his heart heavy with foreboding, Montezuma left his palace and crossed the broad flagstone courtyard to the great temple. He climbed the 114 steps slowly and, as he reached the top, paused to contemplate his beautiful city. What had once been a mud island in the middle of a lake was now a metropolis of sixty thousand families. Flat-roofed, whitewashed houses stretched out around the central plaza with its towering temples and palaces. A system of canals and portable bridges crisscrossed the island, and Montezuma could see hundreds of his people poling their canoes through the canal network, carrying food and merchandise to market. Floating gardens ringed the island and supplied Tenochtitlán with an abundance of flowers of every kind. Farther out Montezuma could see the aqueduct that brought fresh water from Chapúltepec to his capital, and stretched out in front of him were the three long causeways that crossed the shallow lake and connected Tenochtitlán with the shore. The causeways, some twenty feet wide, were broken here and there by canals crossed by portable wooden bridges. The hills rising from the lakeshore were almost barren. Montezuma knew that little food could be grown there, but turning southward he caught a glimpse of the fertile lands of Cuernavaca, where maize and other crops were cultivated. To the south he could see a long caravan of slaves, each carrying fifty pounds of grain on his back, laboring along the road toward the city. Reluctantly, Montezuma turned toward the east. Far away on the crest of a hill he saw the glint of metal weapons and the movement of many figures. These were the invincible Castilians, he thought, the much-feared teules. Tomorrow they would finally meet.

Cortés's soldiers and thousands of his native allies were assembled on the shore when Montezuma, accompanied by a huge escort of caciques and warriors, crossed the causeway to receive them. The Aztec prince was carried under a canopy of green feathers embroidered with gold and silver, pearls, and jadeite. On his feet were gold-soled sandals, their tops encrusted with precious gems of every color; his cloak and loincloth were likewise richly adorned. His subjects, forbidden to raise their eyes before his power, wealth, and magnificence, fell back as he passed.

By contrast, the Castilians looked plain and worn. Cortés's red velvet cap provided one spot of color, but his captains and men were dressed as simple soldiers whose weapons were more valuable to them than all the pearls of the sea. Faced with the prospect of entering that glistening city, the more fainthearted of the Spaniards longed for escape. Cortés fully understood the danger, yet he was determined to lead his men even into the enemy's stronghold. When he spoke with Montezuma, no sign of hesitation or fear could be heard in his voice, and Marina, inspired by his composure, calmly translated for the two leaders.

After the welcoming ceremonies Montezuma arranged for the Castilians to stay in large houses built by his own father during a long and fruitful reign. Inside the central palace was a section of wall that had been freshly plastered. Cortés ordered it secretly opened and on the other side discovered a breathtaking hoard of gold and jewels. He had his men carefully close the wall again in a way that would escape notice by his hosts.

Soon after Cortés was established in Tenochtitlán, an Aztec messenger arrived from the coast with news that Cempoala and tribes in the mountains to the east were in revolt against the Spanish. Only Montezuma could have encouraged so widespread a rebellion. Cortés and his captains decided that for their own protection Montezuma had to be taken hostage and forced to live under the watchful eyes of the Castilians to prevent further treachery.

Cortés, his captains, and Marina went directly to Montezuma's palace. Courteously, Cortés complained to Montezuma about his double-dealing and ordered him to move to the teules quarters. Montezuma was astonished at such a request and refused even to consider it. For more than half an hour the two men argued, until one of Cortés's captains lost his temper and began shouting threats at Montezuma. Startled by the outburst, the Aztec emperor turned to Marina for an explanation. She quickly replied that Cortés's soldiers were angry and would kill him if he didn't go with them at once. Under Cortés's protection, she added, he would be quite safe. Marina's words convinced Montezuma, and from that time on he was Cortés's royal hostage—the Castilians' guarantee of safe passage while in Tenochtitlán.

EMPIRE'S END: THE FALL OF TENOCHTITLÁN

While he lived with the Spanish, Montezuma continued to govern his empire, but as prisoner of Cortés his actions were limited. He continued to receive tribute and visits from his priests and allied caciques, and many Mexica leaders urged him to declare war on the Spanish teules. However, Montezuma realized that an attack on them would cause his own death, and for that reason he betrayed each plot to Cortés. The silent but constant threat against Montezuma's life was balanced by the outward respect and constant flattery he received from Cortés and his men. In this way the prince, formerly a fearless warrior, was robbed of his will and became a pawn of the Spanish.

Early in May 1520, Cortés, Marina, and most of the soldiers departed Tenochtitlán for the coast, leaving Captain Alvarado and a band of soldiers to guard Spanish interests in the capital. Soon after Cortés's departure, Alvarado mistook a religious celebration in a nearby temple for the prelude to an attack on his small force. Frightened by the sound of drums and dancing, Alvarado and his men attacked the unarmed revelers and killed or mutilated many of Tenochtitlán's young noblemen. This cruel error of judgment was more than the Aztecs could bear; had Montezuma not calmed them, massacre of the Castilians would surely have followed. On receiving news of the disaster, Cortés returned at once with an army of thirteen hundred soldiers, some recently arrived from Cuba and others indigenous warriors who had joined the Spaniards following Cortés's victories on the coast. They arrived to find the streets of Tenochtitlán deserted and their quarters under siege.

After two weeks of constant fighting, the situation deteriorated to a once unimaginable end. Led by the Spanish, Montezuma took to the roof to implore his people to cease their attack. A stone from an indigenous man's sling struck his head, and after three days the great Montezuma died, betrayed by his own gods, ruined and alone among his enemies. Cortés ordered the regal body to be laid in the street outside his quarters; it was never again seen by the Spanish.

After Montezuma's death, the Aztecs attacked the besieged Spanish with renewed energy. Their food and water were almost gone. Since neither salt nor oil was left to treat the many wounded, Cortés's soldiers rendered the fat of slain Aztecs and applied it to their open wounds. Their situation had become so desperate that early in July the Spaniards decided to leave the city by night in a daring attempt to save their lives. First to depart were four hundred native warriors allied with the Castilians and one hundred and fifty soldiers who were to guard the all-important causeway bridge. Indigenous porters laden with treasure and guarded by Cortés himself, his captains, and many soldiers, filed out next. At the rear were two captains, thirty soldiers, and three hundred warriors who were to guard Cortés's Mexican prisoners and the few women, including Marina, who traveled with that desperate army.

Almost as soon as the Castilians and their indigenous allies left the center of Tenochtitlán, the attack began. By the time they reached the causeway, Aztec warriors had already surrounded it and, filling the air with their screams and taunts, soon succeeded in destroying the bridge, the vital link to safety. So many soldiers and horses were killed or drowned at that spot that some of the rear guard escaped by walking over bodies that filled the shallow lake. Among them was Marina, who, with another native woman, managed to get away unharmed and was soon reunited with Cortés and the few fortunate survivors of the Noche Triste, the "Sad Night "of Cortés's defeat.

When he saw what was left of his army, Cortés sat under a tree on the shore and wept. His trained force that had grown to thirteen hundred Spaniards and indigenous allies was reduced to four hundred, all of them wounded. Not one horse had escaped unhurt, and some of Cortés's most trusted captains had lost their lives in the terrible confusion of that night. Rather than give up his dream of conquering the Aztecs, Cortés regrouped his small army. With Malinche at his side, within a year he recruited many thousand new indigenous allies and again stood at the gates of Tenochtitlán. By that time the city was already much weaker than it had been on the Noche Triste. Late in May 1521, the aqueduct carrying water from Chapúltepec was cut and the siege began. A force of ten thousand and thirteen small ships or launches were assembled on the lake for the long war against Cuauhtemoc, Montezuma's successor, and the inhabitants of what had once been the most powerful city in all Mexico. Cuauhtemoc and his warriors vowed to fight to the death and fight they did. Cortés and Marina pleaded with them time and time again to save themselves, to stop their resistance, but their words went unheeded.

At last the Castilians understood that only by destroying the city stone by stone and filling in the hundreds of canals would victory be theirs. While the work of destruction proceeded, the launches were used with great effectiveness to prevent food from reaching the starving Mexica, and after two months of siege, Spanish soldiers began finding pieces of chewed bark and roots in the streets. The hunger became so intense that late one night a crowd of eight hundred Aztec women and children were captured when they came out of hiding to search for food. Finally, on August 13, 1521, the starving city fell, and Cortés became captain-general and sole ruler of the Aztecs.

POST-CONQUEST FORTUNES

Cortés turned immediately to the task of rebuilding the city and of governing the kingdom that he and Marina had won for Spain. Sometime in 1522 Marina gave birth to Cortés's son Martín, one of the first Mexicans to be born of Spanish and indigenous parents. Strangely, the birth of little Martín seems to have marked the end of Cortés and Marina's intimate relationship. His great successes caused Cortés to lust after titles of nobility. A Spanish nobleman, Cortés reasoned, could hardly continue living with a native woman, even if she was a princess. In short, Cortés's gentle helper of preconquest days became a serious handicap. Just three months after the fall of Tenochtitlán he sent for his wife, Doña Catalina Suárez de Marcayda, who at his request had remained behind in Cuba until then. In public Marina continued to serve Cortés as his interpreter, and her loyalty to him never wavered. In return Cortés gave her enough land, vassals, and gold to ensure her physical comfort for life.

Reconstruction of the Mexican capital, and with it, the arrival of more Spanish, including priests, marked a definitive break from an Aztec past. European-style buildings soon rose over a foundation of broken idols and temple stones, and broad streets replaced the Aztec canal system.

In 1524, twelve Franciscans arrived in Mexico City, including Fray Toribio Benavente. Known as the "poor one," or Motolinía, Fray Benavente interviewed Malinche, going on to become one of the first chroniclers of the conquest of the Aztecs and its aftermath. By 1536 the priests constructed the first school for the indigenous population, many of whose students were children of slain Aztec nobility. Under the direction of padre Bernardino de Sahagún, the best of these students then created the *Florentine Codex*. This multivolume account of Aztec history included descriptions of preconquest life, first encounters of the Europeans, and the destruction of the Aztec empire. One image in Book Twelve depicts Malinche and Cortés on a palace rooftop. There she looks down and translates for Cortés the words of a Mexica speaker, below.

Cortés dedicated himself as intensely to the government and economy of Mexico as he had to its conquest, but political entanglements hampered his efforts. Once he turned away from Marina, his fortunes changed for the worse. Within a few months of her arrival, his young wife died mysteriously in the night. Their marriage had been strained not only due to his extended absence, but also because Catalina was kin to the governor of Cuba, an archenemy of Cortés, whose direct orders to remain on the island Cortés had disobeyed. Seizing Catalina's death as an opportunity to discredit Cortés, the enemies of the conquistador whispered that he was to blame.

The following year, in October 1524, Cortés led a large force to Honduras to quash a rebellion against his rule. Once again, Marina's services were required—only this time, she had to leave her two-year-old son behind, knowing full well she might never see him again. A more difficult journey could not have been imagined, either for Cortés or for Marina. She was still his primary interpreter and had become a major force in the conversion to Christianity of the native population; her presence was therefore a necessity on the long, dangerous expedition.

For reasons that have never been fully explained, Cortés arranged for Marina to marry Lieutenant Juan Jaramillo, a hero of the siege of Mexico and second-in-command to him on the expedition to Honduras. It is possible, however, that she was involved in her own negotiations for a powerful husband. The marriage took place at Orizaba soon after the party left Mexico City. Marina gave birth to a daughter, María Jaramillo, a year and a half later as the torn remnants of Cortés's army sailed back to Mexico. Marina, Jaramillo, and their daughter lived on a comfortable plot of land that the *cabildo* (town council) deeded to both husband and wife—an unusual step and possible indication of respect for her. Marina, by now a person of wealth and standing in Mexico, did not live long after returning to the city she had worked so hard to win. In 1528, she bade farewell to her six-year-old son; Cortés then took him to Spain to secure a papal blessing and possibly acceptance in the prestigious military Order of Santiago. Marina died not long after her son's departure, perhaps from smallpox or the lasting effects of the dreadful trip to Honduras.[6]

In the Castilian code of values, a native woman, however loyal, intelligent, and beautiful, was of little worth in comparison with the glitter of gold and the attractions of noble Spanish blood. Malinche's short life lasted only about twenty-four years, and her memory was not immediately honored after her death. Though in his writing Hernán Cortés made clear that she had forestalled an unexpected attack on his troops, Cortés only mentioned her twice in his long, narrative letters to Carlos V. In his second letter to the king of Spain, Cortés referred to her merely as "an Indian woman from Putunchán." Her husband, Juan Jaramillo, seemed to forget her so quickly that he remarried a Spanish woman of high status just weeks after her death, and he tried in later years to disinherit their daughter, María.

Yet Malinche did secure safety and material wealth for herself and her children. She ended her days as a respected doña and *encomendera*, according to her daughter, María, able to command labor from her own *altepetl* of Olutla as well as Tetiquipaque. María likely had some grasp of Spanish and Nahuatl when her mother died, but she soon forgot the latter. She received at least a rudimentary education and grew up integrated into the quotidian life of her father's thriving *encomienda* of Xilotepec. At age fifteen, and against her father's wishes, she married don Luis de Quesada of Granada. As a result, she and her husband were virtually cut out of her father's will. She and her husband took Jaramillo's second wife, Beatriz, to court, gathering dozens of witnesses who spoke highly of Doña Marina's contributions to the Spanish cause. After more than two decades, the couple lost their case to Beatriz—but the latter's victory proved hollow; upon her death, her *encomienda* passed to the crown.

Martín, separated from his mother at age six and left in Madrid by his father a year later, was nonetheless provided for, trained to knighthood in the service of Carlos V. Upon his death, Cortés left the bulk of his estate to fifteen-year-old Martín, along with the charge of caring for his legitimate and illegitimate half sisters. In 1562, Martín returned to Mexico with the remains of Cortés; it was his father's wish to be buried there. Martín and María were reunited not long before she died. His enemies charged him with complicity in her death. Absolved of the charge, Martín returned to Spain and his military duties. He later died helping put down a rebellion in Granada.

Sixty years after the conquest, chronicler Bernal Díaz del Castillo noted that Marina did not appear bitter about the twists in her life's journey, beginning with forced separation from her family. He wrote that a few years before her death, during an unexpected meeting with her mother and half brother, she spoke openly of the path her life had taken. Rather than seeking vengeance, she forgave her mother for selling her to the Xicalangos so long ago. No happier fate could be imagined than her own, she had said, adding that she would rather serve her lord and master Cortés and her gentleman husband Jaramillo than be the greatest princess of all Mexico. She did indeed secure safety and material wealth for herself and her children and end her days as a respected doña. According to Díaz del Castillo, it was with humility, without bitterness, that this young indigenous woman viewed her role in the conquest.

EPILOGUE

Perhaps Marina/Malinche/Malintzin's feats seem too incredible to be true. For more than five hundred years, scholars have parsed the historical record in order to better understand her role in the conquest of the Aztec.

Figure 2.1 Lienzo Tlaxcala

In the Lienzo de Tlaxcala, an indigenous pictographic account of conquest, Malinche always appears by the side of Cortés (see figure 2.1). She often looms larger than the male figures around her, including the conquistador. Spanish chroniclers highlighted her clear contribution to the event. Through the postindependence upheavals of the mid-nineteenth century, Mexican scholars reviled her as a traitor; by the turn of the century, "malinchismo" came into vogue as a term indicating a betrayal of native values for foreign ones. However, during the 1980s, Chicana writers, in discerning their own identity, claimed Malinche as their own. To them she served as an agent of conquest, a power broker, and one who acted as a historical strategist. Here was a woman who not only survived childhood trauma but used her skills to secure material well-being for herself and her children. The sixteenth-century Spanish and Nahua accounts, to which scholars will always return, have forever marked her as indispensable, a woman whose achievements remain undiminished by time.

NOTES

1. *Codex Azcatitlan*, Library of Congress and World Digital Library, folio 29/27 at https://www.wdl.org/en/item/15280/.

2. Sandra Messinger Cypess, *La Malinche in Mexican Literature: From History to Myth* (Austin: University of Texas Press, 1991), 142; Camilla Townsend, *Malintzin's Choices: An Indian Woman in the Conquest of Mexico* (Albuquerque: University of New Mexico Press, 2006), 2–4.

3. For an accessible online source for Díaz's narrative, see "Doña Marina, Cortés' Translator: Personal Account, Bernal Díaz del Castillo," in *Women in World History*, Center for History and New Media, http://chnm.gmu.edu/wwh/modules/lesson6/lesson6.php?s=2.

4. Camilla Townsend, *Malintzin's Choices*, 25–27.

5. On her beauty and intelligence, see excerpt of source material: "Dona Marina, Cortés' Translator: Personal Account, Bernal Díaz del Castillo," in *World History Commons*, available at https://worldhistorycommons.org/dona-marina-cortes-translator-personal-account-bernal-diaz-del-castillo. From A. P. Maudsley, trans., *Bernal Díaz del Castillo: The Discovery and Conquest of Mexico, 1517–1521* (1585) (New York: Noonday Press, 1965).

6. On the fate of Malinche's children, see especially Camilla Townsend, "Doña Maria" (chapter 8) and "Don Martín" (chapter 9) of *Malintzin's Choices*.

REFERENCES

Codex Azcatitlan. Library of Congress and World Digital Library, online at https://www.wdl.org/en/item/15280/.

Cortés, Hernán. *Letters from Mexico*. Translated and edited by Anthony Pagden, 72–74. New Haven and London: Yale University Press, 1986.

Cypess, Sandra Messinger. *La Malinche in Mexican Literature: From History to Myth*. Austin: University of Texas Press, 1991.

Díaz del Castillo, Bernal. *The Bernal Díaz Chronicles*. Translated and edited by Albert Idell. New York: Doubleday, 1956.

Diel, Lori Boornazian. *Aztec Codices: What They Tell Us about Daily Life*. Santa Barbara: ABC-CLIO, 2020.

"Doña Marina, Cortés' Translator: Personal Account, Bernal Díaz del Castillo." *Women in World History*, Center for History and New Media, http://chnm.gmu.edu/wwh/modules/lesson6/lesson6.php?s=2.

Godayol, Pilar. "Malintzin/Malinche/Doña Marina: Re-reading the Myth of the Treacherous Translator." *Journal of Iberian and Latin American Studies* 18, no. 1 (April 2012): 61–76.

Maudsley, A. P., trans. *Bernal Díaz del Castillo: The Discovery and Conquest of Mexico, 1517–1521* (1585). New York: Noonday Press, 1965.

Prescott, William H. *History of the Conquest of Mexico and History of the Conquest of Peru*. New York: Random House, 1952.

Rodríguez, Gustavo A. *Doña Marina, monografía histórica*. Mexico City: Imprenta de la Secretaría de Relaciones Exteriores, 1935.

Shedd, Margaret. *Malinche and Cortés*. New York: Doubleday, 1971.

Townsend, Camilla. *Malintzin's Choices: An Indian Woman in the Conquest of Mexico*. Albuquerque: University of New Mexico Press, 2006.

Townsend, Camilla. "Burying the White Gods: New Perspectives on the Conquest of Mexico." *The American Historical Review* 108, no. 3 (June 2003): 659–87.

x

Vaillant, George C. *Aztecs of Mexico: Origin, Rise, and Fall of the Aztec Nation*. Baltimore: Penguin Books, 1966.

Chapter 3

Inés de Suárez, 1507–1572?

INTRODUCTION

One August morning in 1540, a woman rode out from camp deep in the Atacama Desert of northern Chile. She may have sought privacy from her companions, a struggling party of male Spaniards whose provisions had dwindled as they pushed their way south into hostile territory. The woman pulled up in front of an unknown plant. She ate one of its fruits, something that would become known in the Old World as prickly pear. Finding it refreshing, she harvested several and took them back for her companions. Not for the last time, Inés de Suárez had saved the desperate group with her keen sense of observation and her survival skills.

This story, like so much of her life, is shrouded in mystery and myth. How—and why—did a single woman from Extremadura, Spain, end up in the Viceroyalty of Peru and in the camp of the conqueror of Chile, Pedro de Valdivia? What was her role, and why was she revered nearly five hundred years ago but is almost forgotten today? Wife, widow, mistress, conqueror, philanthropist, and heroine, the historical record indicates that Inés de Suárez assumed all of these roles in her long journey from Spain to the southern Chilean frontier.

In her own day, Suárez was in turn respected, vilified, and revered. She crossed the Atlantic in search of her husband only to find she was a widow. In the decades after the fall of Tenochtitlán, European invaders fought desperately in "New Spain's" wars of conquest. Quarter was neither given nor expected in a struggle whose outcome shaped the destiny of two continents. At length the Europeans, with their superior military technology, hammered indigenous peoples they encountered into submission and imposed European social structures upon them.

What emerged was a highly stratified, hierarchical society with theoretical roots extending back to the Roman Empire. The Catholic Church was an institution of fundamental importance in early Spanish America. Another was the *encomienda*, a royal grant of indigenous labor awarded to conquistadores for their service to the crown. Spanish settlers and their children, or creoles as they came to be called, formed a nominally autonomous, landed elite; those of indigenous, African, and mixed descent received less social recognition.

And what was the role of women in this stratified social system? Their place was the home, though few outside the highest aristocracy could afford the luxury of remaining homebodies. The case of Inés de Suárez is illustrative. When faced with the choice of eking out an existence as a proper Spanish widow or seeking adventure and opportunity with Pedro de Valdivia, she unhesitatingly chose the latter. She thus became a protagonist in the drama that earned Valdivia fame and ultimately a ghastly death in the south of Chile. As with many other unconventional women of Latin American history, the least important aspect of her role, as Valdivia's mistress, has been most remembered. But when the story is told objectively, Inés de Suárez stands as high as her consort: Not only was she a chief participant in the conquest of Chile, but she also survived it and went on to become a grand dame of an emerging Hispanic society.

A WIFE'S QUEST

Sixteenth-century travelers who embarked for the New World at Sevilla usually began the voyage with eager expectancy. Behind them lay the old, confining life of Spain; before them, the Americas, a land so recently discovered that its power to arouse hope seemed limitless. Within a day after their ships slipped past the sandbar at the mouth of the Guadalquivir River, the travelers' eagerness and high spirits gave way to a dreadful realization that between Spain and the New World lay a vast purgatory known as the Atlantic crossing. Trapped in small, narrow ships, protected from the ocean's ominous might by tar caulking and a few planks, only the foolhardy failed to ponder their imminent danger.

Seasickness came first, with days and nights of nausea. Men and women too ill to move sprawled on the deck and longed to return to Spain or, better yet, to die at once. By the time seasickness subsided and appetites returned, the supply of fruit and vegetables was spoiled, and passengers resigned themselves to a diet of salted meat and weevil-infested biscuits, made even less palatable by the scarcity of water. During hot summer months the heat and stench from below drove passengers above deck, where they and their lice and fleas roasted in the merciless sun. Time passed slowly; gambling, conversation, and even prayer did little to fill the long days. In addition to the physical discomforts, there was always fear—fear of storms, of being becalmed, of pirates. Not all survived the hardship of crossing. Those who died, defrauded of their hopes, were buried at sea, to rest forever in the salty depths of the Atlantic.

Inés de Suárez was, among those who successfully crossed in 1537, one of the few women—women made up less than 10 percent of all travelers—making the journey that year. When she glimpsed the coast of the New World for the first time, Inés was thirty years old. Had she been a man, she would have been considered to be in the prime of life. But a woman of thirty was thought old, past marriageable age, and usually worn by childbearing. By chance Inés de Suárez, although married for a number of years, had borne no children, and she retained the energy that might have been expended in more traditional ways. Free from ties at home, she left Spain in search of her husband, said to be living somewhere in the Viceroyalty of Peru.

In 1530, Charles V had issued a *cédula real*, or royal decree, stating married men could not depart for the West Indies without their wives. Also, wives were not allowed to join their husbands without proof that they had been summoned by them. Suárez's husband likely defied these instructions by joining the Pizarro brothers' Peruvian expedition in New Spain and subsequently joining in their conquest of Peru.

Inés de Suárez was not deterred by social norms of the day. In 1536 she traveled to Cadiz and formally filed for permission to emigrate, claiming she was in search of her husband. Upon producing witnesses who testified that she was of "pure" blood, neither of Jewish nor Muslim descent, she was granted permission to board a ship departing Spain for the New World. The fleet that carried Inés anchored first in the Gulf of Paria, lying between Venezuela and the island of Trinidad. Undaunted by the steamy heat of that northeastern coast of South America, she gazed at the low coastlines to the east and west and by night looked in wonder at the flecks of light sparkling in the gently swelling water. She may have first thought those millions of minute lights were stars reflected in the dark waters. But she soon understood that tiny phosphorescent sea plants were responsible for the strange effect. If these bejeweled waters were any indication, then the New World would prove more bizarre, more wonderful than she had dreamed possible.

Inés de Suárez found no trace of her husband in Venezuela, only vague rumors that he had gone to Peru. She decided to follow him there. In Venezuela she had learned much about Peru, about its rich mines, fertile land, and dense population of indigenous peoples busy paying tribute to the conquering Spaniards. Peru was a powerful magnet that drew adventurers from Mexico, the Caribbean islands, and Panama, not to mention Spain itself. In 1538 Inés joined that hardy procession, traveling by ship to Panama, then by foot or horseback across the isthmus to the Pacific, first seen by Europeans only twenty-five years before. There she again boarded ship, a crude vessel constructed in Panama or Nicaragua, and at last reached Peru.

A deep uneasiness pervaded Lima when Inés de Suárez arrived. Only two years earlier the Spanish had narrowly escaped defeat when Manco Inca Yupanqui besieged Cusco and trapped Francisco Pizarro in Lima. Then, in the spring of 1538, war again broke out, not between Spanish and Inca but between the forces of Francisco Pizarro and those of Diego de Almagro, partners in conquest turned into enemies by greed and mistrust. Almagro suffered defeat, and in July Hernando Pizarro ordered him garroted in a Cusco dungeon. Hundreds of Almagro supporters still roamed the Peruvian highlands spoiling for renewal of the conflict.

As a recent arrival and a woman, Inés de Suárez was not expected to take sides in such struggles. That was her only advantage, for her position in an armed camp placed her honor, if not her life, in constant jeopardy. Although many men treated her respectfully, others may have assumed she was easy prey. To them her answer would be "no," a "no" accompanied by the glint of a polished steel dagger and, if need be, by a timely call for help. Inés was not flattered by less-than-honorable attentions; she had not come to the New World to indulge some rowdy soldier's lust. As a married woman descended from a family of some standing in her native Plasencia, her sights were set high. Like other Spaniards from Extremadura province, Francisco Pizarro himself among them, who came to win wealth and glory through conquest, Inés hoped to have a share in the riches of Peru. She hoped to find her husband well established, perhaps already an *encomendero*, one who commanded local labor and land, or a respected captain of Pizarro, a leader of men. The men who approached her were brushed aside like minor irritants as she looked ahead to far better things.

In Lima, Inés learned that her husband had last been heard of in Cusco, where he had perhaps helped defend that large, wealthy city first from Manco Inca's warriors and then from Almagro's forces. Understanding that she would not find peace until she found him, Inés decided to travel the six hundred miles to the Incan capital. Sometime in 1539 she reached that high, mountain-ringed city and discovered that she was a widow. Her husband had died after the siege of Cusco, and all Inés had to show for her months of travel was confirmation of her widowhood.

The *cabildo*, or town council, of Cusco recognized the services of Inés's dead husband by awarding her a small dwelling and a few *encomienda* laborers to provide a modest income. This was hardly the fortune she desired, but Inés was confident that she could soon improve her position. Ambitious and highly practical, she displayed an independence of spirit that few could equal. Eager for hard work, even the manual sort so despised by Spanish hidalgos, or aristocrats, Inés was spurred into action by her bad luck and disappointment. She settled into her new home with some pleasure, for she relished the chance to set up a kitchen of her own and to raise a few chickens and sheep, perhaps a pair of goats and pigs. For the first time in two years, she enjoyed wholesome, carefully prepared food. She established herself as a nurse and soon found great demand for her services. Cusco was almost bereft of European-style medical care, and while native medicines and indigenous women skilled in their application were available, the Spanish mistrusted them and tended to label their cures as witchcraft. Inés trained her servants, or *yanaconas*, to help her. She also had them baptized and saw to it that they attended Mass regularly. Doña Inés soon had a thriving business dispensing first aid and, if all else failed, consolation to the ill and dying.

Although her life had improved since the days of hard travel, Inés was still vulnerable. A woman who hoped to be reunited with her husband could defend herself in his name, but a widow had only her own strength, moral and physical, to protect her. The little dagger continued to be her faithful companion. She kept it polished and wore it conspicuously at her waist to discourage men who understood violence far better than pleas of the defenseless. Inés was able to convince most suitors of her lack of interest. Others she simply avoided by never going out alone during the day and staying at home after dark. But among the multitude of adventurers who roamed Cusco was a certain Fernán Núñez, who was not so easily put off. Although she rebuffed him at every opportunity, he refused to admit defeat. Late one night, when most people were already in bed, windows securely shuttered against the cold mountain air, Núñez and a pair of servants approached Inés's little house. They banged on the door and she, accustomed to late-night visitors in search of first aid, moved sleepily to open it. By the time she realized who waited in the shadowy street, it was too late. The three men barged through the door, slamming it shut behind them. While Núñez watched, his lackeys seized Inés and tried to overpower her. Defending herself with fingernails and teeth, she struggled against their superior strength.

Soon her cries were heard and the door flew open a second time. There in the doorway stood an elegantly dressed man of military bearing who glanced around the room and barked a command to his companions outside. The odds suddenly reversed. Núñez's henchmen released Inés and retreated awkwardly through the gathering crowd. Despite her rage and panic, Inés recognized her rescuer. He was Pedro de Valdivia, Pizarro's famous lieutenant, hero of the recent battle against Almagro's forces. Valdivia, for his part, turned on Núñez and promised that he would pay with his life should he so much as look at Señora de Suárez again.

By all accounts, Inés Suárez was a beautiful woman, and Valdivia a soldier in his prime. They began keeping company, their initial attraction strengthened by respect. Inés, like Valdivia, was descended from a noble family of rural Spain. And like Valdivia, she possessed courage and independence of spirit. Inés and Valdivia were well matched, and it was only a matter of time before their relationship became an intimate one.

Only one problem disturbed the liaison of Inés de Suárez and Pedro de Valdivia—Valdivia was married, eternally bound by holy sacrament to Marina Ortiz de Gaete, whom he had left behind in Spain almost five years before. His marriage, like that of Inés, was childless. Although he stayed in touch with his wife and sent her money, Valdivia was not eager to send for her, and she was justifiably reluctant to leave home for the dangers and uncertainties of the New World.

Pedro and Inés were in a difficult position. Had Valdivia been free, they would probably have married. Since he was not, they decided to ignore the inflexible rules governing such matters, although it meant Inés's reputation would suffer irreparable damage. They hoped that somehow Valdivia's constancy and protection would shield her from unpleasantness, for he was without doubt one of the richest men in Cusco. So valuable had been his support of Francisco Pizarro in the mortal struggle with Almagro that only a few months earlier Pizarro gave him the right to exploit the entire Canela Valley, its indigenous population, and the Porco mines as a reward. The estate was more than enough to make three men rich, and it rivaled Pizarro's own holdings in wealth. The income Valdivia could expect to earn from his *encomienda* amounted to almost half a million pesos a year, perhaps more.

A few months as landowner and overlord were sufficient to convince Pedro and Inés that luxurious monotony was no less boring than the penurious monotony both had experienced in Spain. Valdivia protested that he had not come to the New World to fight for a mere five years and then hang up his sword and retire. Surely that great continent had room for one more conquistador of the stature of Hernán Cortés or Francisco Pizarro. Never did Valdivia doubt that by conquering new lands he could join that select company. And if the fire of conquest raged unchecked in Valdivia's veins, Inés was equally alert to the call of adventure. Both were ambitious on a grand scale. At last, their attention settled on the untamed lands to the south: Chile.

TOWARD THE STRAITS OF MAGELLAN: SOUTHWARD TREK AND STRUGGLES

When Francisco Pizarro learned that Valdivia wanted to lead an expedition to Chile, he was dumbfounded. It was impossible to understand why Valdivia should abandon holdings equal to Pizarro's own and devote himself to so risky an undertaking. Several years earlier Diego de Almagro, with ample money and five hundred men, had tried and failed to conquer Chile. The native population, the Reche-Mapuche, or Araucanians as they were then called by the Spanish, had taken courage from Almagro's failure and was not likely to submit easily to a second expeditionary force.[1] For these and other reasons, Chile was the least promising of all the regions to be claimed for the glory of King Carlos V.

In April of 1539 Pizarro was at last persuaded to let Valdivia attempt the conquest of lands lying between the Copiapó River and the Straits of Magellan. With the grant came a series of problems that Valdivia later described in a letter to the king:

> When the Marquis Don Francisco Pizarro gave me this undertaking, there was no one willing to come to [Chile], and those who were most reluctant were those who accompanied Commander Don Diego de Almagro. Once they abandoned [Chile] it became so infamous that they avoided it like the plague; and even many people who thought well of me, and who were taken to be sane, began to doubt my sanity when they saw me spend my income on an undertaking so far from Peru.[2]

But Valdivia seemed to take courage from adversity. He was unruffled by the reluctance of investors to take a chance on the venture, and he was unconcerned that scarcely seven soldiers agreed to depart Cusco with him in January 1540. He believed that more soldiers, drawn especially from the defeated Almagro faction, would join him as the expedition moved south.

Inés was likely not so confident. Indeed, for a time she feared she might be left behind altogether. As the only European woman and, it was whispered, his mistress, she was the object of increasing gossip. In order to silence the malicious rumors, Valdivia asked Francisco Pizarro to grant her a license to accompany the expedition as a *criada*, a domestic servant and nurse, who would oversee the indigenous carriers and manage Valdivia's domestic affairs. Inés would go not as Valdivia's favorite but in an official capacity, as a legitimate and indispensable member of the expedition. This Pizarro granted, clearing the way for Inés's next long journey.

A few months before their departure, an obstacle far more serious than any other appeared in the person of Pedro Sancho de la Hoz. An untrustworthy character, a former secretary to Francisco Pizarro in the early years of conquest, Sancho de la Hoz returned from a trip to Spain with a document from Charles V purportedly giving him the right to conquer Chile. Although Pizarro had never learned to read, he soon discovered that the king had given de la Hoz permission to make an exploratory expedition by sea down the coast of Chile as well as certain rights to territory south of the Straits of Magellan. There was no legal conflict between Valdivia's commission and that of de la Hoz. But Pizarro feared that Spanish supporters of Sancho de la Hoz might cause trouble at court if his unfounded claims to a piece of Valdivia's expedition were not respected. Therefore, on December 28, 1539, Pizarro called both men to his house, where they signed a binding agreement. Valdivia would lead the expedition to Chile as already planned, and de la Hoz would become a partner in the undertaking by providing within four months a number of horses and two shiploads of equipment. Valdivia lost no sleep over the contract, but Inés likely worried about de la Hoz, whose opportunistic character was all too clear.

There was little time even for worry in the last days before leaving Cusco. A thousand indigenous *yanaconas* were assembled to carry supplies for the pitifully small force, for neither Spanish soldiers nor their precious horses could be expected to carry baggage. Inés saw to it that chickens, goats, and pigs were gathered for the journey, that seeds and grain were packed, and that food and remedies were in good supply. After all, the expedition was not merely one of conquest but one of settlement. Valdivia and Inés hoped to build a kingdom, establish cities, and attract Europeans to populate the countryside. Nor were wealth and conquest the only elements in their ambition. Settlement on a grand scale came first. The seeds and livestock were almost as important as swords and guns, for the former would feed settlers and their descendants long after arms had become unnecessary.

Valdivia was correct in his belief that Almagro's discredited supporters would join him. Understanding that they would never be welcome in Pizarro's Peru, the *almagristas* were obliged to seek their fortunes in Chile, under Valdivia's command. In the first days a number of men joined the group, each with his own servants and supplies. But by April 1540, after four months on the road, Valdivia's expedition had grown to twenty men. Further progress was impossible without reinforcements, so the expedition halted in Tarapacá in the hope that more men would join them.

At last the long-awaited soldiers arrived: first a group of sixteen, then a force of seventy men loosely organized under Francisco de Villagra. The new arrivals transformed Valdivia's expedition. They swelled his forces to more than one hundred armed men, each of whom had invested his money and his future in the undertaking. None of them had received monies from Pizarro or the government of Charles V, for whose glory the expedition was undertaken. Each soldier was an independent adventurer who paid his own way and who hoped by his daring to win *qué comer*, or "something to eat," and, by implication, wealth. The desired reward was tribute: tribute paid by indigenous peoples whose land produced abundant food and livestock, whose mines glittered with gold and silver, and whose labor would yield easy wealth for each *encomendero* and his descendants.

In May 1540 Valdivia and his expedition left Tarapacá and started the dreaded desert crossing. Between Bolivia and the Copiapó Valley lay the Atacama Desert, a seemingly endless stretch of sand and pebbles along Chile's northern coast. The region was virtually uninhabitable. Scorched by a blazing sun during the day and chilled by the night's cold, the expedition traveled four painful leagues a day. Grumbling was common among those free-spirited soldiers. On one occasion Inés warned Valdivia that a young soldier named Escobar was making trouble for his captain Juan Guzmán. Fearing rebellion, Valdivia made an example of Escobar, hanging him for disobedience. Pleas for clemency were ignored. The rope was placed around the terrified Spaniard's neck and then pulled taut. His body rose into the air, his face turned purple, eyes bulged. Then, as the last shuddering breath escaped the man's throat, the rope snapped and he fell gasping to the ground. Saved by the grace of God, Escobar was freed immediately and ordered to Spain, where he spent his remaining years as a monk. Idle complaints and hints of revolt were for a time effectively silenced.

Early in June the expedition stopped two days north of Atacama la Chica. Leaving chief of staff Pero Gómez in charge, Valdivia and ten soldiers continued on to Atacama la Grande to secure supplies for the expedition. There Valdivia met Francisco de Aguirre, Rodrigo de Quiroga, and some twenty-three men who had been awaiting the expedition for two months.

While Valdivia was away from camp, another addition, much less welcome, joined the expedition. Late at night intruders entered the tent Inés shared with Valdivia. Frightened, Inés de Suárez demanded they identify themselves. By that time, the guard was alerted and came to the tent bearing lights. The intruder was Pedro Sancho de la Hoz. Given the sinister way that Valdivia's long-awaited partner had chosen to arrive, Inés was suspicious, especially when she noticed de la Hoz and his men carried daggers in their boot tops. But Inés let the matter drop. She sent for Valdivia and ordered supper for the men to keep them in camp pending Valdivia's arrival.

The next morning the expedition moved on. Sancho de la Hoz soon confirmed Inés's suspicions of the night before. Seeking out the most dissatisfied members of the expedition, he claimed to be its true leader and promised land, native labor, and special rewards should the men switch their allegiance to him. Revolt was squelched only when Valdivia and the new reinforcements arrived the next day. Valdivia followed Inés's lead and, hiding his true feelings, greeted de la Hoz cordially. But as soon as the expedition arrived in Atacama la Grande, he had de la Hoz and his accomplices jailed. The truth behind their midnight arrival—for they had plotted to murder Valdivia as he slept—was soon revealed. A gallows was built in the main square. Still, Valdivia had little desire to hang a man whose friends at court might cause him trouble. For that reason, he banished three of the plotters to Peru and allowed de la Hoz and another of his men to remain with the expedition. De la Hoz was kept under guard until August 1540, when he signed documents releasing Valdivia from their partnership and renouncing his claim to the territory of Chile. Sancho de la Hoz continued with the expedition, no longer enjoying any claim to partnership in it.

After the expedition left Atacama la Grande, the travelers experienced the desert in all its intensity. What little food was normally to be found there had been hidden or destroyed by indigenous people hoping to discourage the Spanish from continuing south. Supplies ran low, threatening the expedition with slow death. Inés discovered that certain parts of the desert produced tuna, or prickly pear. For a while the fruit slaked their thirst. But then it grew scarce. Finally, one night after camp was set up, Mass had to be suspended because the faithful could not croak out the necessary responses. Suddenly Inés ordered several *yanaconas* to dig in the dry desert sand at her feet. Several feet down, the sand turned darker and heavier. A few more feet and hoarse cheers rose from the ragged crowd. Pure, cool water bubbled from the sand. By some incredible coincidence, perhaps by a miracle, Inés de Suárez had found a freshwater spring deep in the Atacama Desert. And not a small one, either, but the source of enough water to satisfy the *yanacona* porters, soldiers, horses, and even the livestock. The spring was called Jagüey Inés, Inés's Pool, and it saved Valdivia's expedition from miserable defeat.

Progress was marked by skirmishes with local warriors. Once the desert was behind them, indigenous attacks became more frequent, and the Spanish were forced to remain on guard as they moved through the northernmost reaches of the lands they would soon conquer. Confronted by bands of warriors at narrow passes, fighting pitched battles every time a detachment scouted territory ahead, harassed by ambushes, the Spaniards could proceed only because of their horses and the immense superiority of their arms and armor. As they approached the Mapocho Valley, Valdivia realized that the time had come to found a settlement. After eleven months of deprivation and ongoing encounters with hostile indigenous tribes, his exhausted forces clamored for the *qué comer*, the rewards they had come so far to win.

SETTLEMENT AND SAVAGERY: THE BATTLE OF SANTIAGO

The valley of the Mapocho River was ideal for their needs. It boasted rich soil, a large indigenous population, and a system of irrigation constructed by the Picunche tribe to carry water from the Mapocho River to fields up and down the valley. Fresh from spring rains, with crops coaxed into extravagant growth by the warm December sun, the valley offered blessed relief to the homeless, exhausted Spaniards. Their new city, Santiago del Nuevo Extremadura, was founded on February 12, 1541, between two forks of the Mapocho River. The one-eyed soldier Pedro de Gamboa, Chile's first surveyor, laid out the city according to Charles V's instructions. A plaza was staked out first, and streets extended from it at right angles in a grid pattern. Each of the 126 blocks was a perfect square, 350 feet on a side, divided into four corner lots. It was to be many years before the five hundred original lots were occupied.

The Picunches, hiding their distrust of the handful of foreigners, worked with them to build the new city. Wood-frame houses with straw roofs rose quickly on street corners. Around the plaza foundations for more ambitious structures were laid: a cathedral on the east side; government buildings and a jail north and south, and the residences of Valdivia and his officers on the west side of the central plaza. Important buildings were constructed of stone and adobe and furnished with chairs, tables, and cots of rough-hewn wood.

While Santiago was still little more than a military camp, Valdivia appointed a town council, Chile's first *cabildo*. By setting up that municipal body, he showed that he hoped over time to share his own absolute power. Still, Santiago's first *cabildo* possessed little true authority. Its subservience to Valdivia was obvious to everyone and seemed proper to most. Those who needed some action taken on their behalf knew they must persuade Valdivia before sending their requests on to the *cabildo*. And the requests were many. In Santiago's first decade, no matter was too trifling to escape attention. Even prices were fixed, so demand for goods and services, food, horseshoes, tailoring, and the like would not produce inflation. True, Valdivia could not satisfy everyone. Those hoping to curry favor soon learned it was best to approach him through his most trusted adviser, Inés de Suárez.

Inés became adept at reading the pulse of the colony. She was in close touch with the *yanaconas*, with the men whose wounds and illnesses she treated, and, above all, with Pedro de Valdivia and his goals for leading the colony. Valdivia trusted her judgment and her common sense, and he considered her opinions on many matters. She, in turn, relished her role as go-between. When petitioners turned to her for help in winning Valdivia's favor, she would set up an informal meeting with him following dinner. Sometimes, if the night air was cool, Valdivia and Inés would retreat to the comfort of their bedroom while their guests, perched on chairs around the bed, pressed Valdivia for support. Successful petitioners often expressed their gratitude by giving Inés gifts. Although she felt her actions benefited the colony as a whole, there were those who resented her influence.

From the first, Valdivia was eager to find favor for his infant colony at the distant court of Charles V. Of course, nothing ensured a colony's favor at court as much as gold. Fertility of soil, a comfortable climate, and abundant livestock meant nothing to the king. What he desperately needed was money, gold and silver, to carry out his military campaigns throughout Europe. Valdivia understood this, and as a loyal servant of the king he sought to satisfy that need. After a series of military successes in the Aconcagua Valley, the Spanish learned the location of the Marga-Marga gold mines, the same mines that had yielded up tribute for the Inca long before the Spaniards had arrived. Under the direction of two mining experts who commanded a labor force of twelve hundred indigenous men, a modest quantity of gold began flowing from the mines. Not far from Marga-Marga, on the beach of Concón, shipbuilders started work on a vessel needed to transport the king's share of Chile's wealth to the viceregal capital of Lima.

Happiness caused by discovery of the mines and construction of the first ship was short-lived. In August 1541 an indigenous attack reduced the ship to blackened, smoking timbers and took the lives of thirteen Spaniards and numerous native mine workers. Just one Spaniard and an African slave escaped the slaughter. The attack was a warning of things to come. Michimalonco, a cacique of the Aconcagua Valley, assembled a large force of warriors in the Mapocho Valley and waited for the proper moment to attack. The attack came soon. In early September Valdivia, accompanied by close to ninety horsemen, departed Santiago to subdue tribes south of the settlement. Alonso de Monroy, thirty-two horsemen, fewer than twenty infantrymen, numerous *yanaconas*, and Inés de Suárez remained behind to guard Chile's capital.

Before dawn on September 11, the city was awakened by the desperate cries of sentries. As many as ten thousand enemy warriors crept up on all sides, hoping to slaughter the foreigners as they slept. The Spaniards and loyal *yanaconas* resisted their human wave attacks throughout the day. The besieged, most of them wounded, thirsty, and fatigued, fought on desperately. Inés and her servants moved among the defenders with food, water, and first aid, for men and horses alike. Inés watched with mounting concern as the vastly outnumbered defenders were driven back toward the central plaza. As the sun sank in the sky, native warriors torched the wood and straw houses of Santiago, in the process incinerating stores of food, furnishings, and livestock. Inés surveyed the situation. Two Spanish soldiers and hundreds of *yanaconas* lay dead. Almost no one, not even Pedro Sancho de la Hoz, who had fought with the rest, had escaped injury. Of the outstanding fighters, Alonso de Monroy, Francisco de Aguirre, and Rodrigo de Quiroga were seriously wounded. Overwhelming exhaustion sapped the defenders' strength.

In the center of the plaza seven caciques observed the fighting from a makeshift jail. It was they who inspired Inés de Suárez to take dramatic, gruesome action, as illustrated in figure 3. The enemy chieftains had been captured several days earlier and kept alive as potential bargaining chips in the event Santiago was attacked. As the fighting intensified, Inés ran to Alonso de Monroy and proposed a plan. All seven prisoners should be decapitated, their heads tossed at the attacking forces; the defenders would follow that with one last cavalry charge. Monroy opposed the plan, arguing that the hostages represented the only hope for bargaining with Michimalonco. Other officers, too, opposed Inés's plan. But given the desperate nature of their situation and dwindling likelihood that any of them would remain alive long enough to bargain, Inés took action. As daylight faded and red flames of Santiago's burning houses flickered against the sky, she entered the stockade and, shouting over the war cries of the attackers, ordered the guards to behead all seven imprisoned chiefs. Seeing that no one was willing to start the grisly work, she took up a sword and with strength born of necessity beheaded the first captive.[3] Other Spaniards joined in the butchery, and the sodden heads soon hurtled through the air, thudding at the very feet of the attackers. Those who were able, Inés among them, mounted horses and rode out in a final desperate attack.

The plan succeeded. Michimalonco's warriors retreated in confusion. Four days later, when Valdivia returned to Santiago, he found nothing but cinders and ashes where his capital had stood. The few houses that had escaped the flames were hospitals where wounded horses were nursed as lovingly as men. Valdivia looked on mutely as Inés de Suárez showed him what remained of their livestock and seed: two young sows and a boar, a hen and a rooster that Inés herself had saved, and two handfuls of wheat. All their tools, clothing, food supplies, and seed stored carefully for sowing were destroyed. They had only the clothes they wore and the arms they carried to protect them from the elements and further attacks.

Over the next two years, Santiago was little more than an armed camp. Bands of soldiers patrolled the surrounding countryside guarding against attack. Adobe houses rose over the ashes, and Valdivia started the construction of a thick adobe wall that soon formed a fortress four hundred feet square in the center of the city. Much of the work was done by the long-suffering *yanaconas*: they were, said Valdivia, "our very life." They planted wheat but the colonists survived at first on meals based on a variety of oat that grew wild in the valley. It was rumored that some hungry Spaniards quelled their hunger by eating cicadas. Most, however, remained content with the coarsely milled local grains. By early 1542 Valdivia knew he must travel to Peru for needed supplies and reinforcements. Calling on the citizens of Santiago to contribute their wealth to the common good, Valdivia was able to send Alonso de Monroy and five others on the long and dangerous journey. With them went the best horses, a quantity of gold, and the hopes of the entire colony. They were neither seen nor heard from for nearly two years.

Figure 3.1 Inés de Suárez (Chilean National History Museum)

REBUILDING SANTIAGO

During those long months of isolation and constant vigilance, Santiago was gradually knit together. Under Inés's husbandry the livestock reproduced almost miraculously so that four years later Valdivia bragged of ten thousand pigs and chickens as numerous as blades of grass. The fertile soil of the valley produced more wheat than anyone had dared expect and, although most of December's crop was saved for seed, by winter Santiago had bread once again. But many commodities could not be produced in the valley, even by that resourceful band. Mass had to be suspended for lack of wine. Clothing was of the most elementary sort, made of rags and animal skins, and Inés, Valdivia, and the others suffered almost as much from the lack of decent clothing as they did from hunger. Although some possessed silver and gold, little could be bought to satisfy the colonists' desire for a touch of luxury to alleviate the grinding labor and constant dangers of their lives.

Early in the year after Santiago's destruction, Valdivia and the *cabildo* started the process of *repartimiento*: assigning groups of indigenous men and women to members of the expedition. These native peoples were from the relatively small region they had conquered. It was Valdivia who decided which members of the expedition were most deserving of reward, and he had a tendency to favor his most trusted officers and friends, Inés among them, with *encomiendas,* or grants of indigenous workers, around Santiago. Although the Spanish now considered themselves lords of the land and its native peoples, the grim reality of their position remained unchanged. They lived in a besieged outpost in central Chile, far from help, surrounded by native peoples who preferred death in battle to lives of servitude to the foreign invaders.

At last, in September 1543, a ship arrived from Peru loaded with iron goods, military supplies, and, most important, fine cloth. It brought news as well—news of the new governor of Peru, Vaca de Castro, and of Alonso de Monroy's incredible journey in search of help for the suffering colonists. Lines of supply were at last opened between Chile and Peru. Father Rodrigo González said Mass for the first time in four months, and tailors worked into the night to satisfy the demand for fine new clothes. In December a total of seventy men led by Monroy began to arrive in small groups, intimidating indigenous divisions camped close to Santiago and driving them several leagues from the city.

Peace, a new experience for the citizens of Santiago, settled upon the city. Life was still not what it was in most other settlements of the Viceroyalty of Peru. Only one Spanish woman resided there, though many men had started mestizo families with their *yanacona* mistresses. In fact, not one marriage between a Spanish man and woman had yet taken place in Chile, nor had a properly married couple yet established a household there. Nevertheless, with the urgent problems of food and security solved for the moment, the city turned to secondary pursuits. In Inés's case it was a pursuit of knowledge. She was by turns teacher and student, teaching the catechism and Spanish customs to the *yanaconas* and daughters of local caciques, and in less busy moments learning to read and write under the instruction of Father Rodrigo González.

For the first time in many years, Inés and Valdivia indulged their taste for elegant clothing, cut from bolts of expensive cloth brought by sea from Peru. Inés replaced her worn, patched skirts and plain shawl with dresses of rich fabrics embroidered with gold and silver threads. Her sleeves hung in perfect folds from the shoulder, and a multicolored shawl of the lightest wool protected against the chill. Touches of white lace graced her throat, and on Sundays her high headdress was draped with a delicate mantilla. Valdivia was not to be outdone. When not arrayed in armor of burnished steel, he dressed impeccably in rich velvet doublet and knee breeches, a long, heavy cloak, and polished boots of the softest leather. A high lace ruff, starched to a martial stiffness, pressed up against his chin. He kept his hair short but, as if to compensate for its severity, carefully cultivated his narrow goatee and a luxurious moustache that curled up at each end. To celebrate their new plumage, Inés and Valdivia encouraged a festive spirit among the citizens of Santiago by appearing at public fiestas, entertaining friends, and attending musical events with some frequency. Those who wondered at times whether Inés's place in Valdivia's affections was less secure than before only had to witness the mutual sympathy they shared.

During those years the energies of the colony were absorbed in military expeditions to the south and settlement in the north. Valdivia and his lieutenants were confident of success in their plans for expansion. Familiar with the conquests of Mexico and Peru, they expected the native peoples of Chile to resist for a time, perhaps even several years, and then surrender to the Spaniards' superior military strength. This was, in fact, the case in the regions already settled by them. Even the indefatigable Michimalonco and his Picunche warriors saw the futility of further resistance and allied themselves with the Spaniards.

But far to the south, between the Itata and Tolten Rivers, lived the Reche-Mapuche, or Araucanians, as the Spaniards called them. They were a ferocious people, as unyielding as the Carib and the Apache of North America. Relatively recent arrivals themselves, possibly immigrants from the pampas of Argentina, the Reche-Mapuche carved out a territory between the Picunche lands to the north and those of the Huilliches far to the south. Not until February 1546 did Valdivia and sixty heavily armed horsemen first engage the Reche-Mapuche. Although they routed the enemy twice in two days, the

Spanish prudently departed the region under cover of night, leaving blazing campfires to hide their retreat. This incident was the first skirmish in a long series of wars to be waged by ten successive generations of the Araucanian enemy over a span of three hundred years. The intensity of that war, and its long duration, made them nearly unique in the history of European attempts to conquer indigenous Americans. Unfortunately for Valdivia, he did not take full measure of the Reche-Mapuche of southern Chile. He underestimated their intelligence and fighting ability and paid for it with his life.

At length Valdivia decided to take action on mounting complaints about the *repartimientos* that had taken place four years earlier. He agreed that there were too many *encomenderos* and too few native workers to make settler holdings profitable. He pondered the matter for three weeks, consulting with Jerónimo de Alderete and Inés de Suárez. At length Valdivia reduced the number of *repartimientos* from sixty to thirty-two, preserving intact the rights of his advisers and intimates alike, and in several cases markedly improving them. He knew the dispossessed *encomenderos* would be irate. Still, he found their bitter complaints tiring. It was his colony, after all, and he had tried to act in everyone's best interests. Those who lost out this time would receive rich *encomiendas* in the well-populated but yet unsettled south. But the dispossessed *encomenderos* rejected Valdivia's rosy promise of abundant land and labor there and continued to demand restitution of their original grants of indigenous labor. Valdivia threatened to hang them if they didn't desist.

If his handling of the *repartimientos* did little to endear Valdivia to the citizens of Santiago, his bizarre actions of December 1547 made him even less popular. Late that year he decided to aid the viceroy in strife-torn Peru and to lobby for the governorship of Chile. But Valdivia could not afford to underwrite the voyage himself, and the colonists would never have donated the large sums he needed. Finally, he announced that Jerónimo de Alderete would sail to Spain by way of Peru in order to represent Chilean interests at the court of Charles V. Valdivia then told the citizens of Santiago that for the first time, anyone wishing to leave Chile could do so. Sixteen men made plans to sail with Alderete, some hoping to buy goods in Peru for profitable resale in Chile, others expecting to sail home to Spain. They liquidated their holdings in order to collect as much gold and money as possible from business partners and friends.

On December 6, after their possessions were loaded aboard the ship anchored in Valparaiso harbor, the men returned to shore for a banquet hosted by Pedro de Valdivia. During a long address, Valdivia wished them all well and with misty eyes reminded them of the years of sacrifice and hardship they had shared. He hoped they would speak well of him wherever they went and asked each of them to declare before the notary there present how much money he was carrying so that an account of Chile's wealth could be kept. Warmed by Valdivia's kind words and the meal they had just eaten, the prospective travelers gathered around the notary as Valdivia moved casually toward a rowboat that waited on the beach. When their captain leapt into the boat, the men suddenly understood that Valdivia intended to take the ship and their money to Peru, leaving them behind homeless and destitute. A few of the victims jumped in the water and tried to swim after the rowboat but were clubbed when they got near. The rest simply shouted curses at the receding boat.

DAYS OF RECKONING

Valdivia left Francisco de Villagra in charge of the colony as its lieutenant governor. Both men feared trouble as soon as word of Valdivia's trickery reached Santiago, so Villagra rode back to the capital that same day. Their fears were well founded. Within twenty-four hours a revolt led by Pedro Sancho de la Hoz boiled to the surface, a revolt so widespread that dozens of men, many of them previously above suspicion, were implicated. Quick action by Villagra squelched it, and the ringleaders were put to death. Sancho de la Hoz, who had been pardoned so many times, was hanged while Pedro de Valdivia's ship still rode at anchor in Valparaiso Bay.

What Inés de Suárez thought of Valdivia's action is not known, but she probably was aware of his plan and urged him to follow through with it. His absence was nonetheless painful to her. They had endured so much danger and adventure together that her passive role must have been hard to bear. News trickled slowly from Peru, and she welcomed each bit of information about his odyssey. Inés learned months later that Valdivia had arrived safely at Lima's port of Callao in mid-January and that he had immediately taken charge of the king's forces and led them in routing the last Pizarro rebellion in April. She rejoiced when she heard that Valdivia had at last been formally appointed His Majesty's governor and captain-general of Chile, and she confidently awaited his return to the colony.

But formal accusations of misgovernment, drawn up by his numerous enemies in Santiago, followed Valdivia to Peru and formed the basis of judicial proceedings to determine whether he was fit to govern Chile. Some fifty-seven charges of misconduct were considered, charges including his handling of the *repartimientos*, his underhanded methods of fundraising, and, not least, his irregular relations with and favoring of the widow Inés de Suárez. Valdivia defended himself on each count. Those who had lost their first *repartimientos*, he protested, would soon receive far richer grants in Chile's populous south. All monies taken from Santiago's citizens were in reality debts that would soon be repaid by Valdivia himself. And the accusations having to do with Inés de Suárez were nothing but malicious rumors. Valdivia explained that she went to Chile by license of Don Francisco Pizarro and was much loved by the people for her good deeds. True, she lived in his house, but there was nothing wrong in that because Doña Inés was his *criada*, his servant. After almost a month of deliberations, Valdivia was declared innocent of wrongdoing on all but one count. He was reaffirmed as governor and permitted to return to Chile. But he carried with him a document that read in part, "It is ordered that Pedro de Valdivia . . . cease immodest relations with Inés Suárez [and] that he not reside with her in a single house." The viceroy's decree continued, "From now on, all suspicion of carnal relations between them [must] be put to rest . . . [and she must] be married, or sent to these provinces of Peru, where she may reside, or to Spain or other places, wherever she may choose."[4]

Word of the order reached Inés sometime in December 1548. She understandably reacted with fury. How dare they bandy her name about in such a way! How dare they meddle in her private affairs! Hadn't every man been guilty of "immodest relations"? Why should she bear the full weight of the sentence and perhaps suffer banishment when Valdivia shared equally in their illicit love? Later, when she could calmly contemplate her fate, Inés recognized the sentence for what it was: a sop thrown to Valdivia's enemies by his supporters in Peru. It was some time, however, before she could think clearly about her future. When that moment came, she was certain of one thing: She would never leave Chile. Santiago was her home. She was one of its leading citizens and one of its wealthiest as well. In Peru she was infamous; in Spain she was nobody. Far better that she should lose Valdivia than accept banishment.

By the time Valdivia's ship arrived in Valparaiso Bay, Inés had settled on her course of action. Within a few weeks she married Rodrigo de Quiroga, one of Valdivia's leading captains and a close friend of both Inés and the governor. By so doing she regained the respectability she had sacrificed ten years earlier and, incidentally, established one of the wealthiest households in all of Chile.

Valdivia and Inés seemed to have settled into a comfortable sort of friendship. In January 1550 he gave her land on Cerro Blanco Hill, upon which she built the Church of Our Lady of Monserrate. Rumor had it that he soon found a replacement for Inés among the Spanish women who had come with him from Peru. But two years later, bowing to an explicit command from the king, Valdivia liquidated several of his holdings and sent for his wife, Doña Marina, who still languished in far-off Spain. He never lived to see her, for in December 1553 he became the most famous casualty of the Araucanian Wars.[5]

In a sense Inés suffered less at Valdivia's death than did Chile. She was by then quite independent of the governor. Not so the colony, which suffered through several years without a legitimate leader. Calamity seemed to feed on itself. Insecurity in government was compounded by three years of drought and savage epidemics. The Araucanian Wars, as the Spanish named the ongoing conflict with the Reche-Mapuche people, raged unabated; their initial advantage evaporated when the indigenous learned to fight on horseback using European weapons. Still, the will to impose Spanish ways on that alien land remained strong.

EPILOGUE

In the last decades of her life, Inés de Suárez took the lead in fixing Hispanic culture on Chile through her patronage of the Roman Catholic Church and its charitable institutions. Each year she acted with greater piety and generosity. In 1558 she and Rodrigo de Quiroga established a Dominican chaplaincy at the hermitage of Our Lady of Monserrate, where Mass was said each Friday for the soul of Pedro de Valdivia. While her husband was away in Arauco and Tucumán, and during Quiroga's own years as governor, Inés supported the church in its efforts to provide religious instruction to indigenous residents of Santiago and to the new generation of mestizo children. Rodrigo de Quiroga's only child, his daughter, Isabel, was herself a mestiza, born out of wedlock. Inés made sure that she did not reach adulthood unable to read and write as she, Inés, had, and in 1566, with Inés's support, Rodrigo de Quiroga recognized Isabel as his full and legitimate heir.

Valdivia's widow provided a sharp contrast to Inés de Suárez in wealth and prestige. Doña Marina Ortiz de Gaete arrived from Spain just months after Valdivia's death. Expecting to find herself a wealthy woman, she discovered with chagrin that Valdivia had left her debts of some two hundred thousand pesos for which she was responsible under law. In 1555 she received permission from the king to earn what income she could by sending her indigenous servants out to work as day laborers. But it was scarcely an easy existence, for in addition to her financial burdens, she suffered abuse at the hands of those who had been roughly treated by Valdivia. Inés tried to help Doña Marina from afar, fearing that Valdivia's legitimate wife would not welcome the attentions of his mistress, especially when that lady was a leading figure of the colony.

One day early in 1572, Inés de Suárez stepped through the iron gates of her house and, accompanied by the governor and a cluster of servants, walked slowly down the street and across La Canada stream. She was dressed in black, a heavy mantilla covered her gray hair, and her shoulders were rounded with the weight of sixty-four years. As a small crowd gathered around her, Inés laid the cornerstone of Santiago's first permanent church structure, the

Church of San Francisco.[6] The hands that had bound so many wounds, that had been bathed more than once in the blood of battle, now carried out the duty of a philanthropist and local dignitary. Records show that it was her last public act. When she died, Chile mourned its first lady's passing, oblivious of the controversy that had swirled about her decades earlier.

Succeeding generations of Chileans forgot Inés de Suárez, the social arbiter of the early colony. The historic Inés was replaced by the heroic and scandalous mistress of Pedro de Valdivia. Yet to dwell solely on her role in that turbulent decade of conquest is to slight the greater significance of the woman. Like the cornerstone she laid near the end of her life, the conquistadora Inés de Suárez was one of the builders of early Hispanic Chile.

NOTES

1. Spanish colonizers named this indigenous group Araucanians or "wild ones," but since the twenty-first century, scholars have used the term Reche-Mapuche, Reche, or more recently, Reche-Reche-Mapuche, as in Beatriz Marín-Aguilera, Leonor Adán Alfaro, and Simón Urbina Araya, "Challenging Colonial Discourses: The Spanish Imperial Borderland from the Sixteenth to Nineteenth Century," in *Transnational Perspectives on the Conquest and Colonization of Latin America*, ed. Jenny Mander, David Midgley, and Christine Beaule (New York: Routledge, 2019), 85–97 and Nancy E. van Deusen's "Indigenous Slavery's Archive in Seventeenth-Century Chile," *Hispanic American Historical Review* 1, vol. 101 (February 2021): 1–33.

2. José Toribio Medina, *Cartas de Pedro de Valdivia que tratan del descubrimiento y conquista del Reino de Chile* (Santiago: Fondo Histórico y Bibliográfico José Toribio Medina, 1953), número II, 11, 13.

3. Ann Keith Nauman, *The Career of Doña Inés de Suárez, the First European Woman in Chile* (Lewiston, NY: Edwin Mellen Press, 2000), 53.

4. Alejandro Vicuña, *Inés de Suárez* (Santiago: Editorial Nacimiento, 1941), 169.

5. For a map of Valdivia's route to conquest and death and the Reche-Mapuche's resistance in early colonial Chile, see figure 1 in Vincent Clément's "Conquest, Natives, and Forest: How Did the Reche-Mapuches Succeed in Halting the Spanish Invasion of Their Land (1540–1553, Chile)?" *War in History* 22, no. 4 (November 2015): 431.

6. On the contested accountings of this ceremony, see Nauman, *The Career of Doña Inés de Suárez*, 137, fn. 14.

REFERENCES

Clément, Vincent. "Conquest, Natives, and Forest: How Did the Reche-Mapuches Succeed in Halting the Spanish Invasion of Their Land (1540–1553, Chile)?" *War in History* 22, no. 4 (November 2015): 428–47.

Errázuriz, Crescente. *Historia de Chile, Pedro de Valdivia*. 2 vols. Santiago: Imprenta Cervantes, 111–12.

Marín-Aguilera, Beatriz, Leonor Adán Alfaro, and Simón Urbina Araya. "Challenging Colonial Discourses: The Spanish Imperial Borderland from the Sixteenth to Nineteenth Century." In *Transnational Perspectives on the Conquest and Colonization of Latin America*, edited by Jenny Mander, David Midgley, and Christine Beaule, 85–97. New York: Routledge, 2019.

Martínez, Carmen Pumar. *Españolas en India: mujeres-soldado, adelantadas, y gobernadoras*. Madrid: Anayana, 1988.

Medina, José Toribio. *Cartas de Pedro de Valdivia que tratan del descubrimiento y conquista del Reino de Chile*. Santiago: Fondo Histórico y Bibliográfico José Toribio Medina, 1953.

Nauman, Ann Keith. *The Career of Doña Inés de Suárez, the First European Woman in Chile*. Lewiston, NY: Edwin Mellen Press, 2000.

Pocock, H. R. S. *The Conquest of Chile*. New York: Stein and Day, 1967.

Powers, Daren Vieira. *Women in the Crucible of Conquest: The Gendered Genesis of Spanish American Society, 1500–1600*. Albuquerque: University of New Mexico Press, 2005.

Van Deusen, Nancy E. "Indigenous Slavery's Archive in Seventeenth-Century Chile." *Hispanic American Historical Review* 1, vol. 101 (February 2021): 1–33.

Vernon, Ida Stevenson Weldon. *Pedro de Valdivia: Conquistador of Chile*. Austin: University of Texas Press, 1946.

Vicuña, Alejandro. *Inés de Suárez*. Santiago: Editorial Nacimiento, 1941.

Vivir, Jerónimo. *Crónica y relación copiosa y verdadera de los reinos de Chile (1558)*. Madrid: Arte Historia Revista Digital, 1987.

Chapter 4

Saint Rose of Lima, 1586–1617

INTRODUCTION

Lima, capital of the Viceroyalty of Peru, was the leading city of early colonial Spanish America. It achieved its primacy in two ways. First, it was a wealthy city. Santo Domingo and Mexico City, founded earlier than Lima, possessed far fewer millionaires than did their South American counterpart. Second, the city led early Latin America in both the piety of its people and the magnitude of the Roman Catholic religious presence among them.

Lima's wealth sprang from a fabulous deposit of silver discovered high in the Andes south and east of the city. The silver mountain at Potosí was discovered in the highlands ten years after Lima's founding by Francisco Pizarro in 1535. Potosí's silver was so abundant that once it entered the global bullion supply, it changed the world political economy. Nearly all of the bonanza passed through Lima as it departed the viceroyalty. It was by law inventoried at the city's royal mint on its way to export through Lima's Pacific Ocean port of Callao. Francisco Pizarro christened Lima "The City of Kings." By the end of the sixteenth century, it might well have been called "The City Built by Silver."

The conquest of Peru and the founding of its capital coincided with the Catholic Counter-Reformation, a religious reawakening spurred by the rise of Protestant Christianity. One of the movement's outcomes was that Spain's viceregal capital, Lima, and its residents became models of Roman Catholic fervor and orthodoxy. In this regard Lima rivaled any city in Europe's Catholic heartland. *Limeños*, people of Lima, turned their wealth to building and supporting an array of religious institutions and supporting the many religious they housed. These thousands of individuals included priests, nuns, and lay-workers of the Roman church, as well as monks and female religious of the Regular Clergy: Dominicans, Jesuits, and Franciscans, and members of numerous other orders too. Within such setting it is no wonder that Lima, Peru, became the birthplace of the first American saint.[1] Her name was Isabel Flores de Oliva, canonized as Saint Rose of Lima.

BEGINNINGS: EARLY LIMA AND YOUNG ROSE

The story of America's first saint begins with her father's decision to leave Spain for the New World. Gaspar Flores was from the impoverished province of Extremadura, fertile ground only in its production of conquistadores. Chief among them was Francisco Pizarro and his younger brothers Hernando and Gonzalo, all of whom played important roles in the conquest of Peru. Gaspar Flores departed Spain in 1547, reaching Panama in time to join the military force being assembled by royal emissary Pedro de la Gasca. De la Gasca had been sent to America by King Charles I (who was also known as Holy Roman Emperor Charles V) to end an uprising of Spanish settlers against the New Laws of 1542, which had guaranteed protections to indigenous Peruvians. After defeating the rebels, de la Gasca rewarded his military commanders with grants of land and *encomienda* laborers to work them. Unfortunately, infantrymen like Gaspar Flores received little more than thanks from the crown for their military service. This meant that Flores, and later his family, would live their lives as ordinary members of Lima's middle class.

Gaspar Flores continued to bear arms for the crown later in life. In 1572 he helped Spanish forces crush the rebellion of the last Inca emperor, Tupac Amaru (1545–1572). Afterward he served as a member of the honor guard of Viceroy Francisco de Toledo. In 1577, then in his fifties, Gaspar Flores married a young woman originally from Huánuco named María de Oliva Herrera. They began their married life on a small plot of land located on the outskirts of Lima.

In 1577 Lima was a small but dynamic city of perhaps ten thousand inhabitants. It was located on a plain not far from the Pacific Ocean in a region where rain rarely falls and earthquakes often strike. By the late 1570s Lima was taking shape as a city of broad avenues and impressive structures bespeaking its growing wealth. With the discovery of mercury at nearby Huancavelica, used to extract silver from low-grade ores, silver production soared, further enhancing its importance to the Spanish crown. Its silver exports placed Lima at the epicenter of the economic process later known as globalization. Silver flowed throughout both Europe and Asia, linking them in unprecedented ways. In Europe, American silver financed the endless wars of Holy Roman Emperor Charles V, struggling to protect his empire against the Protestant heresy. Potosí silver flowed westward across the Pacific Ocean to Manila, capital of the Spanish colony of the Philippines. There it was exchanged for Chinese silk and porcelain and many other manufactures of the Middle Kingdom. Cargos of smuggled silver from Potosí reached the Americas and Europe in the holds of French, Dutch, and English ships that had anchored in waters off the coast of Peru.

Surrounded by the remnants of the Inca empire and a much-reduced population of perhaps a million indigenous people, Lima's inhabitants came to include people of diverse backgrounds and races: indigenous, Black, European, Asian, as well as an ever-growing population of residents of mixed descent. Gaspar Flores and his family occupied a special place within that demographic mix. As a creole, or white, his race placed him among the capital's *"gente decente,"* people of good birth. María de Oliva was also considered creole, although her mother, Isabel de Herrera, was said to have been born in Huánuco at a time when no Spanish women lived there. Thus she was probably of indigenous descent. María and her husband went on to have thirteen children, among them the good-natured, rosy-cheeked, and golden-haired Isabel. When she was about three months old, a young indigenous servant named Mariana came upon the infant sleeping in her cradle and was astounded to see that her face seemed to glow like a small rose. From that day forward the beautiful child became known as "Rose."

As was customary in Spanish-American towns and cities, the children of Gaspar and María grew up in an atmosphere of strong religious belief reinforced not only by daily habit and ritual but by the very layout of the city. It could hardly have been otherwise. Construction of the cathedral of Lima and the archbishop's palace began simultaneously with the palace of the viceroy, at the dawn of Lima's founding. Even larger were the opulent churches and residencies that soon followed, built by Dominicans, Augustinians, and Franciscans, all mendicant orders charged with evangelizing among the native peoples of Peru. Rambling convents and monasteries occupied prime locations throughout the city. Rose Flores grew up in the midst of this frenetic construction of religious structures: La Merced, San Sebastián (where she was baptized), the cathedral of Lima, the archbishop's palace, Saint Dominic's church and convent, and San Augustín. In such an environment the people of Catholic Lima could not but view the world through a metaphysical lens. Even small events were seen as being laden with divine signs and portents. For a child of that time and place, stories of heaven and hell, the lives of the saints, miracles, and the threat of eternal damnation were as real and near at hand as the gilt altars, the ornate statues of the saints, and the churches that towered over the city.

In 1579, Spanish presses reprinted a biography of Saint Catherine of Siena (1347–1380), the austere Dominican nun whose life story was an important early influence on the young Rose Flores. The biography, along with other religious texts, reached Lima soon after its publication. It chronicled Saint

Catherine's humble origins, her mystical experiences, and her struggle to live a sacrificial life in a time of the Black Death. Young Isabel read it when only eight or nine years old, memorizing extensive portions of the work. She identified some of the details of her mentor's life with features of her own upbringing, among them the fact that Catherine was born into a deeply religious family in medieval Siena, one of twenty-five children, only half of whom survived. When Catherine of Siena was about fifteen years old, her older sister died in childbirth, inspiring the future saint to take a secret vow of chastity. From that moment forward, she avoided every kind of vanity and coquetry, at times engaging in extreme fasts, sleep deprivation, and penitence. Sometimes Catherine of Siena experienced mystical visions, and she was known to lapse into prayerful trances in public. Saint Catherine not only refused to marry, as was her expected duty, but chose instead to become a tertiary—a religious person who lived in her family's home—of the Order of Saint Dominic. This enabled her to seek solitude at home and later to lead an active life free of the confines of both marriage and the convent. After a short lifetime of prolific writing, possibly dictated to scribes, as well as extreme fasting and mortification, Catherine of Siena died in Rome at the age of thirty-three; she was canonized in 1461.

SAINTLY IMITATION, *BEATAS*, AND COLONIAL WOMANHOOD IN PERU

Inspired by her example, Rose began imitating Saint Catherine in every detail of her own life. This resulted in conflict with her family, especially her mother, María, to whom by tradition she owed absolute obedience. Rose's mother, an intelligent, energetic woman, tried to lighten the family's poverty by selling embroidery and teaching young *limeñas*, or ladies of Lima, needlework and how to read and write. She hoped that her beautiful young daughter would marry well, and she saw to it that Rose was literate, knew a little about music, and was accomplished at lace-making and embroidery. But rather than embracing the attributes of a proper young woman, Rose insisted on performing the lowliest chores of the household and garden, shunned every effort to call attention to herself, and preferred to humbly serve other family members, just as Saint Catherine had done. To soften the effect of housework on Rose's hands, María insisted that she wear gloves at night, until Rose protested that the gloves hurt when she put them on. María dismissed that as an excuse, but when Rose claimed that flames shot from the gloves in the dark, her mother finally gave her permission to stop wearing them. María often took her daughter on visits to friends despite Rose's efforts to avoid these social outings, preferring to remain in the small oratory she had built at home. She was said to have rubbed garlic and hot peppers in her eyes and once dropped a rock on her foot so that she would be excused from social visits.

Still María was pleased when older *limeñas* complimented little Rose on her beauty. On one occasion a friend insisted the little girl wear roses in her hair. The earnest follower of Saint Catherine tried to ignore the request since she was sworn to avoid any show of vanity, but her mother at last convinced her. Both obedient and true to her teacher, or *maestra*, Saint Catherine, she fastened the rose to her head with a long pin that she pushed into her scalp, thereby canceling any hint of vanity with an act of mortification. Her horrified mother forcibly removed the pin later that day.

When barely six or seven years old, Rose Flores began fasting, first on Wednesdays, Fridays, and Saturdays, when she consumed only bread and water. At age eight she caused an uproar when she fainted, presumably from lack of food. Yet when obliged to eat meat, she became ill and was unable to keep food down. She often sought help from Mariana, the family's indigenous servant, who became her ally in many of these practices. As her penances increased over time, so did the conflict between mother and daughter. It was during this time that Rose Flores began to practice mortifications using a small metallic paddle and, later, both a *disciplina*, a scourge made of barbed chains, which she used to whip herself, and a *cilicio*, a hair shirt. She also fashioned a belt made of iron spikes that she wrapped around her waist. She refused to sleep on a mattress and instead made a bed out of three planks of varying thicknesses, often overlaid with pieces of broken crockery, that she would hide under her bed in the morning. It was probably at this time that Gaspar Flores said that he was sorry his daughter had ever heard of Saint Catherine of Siena.

In 1597 Gaspar Flores took a position in Quives, a town about seventy kilometers from Lima. There he served as an overseer at an *obraje*, a textile factory operating with conscripted indigenous labor. From 1597 to about 1601, the Flores de Oliva family was one of few creole families living near the mines of Quives. While Isabel rarely left the house during that period, she was aware of the exploitation and dangerous conditions prevailing in nearby mines and knew about the periodic disasters, illnesses, and deaths afflicting the indigenous and enslaved African miners. The future saint's sympathy for the poor and disadvantaged likely dated from that time.

While in Quives, Rose dedicated herself to prayer, obedience, and mortification of the flesh, and she remained fiercely determined to live according to the medieval model of holiness set by Saint Catherine of Siena. Often, she was ill for months on end, doubtless owing to the effects of ongoing penance. Though intent on total obedience to her parents, she was often at cross purposes with her mother, who wanted her to marry well. Rose began to avoid her mother's attempts to arrange her hair and clothes by cutting off her hair and pouring cold water over her clothes to take away the rose color of her cheeks. She became so sick that María insisted she wrap up in animal skins and not remove them. Four days later, on removing the hides, María found her daughter covered in an infected rash that looked like blisters from a burn. She would obey her mother, it seemed, only when it led to extreme physical discomfort.

It was at about this time that Rose secretly began using a small crown of thorns that she wore under a *toca*, or wimple. She turned the crown every day so that the thorns would dig into a new part of her scalp. One day when Gaspar tried to discipline one of Rose's brothers, he struck Rose on the head by accident. When three streams of blood began to trickle down her forehead, the family discovered the secret crown of thorns. María treated her daughter's wounds with warm wine to prevent infection, but she could not persuade Rose to give up this most emblematic of all her penances.

Soon after arriving in Quives, Rose's path crossed that of another future saint, Toribio de Mogrovejo, the archbishop of the Viceroyalty of Peru, who further influenced her spiritual journey. Toribio was famous for his devotion to pastoral work that had led him to travel thousands of kilometers, often on foot and alone, in an effort to reach every part of the immense viceroyalty. Upon arriving in Quives, Toribio found among the three thousand inhabitants only three Christian families living there. When he entered the small local chapel, he found two boys and Rose, then twelve years old, awaiting confirmation. During the service he inexplicably called her Rose, instead of Isabel, her baptismal name. But to Rose, her nickname, by then official in church records, was too flattering. She later modified it to Rosa de Sancta Maria, Rose of Holy Mary, the name that she kept thereafter. Following her confirmation in the church, Rose is said to have reached the highest level of prayer, the prayer of union.

Four years later, when the Flores de Oliva family returned to Lima, Rose, then about fifteen years old, continued to emulate Saint Catherine of Siena in every aspect of her life. All the piety and asceticism she showed as a young girl seemed to intensify during her years in Quives. On her return to the city, she sought out the company of other *limeñas* whose religiosity, mysticism, service to the church, and penitential practices reflected her own. These *beatas* were widely accepted as saintly women whose prayers were especially pleasing to God and who could intercede for others. While a few flaunted their piety in hope of monetary gain, others like Rose were devout to a fault.

And what a contrast these *beatas* made with the other creole women living in the increasingly opulent city of Lima, now grown to some twenty-five thousand inhabitants. Privileged women watched daily life of the city from the beautifully ornate balconies of carved wood and intricate design that were built out several feet from the second stories of houses lining the main thoroughfares. When going out to witness a religious procession, visit friends, or attend parties, they dressed in the *saya y manto*, a long skirt with a cinched waist and a heavy veil that swept over the back and shoulders and adjusted over the face so that only one eye peeked out. Dressed in this fashion, women were relatively free to move about anonymously and engage in flirtations and other interesting pastimes without fear of being recognized, even by their own husbands.

Rose had no interest in such pastimes. She continued her humble service to her family and worked hours every day to help provide for the large Flores de Oliva family. By this time she had settled into a strict routine: ten hours of work, twelve hours of prayer and penance, and two hours of sleep. During the day she worked with her mother sewing and embroidering, working in the garden, and doing housework. When able, she sought solitude in a small cell her brother Fernando helped her build behind the family home. It was a rough shelter built of sticks and banana leaves. Years later she built an adobe oratory measuring barely six feet in height and having just enough room for one person. It had a small door to crawl through and a single window set high in the wall. It gave Rose a place where she could hide from the public eye.

As she worked in the family's garden, Rose showed an almost Franciscan affinity for nature, and many of the portraits painted of her in later years show her surrounded by birds, trees, and flower gardens. In *Tradiciones peruanas (Peruvian Traditions)*, the famous Peruvian *costumbrista* writer Ricardo Palma recounts the story of Rose and a rooster that was much admired by the Flores de Oliva family for its strange and beautiful feathers. One day the rooster fell ill and stopped crowing. Rose's mother said, "If he doesn't get better, we'll have to kill him and stew him for dinner." Rose picked up the ailing rooster and said, "Little chicken of mine, you had better sing quickly, for if you don't, you'll be fricasseed." The rooster shook his feathers and let out a "*quiquiriquí*," thus avoiding becoming the main course at dinner. She loved music and played songs of praise in her garden accompanying herself on the guitar. Some of her verses and songs survive. The most famous is a short verse that plays on her names, Rosa Flores de Oliva:

> Oh, Jesus of my soul!
> How well you look
> Between roses and flowers
> And green olives.[2]

Nightingales and the little birds that came to be known as s*anta rositas* in her honor came to join her in singing duets, and she even found common ground with mosquitos that invaded her rough hermitage in the garden. She is also said to have made a pact with the annoying insects. She pledged not to harm them if they would not bite or make noise while she prayed.[3] These well-behaved mosquitos did not have a similar arrangement with a *beata* who, while visiting Rose in the garden, swatted a mosquito. "Let them live, sister," said Rose, "I offer you the same peace I have with them." After that the insects did not bother her visitor. Another *beata* only reluctantly visited Rose in her hermitage because of the mosquitos. Rose disapproved of her attitude and allowed three mosquitos to bite the other woman, one each for the Father, Son, and Holy Ghost.[4]

Her dominion over the insect world was matched by Rose's ability to cultivate fruit trees and flowers in her garden. She helped support her family by growing flowers for sale to upper-class *limeñas*, and when she needed flowers to adorn statues of the saints, they appeared even when out of season. Among the flowers brought from Europe to the New World, the rose was the most highly regarded for its beauty and medicinal uses. Roses first reached Lima as seeds around 1552, an event celebrated by the saying of Mass in the cathedral of Lima. Some fifty years after their introduction to Peru, Rose Flores cultivated roses along with other flowers and herbs in her garden on Santo Domingo Street.

Local legend had it that the trees in her garden bowed their branches to the ground in prayer, but even as she cultivated natural beauty Rose's penitential practices grew ever more extreme. In addition to fasting and wearing a crown of thorns, she spent hours using small whips and chains in self-flagellation, often in her refuge in the garden. It was not unusual for her to spend hours in the night walking around the garden dragging a heavy wooden cross behind her, and descriptions of her penitential beds take up much of her biographers' attention. Of all these mortifications, perhaps most difficult for her was to sleep as little as possible. At one point she took to tying her hair to a nail placed high on the wall so that she would be awakened any time she dozed off. At another time she wrapped a chain three times around her waist and fastened it with a heavy lock. According to tradition she threw the key into a well in the garden so that she would never be able to unlock it. However, when the pain became unbearable a friend persuaded her to take the chain off. The lock had to be broken, and when the chain was removed pieces of Rose's flesh came with it.

True to Catholic practice, Rose confessed what she believed were her sins on a regular basis; she would then be absolved by a priest. But even as she earned their admiration for her deep resolve and humility, her confessors were concerned with the extremes to which Rose took these penitential practices. One of her confessors filed down the spikes on her crown of thorns to blunt them; another recommended that she should lash her body with a knotted rope rather than chains. Yet another reasoned that she should sleep four hours a night rather than two; a fourth, concerned with her excessive fasting, tried to limit the times she attended Mass as it was on those days that she refused to eat any food at all. These efforts were largely in vain. Rose soon began to use a silver crown of thorns with ninety-nine spikes, continued to use chains in her penances, and endured fasting throughout her life. Soon after her death one of her confessors wrote that Rose of Lima was one of heaven's most illustrious saints in terms of penance and mortification of the flesh.

MELANCHOLIC VISIONS

At about fifteen years of age Rose, the beautiful young *beata*, began to suffer from melancholy brought on by a sense that her prayers went unheard, and she felt alone, surrounded by darkness, and abandoned by God. These spells of depression would descend on her daily and last for several hours. They caused her so much misery that she repeatedly asked for help from her confessors. These were largely Dominicans who, along with her mother, attributed her depression to her excessive penitence that they believed caused mental weaknesses leading to illusions and strange visions. Only later in life was she able to find more sympathetic confessors among the Jesuits. These Jesuit priests spoke to her of saints and biblical figures who suffered similar episodes and who considered them a paradox—the anguish caused by these spells was actually a blessing, a chance to suffer purgatory in life and speed directly to heaven at death.

Even as her daughter struggled with strict religious practices and melancholy, María de Oliva continued to hope that Rose would one day agree to marry the son of a wealthy family and solve her family's economic problems. Rose's rejection of the idea of marriage continued to cause strife and even, on one occasion, a slap from her mother. Rose felt guilt over the conflict caused by her desire to help provide for the family and obey her parents in every way, while at the same time following a path far different from the one they had chosen for her. María seemed unaware of her daughter's vow of chastity taken years earlier, and she encouraged several suitors who gazed at the beautiful and pious Rose as she walked to and from church with her brother Fernando, and who glimpsed her through a window as she embroidered her exquisite floral designs. Among these suitors was a young man named Vicente Montes Venegas. From a wealthy family, Vicente was an eligible bachelor, although he was said to suffer from a lack of piety. After conversations with Rose, however, he reportedly saw the error of his ways and began attending Mass every week. After she held firm against his offer of marriage, the matter was finally laid to rest, just as it had been in the life of Saint Catherine.

Rose's family and confessors then urged her to enter a convent—the only other socially acceptable option available to women at the time. She had plenty of options in Lima, which featured thirteen large and thriving convents by the early 1600s. They occupied a notable portion of the city's best land and attracted large numbers of devout *limeñas*. Convents were run in accord with a strict hierarchy that reflected the importance of wealth and race in Lima's society as a whole. Young women of elite families could enter a convent as nuns of the black veil upon payment of a substantial dowry. Those less well-off became nuns of the white veil and served as housekeepers who were responsible for the proper management of the community. Other religious were the *donadas*, who wore habits but did not profess vows; these were often of mixed race and were essentially servants of the convent. Rose knew that as her family was unable to pay the dowry she would probably enter as a nun of the white veil. In 1604 a new convent, the Monastery of Saint Clare, of the Franciscan order of the Poor Clares, was founded by Archbishop Toribio de Mogrovejo, and an invitation to enter the convent was extended to Rose. The order of Saint Clare was known for its strict rule, solitude, and deprivation, which likely appealed to Rose. But she could not tolerate the prospect of leaving behind her family responsibilities. Rose's mother and her confessors agreed, and she declined the invitation. Not long after she was invited to enter the Augustinian Convent of the Incarnation, without payment of the dowry. Rose's grandmother, who was by then bedridden and dependent on Rose for much of her care, nonetheless encouraged her to take the veil as an Augustinian nun. Thus it was that, accompanied by her brother Fernando, she was on her way to the convent to become a nun when she decided to stop at Santo Domingo church to ask for the blessing of Our Lady of the Rosary. According to her biographer Pedro de Loayza, Rose knelt in prayer before the statue of the Virgin. But when it was time to leave, she found herself frozen in place and unable to move. When at last she promised the Virgin that she would return home and not enter the convent, she was able to stand freely. Speaking to the Virgin, she promised to return to her mother's house and make it into a spiritual retreat.

For her many biographers this episode is full of mystery and divine providence, although Rose's refusal to enter a convent may have been shaped by the life story of Saint Catherine of Siena. As a Dominican tertiary, Saint Catherine wore the black-and-white habit of the order and followed strict fasting and mortification. Meanwhile the nun lived a relatively unfettered life outside the convent. Rose of Lima similarly would not have tolerated the rigid hierarchies of cloistered monastic life where, under the watchful eyes of her superiors, she might well have had to scale back the austerities and physical abuses to which she subjected herself. Then too, she may not have wished to enter the convent because of her goal to found a Dominican convent dedicated to Saint Catherine of Siena in Lima. Her family's inability to pay the fee required to enter one of Lima's convents was yet another reason for her decision. For all these reasons, in 1606, at the age of twenty, Rose of Lima accepted the Dominican habit and in the eyes of the world became a non-cloistered tertiary of that order. Although she was permitted to wear the long-desired black-and-white habit, the Dominican hierarchy in Lima had to apply to Rome for the authority to allow Rose Flores de Oliva to take the vow to formalize her status as a tertiary of the order. Unfortunately, the authorization did not arrive during Rose's lifetime.

With the weighty matters of marriage and the convent largely settled, Rose rededicated herself to her family and her penitential practices, adding a creative dimension to her efforts. She began writing of her religious experiences in a series of notebooks and also created two graphic works of a single page each. She described the many mercies she received from God in *Las mercedes* and a spiritual stairway that led to the divine in *La escala mística*, a work that was not discovered until the early twentieth century. They comprise hearts carefully cut out of paper and pierced by arrows representing spiritual love, with marginal notes explaining the significance of each. As she wrote in the margin of *Las mercedes*, the works were to be reviewed and corrected if they contained faults or errors. Significantly, she referred to her notebooks and claimed that they were the work of the "powerful hand of the Lord, in whose book I read that eternal wisdom confounds the proud and praises the humble, and promises that what is hidden from the prudent and wise is revealed to the unlettered child [*párvulo*]."[5] In *Las mercedes*, Saint Rose describes her tribulations in reaching the decision to remain in the world as a tertiary of the Dominican order:

> These three mercies I received through divine pity before I suffered the great tribulation during the general confession . . . and suffering nearly two years of great pains, tribulations, distress, afflictions, temptations, battles with demons, slanders of confessors and others. [I have suffered] sicknesses, pains, fever and, in fact, all the worst pains of hell that one can imagine, in these last years. It will be five years since I received the mercies that I have put on this half page of paper, by inspiration of a heart altogether unworthy.[6]

The basic calculus of Rose's life is contained in this document: divine mercies come to those who are willing to suffer and the more acute the suffering, the greater the approbation of heaven.

As Rose approached her twenties, she began attracting attention among the people of Lima. Though reclusive by nature, the combination of her beauty, pious demeanor, and remarkable asceticism led other devout *limeños* to admire her. This was especially true of other *beatas*, many of them young like her and dedicated to expressions of extreme piety. Rose likened the devout younger *beatas* to rose blossoms waiting to be gathered into a new convent in honor of Saint Catherine of Siena. In a 1613 letter to a fellow religious in Spain, she explained that she was sending one hundred ducats, given to her by well-off admirers from the secular world, to advance the cause of the new convent. Although she laid out the design of the convent in wax on a wooden pallet, it only came into being five years after her death.

One of Rose's most faithful admirers was María de Usátegui, a member of Lima's elite. The young Rose Flores met her in 1604 after attending Mass at the Jesuit church in central Lima. Their friendship endured throughout Rose's life and led to other, similar relationships: with Gonzalo de la Maza, the accountant for the Holy Crusade and María's husband, with Juan del Castillo, a medical doctor respected for his piety and brilliance, and with the painter Angelino Medoro Romano, among many others. Rose also knew Brother Martín de Porres, a Dominican friar whose mixed-race origins kept him from becoming a full-fledged member of the order but whose miraculous ability to heal the sick and help the poor led to his canonization almost four centuries later, in 1962.

For ordinary *limeños*, however, Rose represented such holiness that she was believed to have the power to intercede on their behalf. In one of only three surviving letters written by Rose, she offered Father Bartolomé de Ayala an interesting proposition. Thanks to her strong desire to suffer for her beliefs, Rose offered to take onto herself the punishment for sins committed by Father Bartolomé. She further offered her prayers, penitence, fasting, and good works to build up heavenly credits for him. As witnesses to this promise, Rose listed Saint Augustin, Saint Dominic, and Saint Francis. Father Bartolomé's response to this offer is not known. Still, this was not the only time Rose offered herself to save another. She expressed regret that as a mere woman, she was not permitted to seek martyrdom by going out to evangelize among the indigenous peoples of the viceroyalty whose souls she feared were in grave danger, and she strongly exhorted male clergy to do so. In another incident, *limeños* flew into a panic when a well-known priest, Father Francisco Solano, was understood to predict from the pulpit that Lima would soon pay for its sins when God visited an earthquake and flooding upon the city. Upon hearing this rumor Rose spent the night in terrible self-flagellation to atone for the sins of the city. It was widely believed that she thereby protected Lima from imminent destruction. Several years later, in July 1615, word arrived from the coast that Dutch warships had anchored in Callao harbor and that Protestant invaders would soon come to destroy the city's churches. Lima was engulfed in panic. Rose, however, took upon herself the role of defender of the church of Santo Domingo, and more particularly of the sacrament of the Eucharist. She called her followers to the church and exhorted them to accept martyrdom in defense of their beliefs. She rolled up her sleeves and trimmed the hems from her skirts so she could leap to the altar prepared to defend it to the death. As it happened, the Dutch commander fell ill and ordered his ships to withdraw, leaving *limeños* in peace and denying Rose the chance for martyrdom. Rose's valiant action did not go unnoticed. Many later portraits reveal her as the patron saint of Lima holding an anchor with a miniature city balanced on it.

María complained bitterly of her daughter's habit of giving food and clothing to the indigent and taking in the sick—this when her family could barely care for its own needs. In answer, Rose often lived for days on a diet of bread and water. Still, she offered comfort to the sick and dying of all classes and races, attributing her kindnesses to the assistance of her "*doctorcito*," a small image of Jesus that she carried with her for its curative powers. But she personally dressed the wounds of the injured and afflicted. On one occasion Rose gave away one of her mother's two cloaks. On being reprimanded for such an act, she told María that she would soon be rewarded three times over. So it was that a few weeks later Rose's mother not only received a gift of silver from an unknown person to buy a new cloak, but she also was given a length of silk by a wealthy matron, along with another length of fine cloth that had been left in Santo Domingo church as an offering.

That was not the only time that the Flores de Oliva family benefited from the largesse of others. These gifts often came at the moment of greatest need, like the serving of chocolate sent to her by María de Usátegui or the bread that appeared out of nowhere when her family was without or the small pouch given to her by an unknown man that turned out to have the exact sum of fifty pesos, the amount of debt her father, Gaspar, owed and had despaired of being able to pay. The fact that *limeños* gave money and gifts to people they believed to be holy and able to perform miracles or intercede on their behalf caused concern among members of the church hierarchy. While understanding that authentic *beatas* did exist, church officials knew that the average citizen could be taken in by false shows of sanctity and outright deception. In both Spain and the New World, it was the responsibility of the Holy Office—the Inquisition—to investigate and punish such frauds. In Lima the Holy Office occupied a building in the center of the city, and its dungeons were infamous and feared. Among those who were found guilty of deception or heresy, some were subjected to public autos-de-fe where they were obliged to confess and reform; others were held in underground cells and subjected to torture. The truly unlucky few were burned to death in Lima's central plaza, the Plaza de Armas.

SINNER OR SAINT? THE INQUISITION OF ROSE

By 1614 Rose's family had become worried that her piety and religious practices would attract the attention of the Inquisition. They so feared this possibility that María de Oliva tried to distance herself from her daughter by publicly berating her as a hypocrite and deceiver, a false saint lacking in virtue. That moved powerful friends to advise Rose to request a hearing before a panel of inquisitors to answer any questions they might choose to ask. This "examination of conscience" was not a formal proceeding of Lima's Holy Office. In fact, the inquisitors were themselves well-known to Rose and sympathetic to her. Dominicans Luis de Bilbao and Alonso Velásquez had each served as Rose's confessors for more than a decade, and Juan de Lorenzana was her confessor during the final years of her life. Del Castillo, Bilbao, and Lorenzana were also associated with the University of San Marcos, and the Jesuits Juan de Villalobos and Diego Martínez were well known to Rose's close friends Gonzalo de la Maza and his wife, María de Usátegui.

The goal of this examination was to determine whether Rose's religious experiences were the work of God or the devil, or perhaps illusions brought on by severe mortification, physical deprivation, and fasting. The panel was well aware that in seeking profit or fame *beatas* could pass themselves off as holy by faking stigmata, pretending to fast, or claiming falsely to receive divine revelations and special favors from God. In other cases, *beatas* could induce false mystical experiences and delude themselves through extreme practices or even insanity, or they could perhaps be victims of the devil. If not diabolical or delusional, the person could be guilty of heresy, particularly of the illuminist, or *alumbrista*, heresy, which bypassed Catholic sacraments by espousing personal prayer and absolution without need for the confessional and the priest's power to cleanse believers of sin.

Rose was clearly at risk: If she failed to satisfy her interrogators, she would have suffered disgrace and even punishment. To every question, however, she gave profound answers that impressed her inquisitors. They came away convinced of her honesty, humility, and purity. Luis de Bilbao said later that he "fell silent considering the depth and erudition of the solid discourse with which she answered the arduous and intricate questions with all promptness, ease and good order; revealing that it was a very superior spirit that spoke in the Virgin." Juan de Lorenzana concurred, saying that he had never seen intelligence as enlightened and perceptive as that of Rose Flores and that as he listened to her he heard not a woman but a fully consummate theologian. Since she was believed to be only an unlettered woman, her questioners attributed her grasp of theology and ability to express complex mystical concepts to divine wisdom and inspiration. When asked if she had learned these things through reading works of theology, she answered that she had not seen any books treating such matters and that she only recounted what she had experienced.[7] That point might have been true as far as it went, but it was reported that as a small child Rose had memorized the details of Saint Catherine of Siena's life and after many years could still recall the long theological sermons she had heard only twice. In addition to her sharp intellect, Rose possessed copies of Luis de Granada's works, *Book of Prayer and Meditation* (1554) and *Sinner's Guide* (1559), both of which were available in Lima in the early 1600s. Since works recounting the lives of the saints were widely available as well, she was probably familiar with works by Saint Teresa of Jesus, Saint John of the Cross, and other saints and mystics. Still, it was safest to allow the inquisitors to believe that she was merely a vessel of divine intuition. The same reasoning was applied to her self-mortification. It was believed that only divine providence could have made it possible for Rose to survive all the forms of physical torment that she visited upon herself.

Once vetted by the Holy Office, Rose entered a period in which she was celebrated by the people of Lima. Although she had always tried to hide from the public, her reclusiveness served only to fuel the high esteem in which she was held. The Dominican Pedro de Loayza, her earliest biographer and confessor, described Rose's demeanor as follows in his *Vida de Santa Rosa de Lima*:

> She was withdrawn such that she never desired to attend parties, nor even go out to see general processions: she not only withdrew physically, but also in her words, her lips, her eyes. She fled from gossip and rejected it with discretion. She always spoke the truth, so that when she was dying, a person called her confessor saying, "Father, your daughter sent for you." To which she said: "I didn't say that, rather: I would like to see him again before I die." The composure of her eyes was great, she never raised them. Her ears were closed to all conversation that was not of God: she spoke with gravity and without movement. She was a virgin who although gravely tempted by the devil never gave him quarter, and for these reasons from childhood she mortified her body.[8]

In 1614, due in part to her increasing celebrity, Rose's friends, confessors, and family agreed that it would be best for her to move from home to the much grander residence of Gonzalo de la Maza and his wife, María de Usátegui, whom Rose loved as a second mother. According to some, Rose's family agreed to the move because her increasing work with the poor and the sick disrupted her family home. Despite the greater comforts of the de la Maza house, Rose continued her mortifications, abstinence, and strict fasts of bread and water that frequently caused her stomach pains and illnesses. Efforts to force her to eat meat, however, had the effect of causing greater suffering. Through it all her closest supporters noted that her beauty remained miraculously intact.

On Palm Sunday of 1615, soon after moving to de la Maza's house, Rose went to the Chapel of the Rosary with other *beatas* to receive their palm fronds. Inexplicably, Rose was passed over and remained behind empty-handed. Thinking she had committed some grave sin and in deep distress, she knelt before the statue of the Virgin Mary depicted with the baby Jesus in her arms. At that moment she heard him say "Rose of my heart, be thou my bride." She hurried from the chapel and asked her brother Fernando to make her a ring inscribed with the words she heard in the chapel. On Thursday she hid the ring on the altar, and on Easter Sunday, while kneeling beside her mother, her confessor Alonso Velásquez, substituting for Juan de Lorenzana (who had begged off at the last minute), slipped the ring on her finger so surreptitiously that her mother later remarked that she did not know when or how the ring appeared. Like Saint Catherine of Siena, Rose had at last married her divine spouse.[9]

By this time years of fasting, austerities, and physical torment had taken their toll on Rose's body. She was less and less able to carry out her works of charity and labors in support of her family and more subject to various illnesses and maladies. By early August of 1617 she fell ill with an unidentified sickness, and although cared for by her mother, María de Usátegui, and a host of friends and supporters, she died at just past midnight on August 24. Word of Rose's death spread throughout the city, and crowds of *limeños* gathered around the de la Maza house. Throughout the night and following days, processions of people of all ranks and classes filed past her bier, many of them seizing shreds of her robes—and even one of her toes—as relics. The press of humanity was such that streets around de la Maza's residence and the Flores de Oliva house on Santo Domingo Street were almost impassable. The Dominican fathers finally understood that they would have to bury her in the Santo Domingo chapter house in the dark of night. This they did on August 28, 1617.

In the days after Rose Flores de Oliva's death it became clear that she was universally recognized as a saint by the people of Lima, and not just any saint, but theirs alone. A fervent religious cult grew up around her memory, astonishing church fathers and causing them some concern as talk of visions, miraculous cures, and visitations by Saint Rose spread. Groups of devotees took to meeting at the Flores de Oliva home to pray daily, and it was reported that Lima ran out of hair shirts and whips as the faithful sought to imitate the austerities of their saint. Within days of her death, Lima's civil and religious leaders began a process, the *proceso ordinario*, that they hoped would lead to beatification and canonization of Rose Flores. The process comprised interviews with some seventy-four witnesses who knew Rose and were able to answer programmed questions about her secular and religious life, her death, and her miracles.

The report that was prepared included the biography written by Pedro de Loayza; the testimony of her many confessors, family members, and friends; and valuable information about aspects of Rose's time on earth. Although much of the testimony gave insight into the actual Rose, elements of hagiography began appearing immediately as the tide of popular belief overwhelmed restraint and witnesses strove to build her life story into one worthy of sainthood. While some described her early education and noted that her musical ability was limited to strumming with one hand on the guitar, others claimed that she became literate by divine intervention at age twelve and became suddenly proficient on many musical instruments. While María de Usátegui and her longtime confessors testified that Rose recounted dreams to them, others described them as mystical ecstasies, visions, and revelations. Many witnesses agreed that she was able to predict future events, including the time of her own death. Rose's mother testified at one point that she experienced no pain when Rose was born, while the births of each of her other children left her near death. Several *beatas* recalled seeing the dying Rose as she entered heaven, where she was greeted by a heavenly host. A young priest recalled that while celebrating Mass, Rose's face sent out blue flames that were so bright he had to avert his eyes. Others claimed that Rose's decision to take the Dominican habit was made when a black-and-white butterfly landed over her heart. Hundreds of miracles were reported, of which eight were later celebrated during her beatification.

Within a few years of her death, church leaders in Lima grew concerned about the intensity of the Rose of Lima cult. In an effort to control local fervor and tamp down on any attendant heresies, they began to pursue some of Rose's closest associates, seizing their writings and subjecting them to examination by the Holy Office. It was during this period, probably in 1622, that Rose's own notebooks were taken by ecclesiastical authorities. Some claim they were sent to Spain to be reviewed for error and deviation from official doctrine, while others believe they were destroyed or buried away in Lima. They have never been found.

As Dominican leaders in Lima debated the wisdom of promoting Rose's cause, her fame had already extended to Spain, where Philip IV and other members of the royal family seized on her life as proof of the success of Spanish efforts in the New World. The image of the Rose carried from Spain to America was a powerful one. The beautiful flower had found fertile soil in Spain's new world. One of the king's first official acts was to write to the Vatican supporting beatification of Rose of Lima. He also commissioned a fanciful painting in which he appears beside Rose as she defends the Eucharist against Moorish invaders. Although Pope Urban VIII had prohibited any sainthood within fifty years of death, a second process was authorized by the Holy See in Rome. This apostolic process (the *proceso apostólico*) of canonization and beatification included church officials' interviews of 147 witnesses from 1630 to 1631. While many of these witnesses were male religious, women and ordinary *limeños* were also called to answer several dozen questions about Rose's life, miracles, and intercessions. The report was sent to the Vatican's Sacred Congregation of Holy Rites in 1634, where it remained stalled for two decades.

By mid-century hagiographical works about the life of Rose of Lima began appearing in Europe, where they were widely read and admired. According to one account, as a new pope was being selected in Rome, Cardinal Rospigliosi (soon to be Pope Clement IX) brought along two books. He opened the first, the seminal biography of Rose by the German Dominican Leonard Hansen, and on opening the second, realized he had brought another book about her life. Yet a third appeared on loan from another cardinal. If this was not enough to move Rose's beatification forward, another tale from Ricardo Palma in his *Tradiciones peruanas* perhaps explains the sudden energy that attended Rose's sainthood. According to this account Pope Clement IX received the petition for Rose's beatification in 1668. He was highly skeptical about the prospect of a saint appearing in Lima and was heard to comment that he would as easily expect a rain of roses—whereupon fragrant rose petals reportedly fell all around him.[10] That same year he approved her beatification and sped up the process of canonization. In 1670 his successor, Clement X, named Rose the universal and principal patron of the Americas and Spanish dominions, including the Philippines, due in part to the influence of Dominican religious in Manila. One year later, he presided over her canonization in the Sistine Chapel.

When word of her canonization reached Lima early in 1672, the city put on a display that reflected *limeños* wealth and devotion. Streets of the city were paved with silver ingots worth eight million pesos, and altars and public spaces were encrusted with gems. It is worth noting that Rose Flores de Oliva rose to sainthood in a carefully managed campaign that emphasized her conformity to the prevailing religious tenets of her time. It was her astonishing asceticism, not the martyrdom associated with early Christian saints, or reports of miracles and intercessions that animate other saintly lives, or even good works and service to the poor and sick, that led to her place in the hierarchy of saints. Inspired by a model of self-denial and mortification of the flesh, Saint Rose of Lima looked back to the Middle Ages, to the life of her seraphic mistress Saint Catherine of Siena. It must be noted, too, that from a young age Rose Flores de Oliva challenged not only social conventions and the authority of her parents, but also the Catholic Church, to practice faith on her own terms. Rose of Lima pushed expectations of traditional gender and class norms aside to transcend the boundaries of what was for early modern Spanish women the most restrictive of environments: home and church.

EPILOGUE

Today, nearly a half millennium after her birth, Saint Rose of Lima is venerated in Spanish-speaking America, from Bogotá to Buenos Aires—and beyond. Throughout Latin America schools, churches, and charitable institutions bear her name. A 2015 forensic reconstruction of her lovely face moved her devotees to tears of astonishment and love (see figure 4.1). This reveals the ongoing power of faith and spiritual steadfastness in a secularized modern world.

Figure 4.1 Saint Rose of Lima (Wikimedia Commons | Cicero Moraes)

NOTES

1. Santa Rosa was also revered as the "principal patroness of the Americas, Philippines, and Indies" and has been credited with saving Lima from natural disaster many times over. See Charles Walker, *Shaky Colonialism: The 1746 Earthquake Tsunami in Lima, Peru, and Its Long Aftermath* (Durham, NC: Duke University Press, 2008), 25, 26, 47.

2. Luis G. Alonso Getino, *Santa Rosa de Lima, patrona de América, su retrato corporal y su talla intelectual según los nuevos documentos* (Madrid: Aguilar Editores, 1943), 162.

3. Stephen Hart, "The Biographical Fashioning of the Americas' First Saint: Santa Rosa de Lima (1596–1617)," *Modern Language Review* 114, no. 2 (April 2019): 240.

4. Ricardo Palma, "Los mosquitos de Santa Rosa," *Tradiciones peruanas*, seventh series, Biblioteca Virtual Miguel de Cervantes, *cervantes virtual.com*.

5. Carolina Ibáñez-Murphy, "¿Primera escritora colonial? Santa Rosa de Lima: sus 'Mercedes' y 'La escala mística,'" (Ph.D. diss., University of Arizona, 1997), 152–53.

6. Ibáñez-Murphy, "¿Primera escritora," 153.

7. Leonard Hansen, *Vida admirable de Santa Rosa de Lima, patrona del Nuevo Mundo*, trans. from Latin by Jacinto Parra (Vergara: El Santísimo Rosario, 1929), 176–77.

8. Pedro de Loayza, O.P., *Vida de Santa Rosa de Lima* (Lima: Santuario de Santa Rosa, 1937), 4.

9. Rubén Vargas Ugarte, S.J., *Vida de Santa Rosa de Lima*, third edition (Buenos Aires: Imprenta López, 1961), 121–25.

10. Ricardo Palma, "El rosal de Rosa," *Tradiciones peruanas*, second series (Mexico: Espasa-Calpe, 1960), 84–86.

REFERENCES

Clissold, Stephen. *The Saints of South America*. London: Charles Knight, 1972.

Getino, Luis G. Alonso. *Santa Rosa de Lima, patrona de América, su retrato corporal y su talla intelectual según los nuevos documentos*. Madrid: Aguilar Editores, 1943.

Giraldes, Arturo. *The Age of Trade: The Manila Galleons and the Dawn of the Global Economy*. New York: Rowman & Littlefield, 2015.

Hansen, Leonard. *Vida admirable de Santa Rosa de Lima, patrona del Nuevo Mundo*. Translated from Latin by Jacinto Parra. Vergara: El Santísimo Rosario, 1929.

Hart, Stephen M. "The Biographical Fashioning of the Americas' First Saint: Santa Rosa de Lima (1596–1617)." *Modern Language Review* 114, no. 2 (April 2019): 230–58.

Ibáñez-Murphy, Carolina. "¿Primera escritora colonial? Santa Rosa de Lima: Sus 'Mercedes' y 'La Escala Mística.'" Ph.D. diss., University of Arizona, 1997.

Loayza, Pedro de, O.P. *Vida de Santa Rosa de Lima*. Lima: Santuario de Santa Rosa, 1937.

Mujica Pinilla, Ramón. *Rosa limensis: mística, política e iconografía en torno a la patrona de América*. Lima: IFEA, 2001.

Myers, Kathleen Ann. *Neither Saints nor Sinners: Writing the Lives of Women in Spanish America.* New York: Oxford University Press, 2003.

Palma, Ricardo. "El rosal de Rosa." *Tradiciones peruanas*, second series. México: Espasa-Calpe, 1960.

Palma, Ricardo. "Los mosquitos de Santa Rosa." *Tradiciones peruanas*, seventh series. Biblioteca Virtual Miguel de Cervantes, *cervantes virtual.com*.

Vargas Ugarte, Rubén, S.J. *Vida de Santa Rosa de Lima*. Third edition. Buenos Aires: Imprenta López, 1961.

Walker, Charles. *Shaky Colonialism: The 1746 Earthquake Tsunami in Lima, Peru, and Its Long Aftermath*. Durham, NC: Duke University Press, 2008.

Chapter 5

The Nun Ensign, 1585 or 1592–1650?

INTRODUCTION

American treasure reshaped the economy of Spain, and of Europe at large, driving international trade and thus binding both Europe and America to Asia. The New World itself was profoundly affected by this bonanza of extracted wealth. Initially the mining boom was based in silver flowing from a fabulous mountain of silver called Potosí, high in the Andes Mountains of Upper Peru (modern-day Bolivia). Below the mountain sprang up the city of Potosí, the world's foremost mining town of its day and one of the largest settlements of Europeans in either North or South America. During its brief heyday Potosí teemed with adventurers from all of Spain's regions. Castilians and Catalans, Basques and impoverished Spaniards from Extremadura, and those from other parts of Iberia jostled and fought for wealth within an atmosphere of unfettered freedom. Fortunes were made in a day and lives lost overnight as young adventurers, intoxicated with life, made wanton challenges to the death.

Women as well as men joined in the chase after riches and fame, suffering all the same dangers in equal, and sometimes greater, measure. When gender proved a hindrance, some simply disguised themselves as men. Records of the era yield many such examples. The *Annals of Potosí*, for instance, chronicle the case of two young women who for fourteen turbulent years traveled throughout Peru dressed as men, returning home only at the point of death and announcing to incredulous relatives that they died chaste. The same source tells of the beautiful Doña Clara, who, dressed as a soldier, fought beside her brother in the wars between Basques and Castilians. Only as the enemy prepared to behead her did she escape death by revealing her identity.

No tale of unconventional womanhood can rival that of Catalina de Erauso, a nun and a proud Basque. After she fled the convent, Catalina donned men's clothing and mingled with the vagabonds traveling Spain's highways. Making her way to America, she earned the esteem of her peers through sheer audacity and mastery of the martial arts. She was breveted ensign on the field of battle and later, when her true identity was discovered, became famous as *la monja alférez*, or the Nun Ensign.

The Nun Ensign's story is one of high adventure spanning an epic phase in the expansion of Iberian civilization. It also provides an unfolding microcosm of a rude society in flux. Because Catalina was Basque, from a region brought unwillingly into the kingdom of Castile, she held regional loyalties far transcending any sense of "Spanish" subjecthood. Basque country spanned the region between Spain and France, its denizens distinct from both by their language, traditions, and exceptional seafaring skills. The early supremacy of Basque sailors, whalers, and shipbuilders helped drive Spanish expansion in the Western hemisphere. Yet decades later, and across the Atlantic, Basques remained distinguished by their own almost impenetrable language and their dislike of all things Castilian. Catalina de Erauso and many others from Spain's diverse empire sowed seeds of regionalism in an American soil already geographically conditioned to receive them.

Catalina's odyssey is also marked by ecclesiastical privilege and the related issue of church-state conflict. Time and again Catalina sought and received religious sanctuary, thus escaping punishment by the secular arm of government. Often those granting sanctuary were her own Basque countrymen. Finally, when appeal for clerical intercession could not save the hot-headed ensign from punishment by the secular state, Catalina played her unbeatable trump card. Not only was she a woman and a nun, but, most incredibly, she was a virgin!

The history of Catalina de Erauso arouses conflicting emotions: admiration for her rejection of a stereotype that frustrated her, amazement that she succeeded in her heroic masquerade, and wonder at her unchecked thirst for blood. Finally, one is bound to be a bit skeptical that she experienced all the adventures that historical sources attribute to her. One wonders whether some details of her life story weren't tailored to fit the picaresque convention that had by her day captured the Spanish imagination. But there can be no doubt that Catalina de Erauso, the Nun Ensign, lived. Nor can it be disputed that she was one of the most remarkable women of her time.

CONVENT BREAK: "DON ANTONIO'S" ADVENTURES IN SPAIN

Although Catalina de Erauso writes in her autobiography that she was born in 1585, her birth certificate, found many years after her death, lists 1592 as her date of birth. Scholars have been unable to resolve this mystery. Still, most of her life's story connects to important events of that time, events that were well known to her readers and that have come down in the historical record.

Her story begins in San Sebastián, a city in northeastern Spain. As was the practice with most sixteenth-century Basque families of means, at the age of four Catalina was sent from her large family to be raised in San Sebastián's Dominican convent. Boys were trained for conquest, to expand family wealth; girls were brought up in convents until they were of marriageable age. Catalina de Erauso remained in the convent for the next eleven years, under the eye of her stern aunt, the mother superior.

When she was fifteen, Catalina quarreled with a nun, a conflict that escalated into physical punishment. It may not have been the first time Catalina experienced such punishment. "When she beat me, I felt it," she noted in her autobiography.[1] So it was that after more than a decade of the cloistered life, as a novice on the verge of taking her vows, Catalina decided to break free. One night her aunt ordered Catalina to fetch the heavy ring of keys from her cell. Understanding that freedom lay in possessing one of her aunt's keys, Catalina slipped one from the ring and dropped it into the deep pocket of her novice's habit. The dream of many long nights was suddenly within reach, and a half-conceived plan of escape suddenly crystallized. From a blue wool overskirt, she cut and sewed a pair of knee breeches and transformed a coarse green petticoat into a doublet with long sleeves. The remodeled clothes cost her a mere three days' work. On the third night Catalina put on her disguise and, without a moment's regret, cut off her long, black hair. The petticoat and veil that had confined her since earliest childhood lay abandoned on her cot. Scarcely daring to breathe, she opened the door to her cell and crept into the hall and then down the stairs to the side entryway. Turning the key in the high iron-hinged door, she opened it and, casting a wary eye at the moon riding high over the convent garden, made her way to the outer gate and stepped into the street beyond.

In those first few days of freedom, Catalina traveled south from San Sebastián, a provincial capital in the heart of Basque country. Her destination was Vitoria, another Basque city lying almost sixty miles inland. As she walked, she practiced the small gestures and forms of speech that went with her new identity, replacing the feminine words she had used all her life with masculine ones. Her body, free from the heavy skirts and tight bodice of her convent clothes, soon relaxed into the swinging stride of the long-distance traveler. By the time she arrived in Vitoria, her convent paleness had been burned away by the sun, and with it every trace of the femininity that had held her captive since birth. Longing for anonymity, she exchanged her illustrious Basque name for a more common one that was far less likely to betray her. Catalina de Erauso y Pérez de Galarraga thus became Antonio Ramírez de Guzmán, a name as rootless as its new owner was determined to become.

Hunger was the first by-product of her new freedom. Little food grew in the Basque countryside of early spring, and by the time she approached Vitoria, her courage was strengthened by the demands of an empty stomach. On arrival, the new Antonio went to the home of a distant relative, Don Francisco de Cerralta. Her disguise easily protected her true identity, and for a few weeks she did odd jobs in the Cerralta household. Soon, however, the taste for trouble that had so exasperated the nuns of San Sebastián reappeared on a more ambitious scale. Tempted by her master's purse lying unguarded on a table, she stole it and fled.

The few weeks' success as Antonio Ramírez gave Catalina confidence, and she traveled the highways of Spain with a new boldness, toward Valladolid, a city some 130 miles south of Vitoria and close to the center of the Iberian Peninsula. In Valladolid she became a page in the household of a duke, Don Juan de Idiáquez, who as secretary to the king was a member of Spain's highest nobility. Principal among her duties was to accompany the ladies of the house to Mass, the irony of which was not lost on her. Now using the alias Francisco Loyola, Catalina lived in Valladolid for seven months, learning to be an adequate servant and demonstrating her skill for seeking out trouble. She started arguments with the other servants and gambled away the nights in the servants' quarters. These tendencies, alien to young middle-class ladies of that day, were appropriate in a duke's page who was considered agreeably high-spirited. All was well, in fact, until Catalina's own father came to call on the duke. Fearful that she would be discovered, she stayed only to hear him tell the story of his daughter's escape from the convent.

Catalina was almost seventeen years old when she fled Valladolid. She was large-boned for a girl, athletic, strong, and gifted with an abundance of physical energy that had caused her many a problem in the close environment of the San Sebastián convent. But it was her Basque audacity and willingness to dive into action, above all else, that kept her small hands and smooth face from becoming features that called her "masculinity" into question.

For two years Catalina wandered the Basque provinces of northern Spain. She stayed for a time in Bilbao, most of it in jail. When she arrived in the town she could find no lodging, and as she wandered from street to street, a growing group of youths dogged her every step. Fed up, she threw a stone at them, injuring one badly enough to merit arrest. Authorities jailed her for the month that it took the wound to heal. Somehow, she maintained her disguise during the days in prison—and fought back the impulse to gain release by confessing her true gender. She realized all too well that such a confession would lead her back to a prison of a different sort, constructed not of iron bars but of long, heavy skirts, endless household chores, and cloistered confinement. So she endured the ignominy of prison without revealing her secret to anyone.

Free once again, Catalina journeyed almost a hundred miles to the city of Estella de Navarra. There she found employment as page to one Carlos de Arellano, in whose household she lived for almost two years. During that time she perfected a style that complemented her youthful good looks. Her original knee breeches and doublet were replaced by an elegant black suit trimmed in silver, high boots of crimson morocco leather, and a soft, broad-brimmed hat, bright red and adorned with a single black ostrich feather. The "handsome Antonio," dressed in that red and black costume, attracted the admiration of many a Spanish maiden. Catalina enjoyed their attentions and began to adopt a swagger, an exaggerated braggadocio, that fed on her natural boldness.

In the years after her escape from San Sebastián, Catalina de Erauso lost herself in the life of vagabonds who roamed the heart of Spain. Like the pícaros, or rogues, who peopled Spain's popular literature of that era, Catalina lived by her wits and paid homage only to her own freedom. The fraud she lived was her most prized possession, for it permitted her to shape a destiny entirely different from the one prescribed by society. Most important, by dressing as a man, she could contemplate an active role in the greatest adventure of her day: the one to be had in Spain's New World colonies.

EARLY AMERICAN ADVENTURES

For a full century, the New World had served as an escape valve for the Spanish population. Spain offered neither wealth nor honor to the average person, while the New World offered both to those with sufficient energy and endurance to fight for it. Simple adventurers escaping bonded servitude, second sons of noble families, friars and priests anxious to convert an entire continent to Christianity, and soldiers of fortune in search of a battle—these were the men who flocked to the New World. And with them, distinguished only by an accident of biology, went Catalina.

The escaped novice could never be satisfied to spend her days as some nobleman's servant chafing against the limitations of a calcified social system. Then too, she had long heard stories of Basque youths who left for the New World and returned home wealthy. Her brother Miguel de Erauso, a dozen years her senior, had gone to the New World when Catalina was a child. Even Friar Lope de Altolaguirre, chaplain of the San Sebastián convent, had abandoned his religious vows in favor of New World adventuring. Convinced that her future also lay in those outer fringes of Spain's empire, Catalina packed her things and took the road north to San Sebastián and the coast. There, once again she walked the streets of her childhood and entered the cool, dimly lit chapel of the Dominican convent, her plumed hat in one hand, a sword of polished Toledo steel at her side.

It was there in the convent of San Sebastián that Catalina's decision to leave for the Americas became final. As Mass began, she noticed a familiar, mantilla-clad head bowed a few feet from where she stood. Catalina recognized her mother. But when Doña María glanced at her daughter, she saw not a trace of the young novice who had run away three years before. Without a word Catalina backed out of the church. All ties with her parents irrevocably cut, Catalina boarded ship and sailed down the coast to the great Spanish port of Sevilla. There, on Easter Monday, she boarded a second ship, sailed down the Guadalquivir River, through the marshy delta lowlands, and out into the broad Atlantic.

Working as a cabin boy, Catalina remained with her ship until it reached Panama. There, having pocketed the purse of the captain, she jumped ship, crossed the isthmus, and sailed south along the Pacific coast of South America. Her destination was Peru, the vast viceroyalty that reached from Panama in the north to Chile and Rio de la Plata in the south. Soon after her arrival at the port village of Paita, on Peru's northwestern coast, she was hired by a shopkeeper named Juan de Urquiza. Urquiza was a Basque, one of a small army of merchants and landowners who, blessed with characteristic Basque industriousness, were busy accumulating wealth everywhere in Peru. Catalina served her master well in the arid villages of Paita and Saña and was rewarded with two new suits, several servants, and an allowance of three pesos a day. After a time, however, these physical comforts and the routine of minding the store for Urquiza started to bore her. She became increasingly touchy and quick to pick a fight. Urquiza, misinterpreting the cause of his countryman Antonio's restlessness, suggested in a friendly manner that he court the lovely Beatriz de Cárdenas, a lady whose enthusiasm for romance Urquiza already knew well. Beatriz, a frequent visitor to the store, had openly admired young Antonio. Catalina, seeing her own interest in Beatriz returned, became bolder in her advances, even accepting invitations to visit Beatriz at night.

As Catalina became tangled in the sticky web of love, she slipped into indiscretions of a different sort. One night at a local cantina, a man named Reyes pulled his chair in front of hers, blocking her view of the entertainment. Catalina, her temper rising, told him to move. Words were exchanged and Reyes refused to budge. Furious, Catalina took her sword to the barber to be sharpened and the next night returned to confront Reyes. In the ensuing brawl, Catalina laid open Reyes's face and stabbed one of his friends for good measure.

Pleased with her first taste of armed combat and with the insignificant jail term that it earned, Catalina thirsted for further encounters. However, her success in the boudoir had just the opposite effect. As her lover, Beatriz, became aggressive, Antonio grew reticent. At length Beatriz locked Antonio in her room, opening the door only after exacting a proposal of marriage. Catalina grew alarmed. Romance was delightful, and flirtations stimulating; even duels over the love of a beautiful woman were pleasant entertainment. But marriage was, to say the least, out of the question. Finally, Catalina's employer, Urquiza, resolved her problem by sending her to open a shop in the city of Trujillo, 250 miles down the coast.

The transfer to Trujillo offered welcome release from the passionate Beatriz, who was making wedding plans even as Catalina plotted her escape. Trujillo offered little peace, however, for her enemy Reyes and two companions followed Catalina there, eager for revenge. In a matter of days, confrontation became unavoidable, forced to a head by universal obedience to a code of honor that claimed life itself as surety. When the brawl began Catalina and a friend managed a good defense against the three men from Saña. At length, urged on by the shouts of onlookers and her own excitement, Catalina ran Reyes's friend through with her sword. Companions of the dead man accused Catalina of murder and demanded that she be hanged. But Trujillo's magistrate, Ordoño de Aguirre, was a sympathetic man. Like Catalina he was a Basque. He recognized the incident for what it was—an affair of honor—and permitted her to seek sanctuary in the cathedral of Trujillo. There, safe from civil authorities and from further revenge, Catalina sent word of her troubles to Urquiza, who washed his hands of her—although not before sending pocket money, two new suits, a letter of recommendation, and his best wishes.

Soon thereafter, Catalina slipped out of Trujillo and traveled down the coast to Lima. At that time, and indeed throughout the ensuing century, Lima was the primary seat of government and center of trade for the entire South American continent. It boasted large, impressive buildings that housed the viceroy, the archbishop, many churches, monasteries and convents, and the continent's first university. Fed by a constant flow of silver from the mines of Potosí, Lima was a plump and prosperous city, full of ostentation and vainglory, peopled by soldiers of fortune, professional bureaucrats, and ambitious merchants.

Not long after arriving in Lima, Catalina presented her letter of recommendation to a businessman named Diego de Solarte, who hired her on the spot—and Solarte's sister-in-law promptly fell in love with Antonio. For nine months Catalina worked for Solarte, barely enduring the boredom and confinement of city life. Convinced that Lima promised little more than another unwelcome betrothal, she let her thoughts turn to the possibility of new adventures. Had the nights not been sweetened by secret flirtations, it is doubtful that she would have suffered Lima's bourgeois society as long as she did. When word of the infatuation at last reached Solarte, he threw Catalina unceremoniously into the street and closed the door firmly behind her. With no reason and less desire to stay in Lima, Catalina persuaded some gambling companions to join her in enlisting as soldiers in the Araucanian Wars of Chile.

OF MEN AND MURDER: SOLDIERS ON THE SOUTHERN FRONTIER

When Catalina and her friends left Lima, the war against Chile's Mapuche people had already raged for more than half a century, consuming the constant stream of soldiers sent from Peru to the viceroyalty's distant southern frontier. Only the roughest, most rootless of Iberia's sons were drawn to that battlefield. Unlike much of the New World, the colony, established by Pedro de Valdivia and his consort Inés de Suárez nearly seventy years before, offered neither silver nor easily exploited native peoples. Chile had become an agricultural colony, and the irrigated valleys that spread out from Santiago supported vineyards and orchards, domestic animals, and crops of wheat, maize, and other grains. But such economy never contributed great wealth to the Spanish crown. In fact, Chile had a negative impact on the viceroyalty's ledger books due to the long and costly Araucanian Wars. South of Santiago, the provincial capital, in a region bound on the north by the River Maule, lived unconquered peoples that incessant military campaigns had yet failed to secure for Spain. Far different from the Inca, the Mapuche were nomads, intensely warlike and independent. They, in fact, resisted Spain's encroachments far into the nineteenth century. Traveling to Chile by sea or over high cordilleras and through coastal deserts, young men arriving there thirsted for war and glory.

Catalina de Erauso departed Lima for Concepción by sea. Concepción was little more than an armed camp located some two hundred miles south of Santiago. It was November and late spring probably in the year 1605 when the soldiers disembarked at the port of Concepción, then administered by Governor Alonso de Ribera, whose fame as an iron-willed commander had spread throughout Spanish America. Located close to the Pacific, on the banks of the Bío-Bío River, Concepción was distinguished both as a center of military operations and by the fact that a bishop resided there. On all other counts it was an inhospitable place. Its muddy streets were lined with gambling houses, and its nights were pierced by clashing swords and the muffled cries of soldiers playing their deadly games.

Catalina fell in with a group of hard-drinking Basques and soon became known as one of the worst of the lot. Upon arriving in Concepción, she learned that the governor's secretary was another Basque, Captain Miguel de Erauso, who was none other than her older brother. As he was twelve years older and had last seen her as a small child, Catalina was able to keep her identity a secret. They spoke only of their common ancestry and of the mutual sympathy existing between sons of the same Spanish region. For three years Antonio and Miguel were constant companions who ate together, gambled together, and, after petitioning the governor for Antonio's transfer to Miguel's company, fought together.

Soon after the arrival of troops from Lima, word came of serious indigenous attacks in the untamed lands between Santiago and Concepción. Spanish settlers from Nacimiento, Temuco, Villarrica, and the plains of Valdivia straggled into Concepción with word of defeats by indigenous war parties. Then came the news that Cacique Huenchullán, leader of Mapuche forces in the area of Temuco, had laid siege to the fort at Villarrica. The entire region south of Concepción was close to falling to his warriors. Governor García Ramón, newly arrived in Chile, mobilized Concepción's fighting force of five thousand men and ordered it to the plains of Valdivia, more than two hundred miles to the south. He had a camp established there, and from it the Spanish troops undertook forays into the surrounding countryside.

Fifty soldiers made up Miguel's company, and among them was his sister, known to them as Antonio Ramírez de Guzmán. Receiving their marching orders, the company broke camp and traveled east into the foothills of the Andes. For several days they saw no one and heard nothing but birdsong and the sound of their own horses' hooves. On the third day a young Mapuche warrior, mounted bareback and seemingly alone, appeared from a stand of trees, galloped toward Captain Miguel, and thrust his lance into the ground. Even before the lance had stopped quivering, the Spanish were set upon by an indigenous force twice their number. The Spanish held their own for a while, shielding themselves from the enemy's lances and arrows and charging again and again into their ranks, cutting down the Mapuche with their swords. Spaniards fell from their horses, their bodies bristling with arrows. Many died instantly as an indigenous lance found a vital spot; others, severely wounded, lost consciousness and lay helpless under the feet of the plunging horses. One soldier, wounded by ten lance-thrusts, dragged himself to a protected spot and, drawing a cross on the ground with his own blood, kissed it and died.

As the Spanish were driven back, Catalina sensed they were about to be routed. Seized by sudden inspiration, she rode among the surviving soldiers shouting the ancient battle cry of Catholic Spain: "Santiago! Santiago and attack!" She rode down the Mapuche warrior who had captured the company's battle flag, killed him, and retrieved the banner. She was a fearsome sight. Bleeding from the shoulder and from several arrow wounds, her face covered with dirt and sweat and her sword flashing in the dusty air, Catalina de Erauso turned the tide of battle and raised high the battle flag. The Mapuche line wavered and broke. They disappeared as suddenly as they had appeared.

Captain Miguel wept with fury as he surveyed the wounded survivors. Of his fifty soldiers, thirty were dead and all of the survivors were wounded. On that same bloody battlefield, he promoted Catalina to the rank of ensign, recognizing that only his companion's heroism had saved his division.

During the months following her heroic actions, Catalina participated in several other skirmishes across the plains of Valdivia. On one occasion she captured and killed the son of one of the Mapuche's most important leaders. Their numerous reverses convinced the Mapuche that further attacks were futile, and they withdrew for a time, some to the eastern fastness of the Andes, while others withdrew to the cold lake district far beyond the reach of even the most fearless Spaniard. This retreat and the onset of winter brought peace to frontier Chile. Catalina and her comrades undertook the painful and tedious journey north. Hundreds of veterans nursed wounds, and many whose horses had perished struggled along on foot. By the time the army reached Concepción, they were more than eager for pleasures denied them in the field. When she returned, Catalina learned that Governor García Ramón had approved her promotion and assigned her to serve under Captain Rodríguez, where she spent the subsequent five years.

Once the Mapuche recovered from the blow dealt them at Valdivia, they renewed their attacks. A Spanish expeditionary force was sent south, stopping briefly at the encampment of Nacimiento and continuing on to the center of hostilities. Late in 1609, as several hundred Spanish troops neared the plains of Purén, three thousand indigenous warriors attacked from all quarters, filling the air with battle cries and a hail of arrows. Closing ranks at the order of field commander Gonzalo Rodríguez, the mounted soldiers began the sallies and sword thrusts that slowly wore the attackers down. Four times during the course of the battle, Catalina's mount fell dead under her; each time she leapt to the back of a riderless horse and continued the attack. Captain Rodríguez was among the fallen. Although the Spanish lost their commander and many men, heavy indigenous losses forced their withdrawal. After that initial battle, they resorted to ambushes and continual attacks on Spanish scouting parties.

The Spanish army remained in the Valley of Purén for six months, often skirmishing with the enemy. It was during one such fray that Catalina lost her chance at further promotion in rank. After the death of Captain Rodríguez, she was placed in command of a company and led them on frequent excursions into indigenous territory beyond Purén. On one sortie Catalina captured and summarily hanged a Christian cacique named Don Francisco Quispiguancha. Unfortunately for both of them, the governor wanted the chief taken alive to Concepción. By executing him Ensign Catalina de Erauso had overstepped her authority. The captaincy she had long desired was given to another.

The expedition to Purén was Catalina's last. Soon after returning to Concepción, her habitual violence passed the bounds tolerated even in that frontier town. Boasting a new rank and outfitted with new clothing bought with combat pay, Catalina returned to the grimy gaming rooms of Concepción. She continued to take meals with Captain Miguel, but friction developed when her battle-ripened handsomeness turned the head of Miguel's own mistress. For a time Catalina stayed away, seeking amusement in other gambling dens and cantinas, where she became notorious as an exceptionally dangerous man. The most innocent comment was enough to provoke her anger, sending her rapier from its scabbard. At a party given by the governor, Catalina was drawn into a petty squabble; words were exchanged, then insults. Swords so recently bloodied in battle were drawn against friends. Catalina caught an opponent off guard and fatally wounded him. The governor himself witnessed the murder and ordered her capture. Surrounded, Catalina leapt to a table, jumped outside through a bank of windows, and ran down the darkened streets to the San Francisco church, where she sought sanctuary.

For eight months she remained under the protection of ecclesiastical authorities. The governor placed guards around the church to keep her from escaping. But as time passed the guards gradually relaxed their vigilance, and Catalina was able to receive visits from her friends. One day a friend named Juan de Silva came by the church with a request. He had quarreled with another soldier and had challenged him to a duel that same night. Would Catalina serve as his second? She reluctantly agreed and at ten o'clock that evening she slipped out of the church to meet de Silva at his quarters. The night was so dark that they could scarcely see two feet ahead, but they made their way to the agreed-upon meeting place. Two men showed up, de Silva's opponent and his second. Only the principals spoke, and the duel began. When she saw her friend was losing ground, Catalina leapt to defend him. That caused the man's second to lunge at Catalina with his own sword. Catalina turned and wounded the second near his heart. As he fell, a familiar voice choked out the words "Traitor, you have killed me!" Her brother! She had slain her brother Miguel! Dazed, but certain she would be hanged if captured, Catalina fled the scene and sprinted back to the San Francisco church. Once inside she was again safe from capture. That also meant she witnessed her brother's funeral service—"God knows in what misery," she wrote in her memoir.[2]

Chapter 5

STRIKING SILVER: FROM TUCUMÁN TO POTOSÍ

Time passed and Catalina de Erauso planned her escape from the church. One moonless night when the guard posted outside was less than vigilant, she fled the church and made her way to a sheltered spot where a friend waited with a horse and weapons. She mounted the horse and with a terse farewell headed northeast toward the Andean cordillera and, beyond that, the city of Tucumán, in present-day Argentina.

She traveled alone for several days and then fell in with two renegade soldiers who were as anxious to leave Chile as she was. Together they ascended into the mountains, climbing higher and higher until they reached cold country. Their provisions were soon exhausted, and there were few homesteads to offer hospitality in the desolate region. Even water was scarce, and, as they climbed, everything but the coarsest grasses ceased to grow. As the days passed, the travelers grew desperate for food. They killed and ate their horses one by one, until they were forced to continue on foot. The journey began to exact its toll. First one, then the other of Catalina's companions died. Before moving on alone, she searched the corpses and found eight pesos and a small supply of gunpowder for the heavy arquebus the dead soldier had carried. Her clothes torn, her boots long since worn through, Catalina traveled on, driven by her will to survive.

At last, months after her escape from Concepción, she saw what must have seemed a mirage. Down the slope a herd of sheep grazed before a rustic shelter. A slender line of smoke rising from its chimney signaled the end of her ordeal. The two shepherds whose hut she had stumbled on scarcely concealed their amazement when Catalina appeared, shouting hoarsely and dragging the arquebus behind her. They were even more amazed when Catalina told them how she had survived the thousand-mile journey from Chile to their hut at the western edge of Tucumán province. The shepherds fed her a little hot soup, bound her bloody feet, and took her to a nearby ranch for rest and care.

Tucumán, bound on the west by the Andes Mountain range and south of Upper Peru, was only slightly less remote from Lima than Concepción. Yet, unlike the Chilean fortress-village, Tucumán formed a vital link in the silver chain that bound the New World to the king's treasury in Spain. This was because Tucumán, along with its sister cities Córdoba, Salta, and Jujuy, bred the mules that were the single most important form of transportation in the New World. In exchange for mules, the towns of western Argentina received a share of the silver that their mules transported from the Andean fastness down dangerous mountain trails to the coast.

The comfortable ranch where Catalina recuperated was the property of a mestiza widow whose pocketbook bulged with cash earned from the mule-breeding industry. Doña Encarnación had one child, a daughter of marriageable age. Thus, the welcome she gave Catalina was not entirely disinterested. Believing Catalina to be, as she claimed, Ensign Antonio Ramírez, a battle-scarred veteran of the Araucanian Wars, Spanish-born and unmarried, Doña Encarnación had reason to be overcome with delight. After scarcely a week she made Catalina foreman of the ranch hands and administrator of the property as well. In exchange it was understood that the ensign would soon become her son-in-law.

Catalina pretended great happiness but was secretly repulsed by Doña Encarnación's singularly homely daughter. For several months she managed to please everyone, pretending to woo the heiress, all the while resisting a dash to the altar. During that time, Catalina became acquainted with a priest who had an unmarried niece in need of a husband. Catalina found herself besieged from all sides. Favors, gifts, and special attentions flowed from both, and a bit of quick thinking now and then was needed to keep her duplicity a secret. The priest was as generous as was Doña Encarnación, giving Catalina an excellent dowry that included a velvet suit, a dozen shirts and stockings, collars of fine linen, and two hundred pesos. Catalina adopted a posture of humble gratitude toward her patrons, understanding all the while that the situation was volatile. Thus she was prepared when an annoyed Doña Encarnación finally insisted that the wedding be celebrated immediately. That same night Catalina slipped away as she had so many times before, riding away before dawn and leaving behind two unhappy benefactors and two disappointed fiancées.

The trade route from Tucumán to Potosí covered a torturous, mountainous six hundred miles. Along the way, Catalina fell in with another solitary traveler. Thus accompanied, she traveled the weary miles to the rich highlands of Potosí. The journey took three months. Once in the city of silver, Catalina and her traveling companion parted company, to make their way as best they could.

The Potosí that greeted Catalina de Erauso was a large, unfortified city extending over the New World's richest silver mines. Its varied population of more than one hundred thousand was made up of Spaniards from eleven different regions or "nations" of Spain and their creole children, indigenous peoples, Blacks, and all possible ethnic mixes of these groups. The wealthiest residents lived in elegant stone houses several stories tall. They, and even members of the middle class, dined on plates and tableware made of pure silver. Wealthy by world standards of the day, they dressed in the finest brocades, laces, and linens. In Potosí a Sunday-afternoon stroll became occasion for the display of jewels and finery, and the simplest celebration became a weeklong carnival, with elaborate floats, open-air plays, and religious processions that wound through the streets. Yet that same exuberance had a darker side. A casual affront festered for a lifetime; a quarrel between friends easily became a neighborhood brawl; and political jealousies among groups became cause for civil war.

Conflict verging on civil war was epidemic when Catalina arrived in Potosí. Two warring factions had clashed again and again throughout a period of twenty years. On one hand were the Basques—merchants, administrators, and elected officials—who tenaciously maintained their position of preeminence during Potosí's richest years. More silver merchants, more craftsmen, more mayors and magistrates, and more officers of the mint and the royal treasury were from the Basque provinces than from any other region of Spain. Jealousy and suspicion born of this disproportion were widespread. Yet the Basques did little to placate their fellow citizens and seemed instead to use their positions to their own advantage. Other groups, among them Andalusians, Extremadurans, and Castilians, wanted to destroy Basque power. Basque-owned businesses suffered frequent boycotts; young men from non-Basque groups were discouraged from courting Basque daughters. Within this setting civil disobedience and violent forms of protest were the order of the day

It was only a matter of time before Catalina was drawn into the strife. She was hired by the Basque Juan López de Arguijo, a merchant in La Plata who was in the highly profitable business of transporting food to Potosí. As one of López's principal overseers, Catalina was responsible for twelve hundred pack animals and eighty carriers who plied the route from the lowland agricultural plains of Cochabamba to Charcas and on up to Potosí, more than 13,200 feet above sea level. In Cochabamba she commonly bought eight thousand bushels of wheat for four pesos a bushel, had it ground, and then transported it to Potosí, where it was worth four times its lowland rate. Her work with López quickly earned her a reputation as an efficient worker by day and an incurable brawler by night. The frequent attacks on Basques gave her constant cause for swordplay. In those clashes she earned an informal rank of assistant to the local sergeant major, who was a Basque. For two years she played a double role: supervisor of López's teamsters on one hand and defender of Potosí's Basque power structure on the other.

REVELATIONS: CATALINA, THE NUN ENSIGN

By 1617 Catalina had made so many enemies that she was forced to leave Potosí. But everywhere she went in Upper Peru—Chuncos, Charcas, Cochabamba, Piscobamba—she carried along the fiery temper that injury, loss, and death were unable to curb. In La Paz a servant of the sheriff insulted her, and she responded by stabbing him. Seized, jailed, and tried, she was summarily sentenced to hang.

On the morning of what was to be her last day, Catalina de Erauso was taken from her cell to an anteroom where the priest waited to perform final religious rites. A portable altar stood to one side, and after confession, the priest began Mass, placing the Host on the ensign's tongue. To his horror, Catalina leapt to her feet, took the Host from her mouth, and ran into the street, Host held high, crying "Sanctuary, sanctuary!" The crowd that had gathered was aghast. No one dared seize her, so awful was her sacrilege. Instead, they followed her down the street into the central plaza and watched as she sprinted into the cathedral. Once inside, secure in the comforting shadows of the church, Catalina knelt at the high altar and handed the Host to a priest. Next, she submitted docilely while the ritual cleansing was performed. The hands that had touched so sacred an object were washed with holy water and then scraped and dried. She was kept locked in the church for a month, and then, thanks to help from a supporter, left quietly for Cusco.

When she reached Cusco, Catalina de Erauso was jailed for a murder she did not commit. Five months passed before witnesses came forward and swore that she was innocent of the crime. Soon after her release, however, she did in fact commit murder, stabbing to death the bandit El Nuevo Cid in a brawl and suffering serious injury herself. After convalescing for four months, she attempted to leave Cusco undetected. But her enemies followed her. Along the way three soldiers recognized her as the infamous Ensign Antonio, but she was able to bribe them with three gold doubloons and continue on her way to the city of Huamanga (later renamed Ayacucho). Friends of El Nuevo Cid and officers of the law trailed along behind her. Upon reaching Huamanga, Catalina had the bad luck of attracting the attention of Corregidor (regional administrator) Baltazar de Quiñones. The official questioned her: Where are you from? Where are you coming from? He ordered the surly, battle-scarred Catalina arrested. But she drew her pistol and fled to a Basque-owned inn, and from there into hiding. A few days later she tried to flee Huamanga early in the evening. But just as night was falling, she ran into two bailiffs who tried to arrest her. Several Basques appeared out of nowhere, and another brawl ensued. Suddenly, in the midst of the fight, Huamanga's saintly Augustinian bishop Agustín de Carvajal appeared on the scene. Accompanied by four men carrying torches, he convinced Catalina to throw down her weapons and personally escorted her to the city's principal church. Civil officials demanded return of the criminal. But the bishop insisted on interviewing Ensign Antonio. For her part, Catalina de Erauso knew she had reached the end of the road. There was no way she could escape; there were no strings to pull, no influential friends to arrange a timely pardon. Her infamous past had become a nightmare she could not shake. No longer would there be pardon for her crimes.

Bishop Agustín de Carvajal looked up from his desk when Catalina entered the room. He gazed thoughtfully at the figure standing before him, noting the stiff military bearing, his proud head and slender neck, his sun-blackened, clean-shaven face, and his hard, suspicious eyes. This man was obviously a fighter, a loner, probably dangerous, but surely not beyond the reach of spiritual guidance. The bishop dismissed his aides with a gesture and, in a deep, kindly voice, began speaking of life and death, of sin and salvation, of the horrors of hell and the glories of heaven. Then he asked questions—direct, unavoidable questions—his eyes fixed on the scarred face of the person who listened to him intently. "Who are you?" he asked. "Where are you from?" "What brought you to Peru?" Suddenly Catalina fell to her knees. As she recalled in her autobiography, "It was if I might already be in the presence of God."[3] She started to talk. One by one the long-hidden details of her true identity poured forth in a confession that left the bishop shocked and bewildered. Her story ended at one o'clock the following morning. After Catalina was returned to her cell, the bishop likely meditated into the night on the perverse miracle that had transformed a bride of Christ into an infamous but now-repentant soldier. Could this all be true?

The next day Bishop Carvajal took Catalina de Erauso by the hand and led her out of the church. The hushed whispers of onlookers became a confused babble when the cleric and the outlaw pushed through the crowd and proceeded to a nearby convent. Shocked silence descended as the two figures stepped inside and closed the high wooden doors behind them. While the bishop conferred privately with the prioress, ten quaking nuns examined the fearsome Antonio. At length, one of them appeared with astonishing news that the condemned criminal was not only a woman, but a virgin as well! This was a person who could not be hanged. But neither could she be allowed to leave the cloister.

Dressed awkwardly in nun's habit, Catalina de Erauso was held prisoner in the Huamanga convent while the bishop tried to decide what to do with her. He dispatched detailed letters about Catalina de Erauso to Pope Urban VIII and to King Philip IV of Spain, and to the Basque convent of San Sebastián as well. What advice could they offer on this bizarre case?

Several months passed as Catalina awaited word on her fate. Outside the walls of the convent, and across the Viceroyalty of Peru, exploits of the Nun Ensign became a favorite topic of conversation, those who had known her becoming minor celebrities in their own right. Five months after her arrest, Lima's archbishop Lobo Guerrero called for Catalina to appear before him. Catalina arrived in Lima escorted by six priests, four nuns, and five swordsmen, none of whom, she protested, would last long against her in a street fight. Offered the choice of living in any one of the capital's numerous convents, she selected the largest, the Holy Trinity Convent of St. Bernard.

There she resumed her wait for word on what fate held in store for her. After two long years a report arrived from San Sebastián explaining that Catalina de Erauso had indeed been a novice there but had never taken perpetual vows. The archbishop therefore granted her permission to return to masculine dress. He also made arrangements for her to travel to Spain for an audience with the king.

Catalina de Erauso made the transatlantic crossing back to Spain in 1624. Once in Cadiz, she dined with numerous illustrious figures, including don Fadrique de Toledo, head of the Spanish armada, which at the moment was preparing to challenge the Dutch in the New World. In Sevilla, she dodged mobs of curious people. Her audience with King Philip IV took place in August 1625. Shortly thereafter she submitted patiently as Francisco Pacheco, a noted artist of the period, painted the portrait of her that long hung in a San Sebastián café with other paintings of illustrious sons of the Basque provinces. Meanwhile, Catalina composed a petition to the king recounting her numerous courageous acts and requesting a pension in return for her years of faithful service in the Araucanian Wars. Philip IV surely mused that the petition seemed more a picaresque novel than an authentic account of Catalina's adventures. Nevertheless, he forwarded her petition to the Council of Indies, which awarded her a lifetime stipend valued at more than four times the normal ensign's wages. Additionally, she was awarded a handsome bonus of thirty ducats, payable by the royal treasuries of Lima, Mexico City, or Manila. While less than she had hoped for, the money more than covered her future expenses. Realizing that further requests were useless, Catalina de Erauso proceeded with plans to visit Rome.

In 1627 she was received by Pope Urban VIII, who found her story as intriguing as had Philip IV. After hearing her story, he reaffirmed her ecclesiastical dispensation to wear men's clothing, going on to require that she live an honest and peaceful life. Armed with the papal dispensation, Catalina returned to Spain en route once again to the New World. On July 21, 1630, she departed Sevilla for Mexico. There, far from the enemies of her youth, free from the social restrictions she had endured in Spain, and with a measure of financial security, she settled into the way of life most suited to her. (See figure 5.) Dressed in the Spanish style, a silver-handled sword and matching dagger at her side, she became a muleteer on the royal highway from Veracruz to Mexico City and spent the remainder of her days transporting goods between the coast and the capital.

122 Chapter 5

Figure 5.1 Catalina de Erauso, "Nun Ensign" (Collection of Fundación Kutxa Fundazioa)

EPILOGUE

The last account of Catalina de Erauso was recorded in 1645 when a Capuchin friar wrote that he had seen her in Veracruz, where she was universally respected for her fearlessness and piety. About her death little is known. Whether she died by the sword or expired peacefully at age sixty, as various writers have suggested, will perhaps never be known. Her own memoir ends prior to her return trip to the Americas. It reveals that she shaped her own destiny far more than most other women of her time. Escaping from the narrow role assigned her from birth, Catalina de Erauso emerges as an abiding symbol of a bizarre and extravagant age. When in Rome, she had met with all the cardinals at St. Peter's Cathedral and shared her story. One of them, Cardinal Magálon, mused that theft, gambling, and murder aside, Catalina's only fault was that she was a Spaniard. Perhaps thinking on how she chose her own fate while remaining true to Spain and the Catholic church, *La Monja Alférez*—the Nun Ensign—issued a sharp retort: "With all due respect, your Holiness, being a Spanish citizen is my only virtue."[4]

NOTES

1. Catalina de Erauso, *Lieutenant Nun*, translated by Michele Stepto and Gabriel Stepto (Boston: Beacon Press, 1996), 3.
2. Catalina de Erauso, *Historia de la Monja Alférez, Catalina de Erauso, escrita por ella misma*, ed. Ángel Esteban (Madrid: Ediciones Cátedra, 2018), 117–18.
3. Erauso, *Historia*, 160.
4. Catalina de Erauso, *Lieutenant Nun*, 79; Erauso, *Historia*, 174.

REFERENCES

Erauso, Catalina de. *Historia de la Monja Alférez, Catalina de Erauso, escrita por ella misma*. Edición de Ángel Esteban. Seventh edición. Madrid: Ediciones Cátedra, 2018.
Erauso, Catalina de. *Lieutenant Nun*. Translated by Michele Stepto and Gabriel Stepto. Boston: Beacon Press, 1996.
Heredia, José María de. *La monja alférez*. Santiago de Chile, 1906.
León, Nicolás. *Aventuras de la Monja Alférez*. Mexico City: Colección Metropolitana, 1973.
Leonard, Irving A. *Baroque Times in Old Mexico*. New York: Alfred A. Knopf, 1972.
Morales-Álvarez, Raúl. *La monja alférez: Crónica de una vida que tuvo perfil de romance*. Chile: Editorial Nuñoa, 1936.
Palma, Ricardo. *"¡A iglesia me llamo!" Tradiciones peruanas: primera selección*. Buenos Aires: Espasa-Calpe Argentina, 1956.
Pérez Villanueva, Sonia. *The Life of Catalina de Erauso, the Lieutenant Nun: An Early Autobiography*. New York: Rowman & Littlefield, 2014.
Velasco, Sherry. *The Lieutenant Nun: Transgenderism, Lesbian Desire, and Catalina de Erauso*. Austin: University of Texas Press.

Chapter 6

Sor Juana Inés de la Cruz, 1651–1695

INTRODUCTION

During the 1970s renovation of the San Jerónimo convent in Mexico City, workers unearthed bones and a bronze medallion worn by a seventeenth-century nun. The *escudo de monja*, as it was called, and the remains with which it was found were of the convent's most celebrated religious person, Sor Juana Inés de la Cruz. More than three hundred years earlier, the Tenth Muse, as she came to be known, was recognized as the preeminent Baroque poet of the Spanish-speaking world.

At the time of the famous nun's death, Spain and its far-flung colonies were under attack from every quarter. Dutch, English, and French ships harassed Spanish vessels on the high seas, and Protestant settlers from those same countries began carving out settlements on American soil long claimed by Spain. In 1643 the renowned Spanish infantry was beaten by the French at Rocroi—a defeat as shocking as that of the "Invincible Armada" some half century before. Deteriorating conditions within Spain paralleled the unrelieved disasters occurring outside the country. The American gold and silver that helped make Spain supreme during the sixteenth century ended up in northern Europe, where they served to fuel economic prosperity. Spain's short-lived bullion bonanza had wrecked the national economy by driving up prices, leaving the ordinary person worse off than ever before. It had also bankrupted the economy on several occasions in the fifteenth and sixteenth centuries.

Unable to halt these military and economic reverses, Spain adopted defensive policies to shore up imperial claims. Its strategy to stem its losses included the building of great fortresses at strategic points throughout the empire; this was meant to enforce the closed economic system known as mercantilism. The defensive measures were not only military and economic but intellectual as well.

The Spanish way to knowledge had long rested on the belief that all truth was revealed by God through the teachings of early church fathers. But truth by revelation was also under attack. Thinkers in the rising nation-states of Protestant Europe advocated the scientific method as the proper way to arrive at knowledge. Even in Catholic France, philosopher René Descartes advocated empirical observation as the best way to learn about the world. Should the Cartesian method contaminate Catholic Spain's kingdoms, the religious wisdom of the ages might come into question. To guard against that possibility, church and state collaborated to police the thoughts of the people. The Holy Office, or Inquisition, constituted by Isabel I of Castile, was now an institutional watchdog, a censor whose duty it was to ferret out any person, at home or abroad, who failed to think along acceptable lines.

Under such conditions it seems incredible that creative intellectual activity was possible. Yet Spain's troubled seventeenth century witnessed a spectacular outpouring of artistic genius. Throughout the empire the Age of the Baroque manifested itself in exuberant, ornate, and colorful poetry, prose, art, and architecture. Literary works also highlighted societal tensions and celebrated a uniquely Spanish style. For instance, Cervantes published his improbable *Don Quixote* in 1604; many of Lope de Vega's two thousand dramas, including his witty, action-oriented *comedias*, appeared during the first thirty-five years of the century; and the intricate poetry of Luis de Góngora set a style that was extensively imitated in the Spanish-speaking world. In Spain's distant Mexican kingdom, the remarkable nun Sor Juana Inés de la Cruz won a place among those Spanish luminaries by crafting lyric poetry rivaling any in the Spanish language. Confronted by obstacles that would have overwhelmed a lesser genius, Sor Juana Inés struggled for a lifetime against enemies who demanded that she conform to conventional standards of feminine and religious behavior. Yet the limitations placed upon her merely drove her to excel even in the face of adversity. Today it is not just for her poetry, but also for her defiance and ongoing creative output that Sor Juana Inés is remembered with affection, even awe, by her admirers.

A COURTLY EDUCATION

In mid-1664 the Marqués and Marquesa of Mancera, only recently arrived in Mexico City, marveled at the intense blue skies and wide expanse of New Spain. The Marqués of Mancera had served Felipe IV of Spain as ambassador to Germany and Venice and, in recognition of his faithful service, had been appointed twenty-fifth viceroy of the kingdom of New Spain. The viceroy was the crown's representative in its New World possessions, having power inferior only to that of the king himself. Mancera was pleased that the new position was important—and one that he was eminently qualified to occupy.

Soon after their triumphant entrance into Mexico City, the marqués and his beautiful wife, Doña Leonor Carreto, began to make their scholarly and aesthetic tastes and interests known within the viceregal court. The viceroy was eager to find aides who could serve him faithfully as counselors and entertain him with intelligent conversation. Doña Leonor wished to surround herself with companions who would sweeten the hours with poetry, art, music, and learned discourses on questions of religious or historical interest. Accustomed to the sophisticated pastimes of the age, both were eager to re-create in Mexico the court life they had known as members of Europe's highest diplomatic circles.

During her first months in New Spain, Doña Leonor received a petition from the family of a young creole girl, Juana Inés de Asbaje, begging that she be admitted to the viceregal court as a member of the marquesa's retinue. Such requests were not uncommon. In fact, Doña Leonor received petitions almost daily from families of young ladies who hoped to find suitable husbands—preferably rich and Spanish-born—in the heady atmosphere of the Mexican court. But in the case of Juana Inés de Asbaje, the request was quite different. Instead of a husband, the Asbaje family sought viceregal protection for Juana as though she were a precious jewel or rare book in need of safekeeping.

Her curiosity aroused by this unusual petition, the marquesa asked for further information about Juana Inés. To her delight, she found that the child was a prodigy, a young genius who had begun to read at age three, and, at eight, had learned Latin in a scant twenty lessons—or so her tutor claimed. At that same age she won a prize for a *loa*, a short piece introducing a play, written in complicated style; her work celebrated the sacrament of Holy Communion. Doña Leonor was not discouraged by the fact that Juana's family was poor, nor that her parents may not have been legally wed. It was enough that the girl was of pure Spanish blood, supremely intelligent, and poetically gifted.

Born out of wedlock to a creole mother and Spanish father, Juana Inés de Asbaje had, in fact, enjoyed a fairly idyllic childhood. That her parents were not married was not unusual, given the circumstances; this was one way that American-born mothers were able to maintain a degree of independence and financial stability. In fact, Juana Inés was one of five siblings by two fathers. Her mother ran one of her grandfather's small estates. As a small child, Juana Inés had tagged along to her older sister's lessons and spent long hours in her grandfather's library. At age ten she was sent to Mexico City for more opportunities for learning, where she stayed for a short while with relatives. In fact, she had shown such an overwhelming desire to learn that she begged to be disguised as a boy in order to attend a proper school. This bizarre idea made her family despair of ever turning her into an ordinary child. The petition to join the Mancera court, they hoped, would afford the prodigy opportunities that would otherwise be stifled.

The first meeting between the gracious marquesa and Juana, then age thirteen, convinced Doña Leonor that Juana Inés would be a delightful young companion. She was as pleased by Juana's adolescent beauty—her pale skin, dark eyes, and long dark hair—as she was by the girl's good manners and elegant speech. Doña Leonor understood instantly that Juana's family was correct. Only in the sophisticated atmosphere of the viceroy's court would Juana's talents develop and receive the applause they deserved. Outside, unprotected by wealth or high birth, she would be subjected to constant criticism from the church and society—from the church because learning was considered a threat to faith, and from society because women were believed to be inferior to men and were expected to act the part. Indeed, Juana would never have been happy in ordinary society. In Mexico of the 1600s, women of the advantaged classes were expected to remain at home, shut away from the evils of the outside world. But for the Marquesa of Mancera, this might well have been Juana's fate.

In late 1664, Juana packed her belongings and left the home of relatives for her new residence in the viceregal palace on Mexico City's central plaza. The change must have been dizzying. From quiet isolation she passed directly into the rarefied atmosphere of New Spain's intellectual and political center. Fortunately for her own sake, Juana was armed with two talents that ensured her success. The first was the powerful intelligence so admired by her contemporaries. If, as it was believed, all knowledge was contained in certain church-approved works, here was a mind capable of reaching into those dusty tomes and pulling out truths guaranteed not to harm a soul longing for salvation. Juana's conversation, her writing, and her contributions to learned discussions at the viceregal court were laced with long and gracefully appropriate quotations from her readings.

Her second talent, that of a skilled and sensitive poet, guaranteed her a place of honor at court. For Juana, writing in verse was, if anything, easier than writing in prose. And since the niceties of court life, and much of its entertainment, were carried along on a cushion of poetry, Juana's singular talent was much in demand. Every occasion, ordinary or extraordinary, religious or secular, called for a sonnet at the very least. The exchange of gifts brought forth a poetic exercise of one kind or another. Love, death, illness, graduation, and birthdays were similarly remembered in poems in honor of the person involved. These poems, often called poems of protocol, or occasional verse, are peppered throughout the more serious works of Juana Inés, much of their value lost as soon as the occasion that inspired them had passed.

The court of the Marqués and Marquesa of Mancera attracted outstanding figures from New Spain and from abroad. Those distinguished by wealth or power, by beauty or noble birth, by intellectual renown or artistic achievement gathered at the table of the viceroy and participated in the social life of the court. Elaborate plays were performed, many of them by acting companies from Spain. Feasts, glittering balls, and opulent dress were commonplace. Learned debates and poetry contests provided entertainment for those fortunate enough to spend time at court.

Juana lived for five years surrounded by the luxury and frivolous play of the Mancera court. During that time she enjoyed the unceasing affection of Doña Leonor, an affection she wholeheartedly returned. She was able to continue her studies, reading works that had not been available to her before. Spanish plays of the Golden Age, the works of Cervantes, Quevedo's somber satire, the complex verses of Góngora, and perhaps even the prohibited writings of Descartes were read and discussed by the worldly members of the viceroy's court in Mexico. It would be hard to believe that Juana, young and beautiful, was not enchanted by a way of life designed to amuse and to banish boredom. Secure in her favored position, pampered and sought after for her talents, Juana Inés was famous throughout New Spain by the time she was seventeen years old.

In 1668, during her seventeenth year, when most of Juana's peers were concerned only with romance, entertainment, and finding a suitable mate, the Marqués of Mancera arranged for Juana Inés to prove once and for all that she merited her fame as a brilliant and skilled debater. To that end he arranged a public examination of Juana by some forty professors who taught at the University of Mexico. The debate would be an oral test of Juana's knowledge of theology, philosophy, mathematics, history, poetry, and other disciplines. She, denied all formal education because of her sex, would face the questions of those who had enjoyed the best education then available. Years later, after Juana's death, the Marqués of Mancera described the historic confrontation. "As a royal galleon would defend itself from the attack of a few small boats," he wrote, "so Juana Inés fended off the questions, arguments and replies that all of them, each in his own field, put to her."[1] Her self-education thus displayed, her fame soundly defended, Juana Inés had the grace to claim that her great triumph had caused her only the slightest satisfaction.

Even as belle of the viceregal court, Juana Inés was faced with a problem of such gravity that it was to plague her, unsolved, throughout her life. Where in the closed and restricted society of seventeenth-century Mexico was she, a woman of the social elite, to find a life congenial to her talents and tastes? She, and her elite sisters throughout the Hispanic world, had but two choices.

They could marry or they could become nuns, married in effect to the church. No other options existed. Her family lacked the wealth to support her in her scholarly pursuits, and she was barred by her sex from earning her own living. Faced with a choice between marriage and the church, and encouraged by her confessor, Jesuit priest Antonio Núñez, Juana Inés chose the convent. As she wrote in self-defense many years later, "I became a nun, because even though I realized that state was (in many superficial ways) repugnant to my temperament, given the total disinclination I felt toward marriage, it seemed the most fitting and decent thing I could do, especially since I wished to ensure my personal salvation."[2]

CLOISTERED CREATIVITY

Shortly before her sixteenth birthday, Juana had left the side of the marquesa and entered the Convent of the Discalced (Barefoot) Carmelites, a strict religious order that had the advantage of owning a large library of some twelve thousand books. The young novice found it hard to adapt to the change from viceregal opulence to the severity of the Carmelite order. Barely three months later, in November 1667, Juana Inés fell ill and was removed from the cloister by her viceregal patrons. For fifteen months she recuperated at the marqués's palace. Yet the harsh experiences of convent life failed to sway her from her course. In February 1669 Juana Inés de Asbaje entered the convent of San Jerónimo, far less rigid than that of the Carmelites, located in the heart of Mexico City.

Convent life in Mexico was not the otherworldly existence that one might expect. With the exception of a few orders such as the Carmelite, most convents were comfortable places that offered a routine not much different from that of a large, well-to-do household. Nuns were permitted to have private rooms customarily called cells but not as austere as that word implies. They were also allowed to have personal servants and even slaves. This practice was carried to such extremes that one large Mexican convent reported that five hundred servants were in attendance on a mere one hundred nuns. Yet these practices were not treated severely when brought to the archbishop's attention. The convents served much too important a function in a society that offered so little to its female members. It was recognized that many who entered the convents were unmarried daughters of well-to-do parents who had no convenient place to live and who may or may not have had true religious vocations. No one seemed to expect outstanding saintliness from such nuns, nor did it seem a waste that a great number of them spent their lives singing in choirs, doing embroidery, cooking sweetmeats, and receiving visitors.

Those aspiring to the religious life were required to bring a dowry when they entered the convent. This, and the celebration similar to a wedding feast that followed the ceremony of taking the veil, placed most convents financially beyond the reach of poorer women. Juana Inés's dowry was provided not by her own family but by Don Pedro Velázquez de la Cadena, a wealthy resident of Mexico City. Juana's confessor, Father Núñez, was only too happy to host a party in honor of the young nun; he was not displeased that self-possessed young lady would now be housed within the confines of the convent. Sor Juana Inés de la Cruz, as she was called from that day forward, did not enter the convent as an ordinary nun. Protected by her friends the viceroy and Doña Leonor, on good terms with Don Payo de Ribera, the archbishop of New Spain, and already famous throughout the colony for her poetry and intellectual prowess, she began convent life as something of a celebrity. The dowry provided by Don Pedro Velázquez was ample, and Sor Juana never suffered from lack of diversion or comfort. She occupied a two-story cell and was attended by her own slave, a gift from her mother. Her visitors flocked to the convent locutory, a comfortable sort of living room, where she held salons, leading learned discussions and courtly conversation with highly placed friends and admirers. Her aristocratic friends often requested her poems for special and informal occasions, and the exchange of delicacies and small gifts was constant.

Even after taking the veil, Sor Juana remained a kind of poet laureate of the viceregal court. Nuns were expected to cover their expenses, and this she did through her literary output. On occasions of secular importance, it was she who was called upon to write official poems, and often she was paid for that service. Should someone noteworthy die, it was she who composed sonnets in honor of his or her memory. When New Spain commemorated events in the life of the Spanish monarch, her words marked the occasion with expected dignity and respect. Sor Juana carried out her function as official poet with great skill and, surprisingly, given the themes she had to deal with, some originality.

Among the gifts that Sor Juana valued most were the books and scientific instruments that she received from friends beyond the convent walls, and she treasured the moments when she could study uninterrupted. The quotidian life of a nun, even in a convent known for relative laxity, was punctuated by a prayerful routine that began in the earliest hours and continued through the night. Most sisters of the convent spent unstructured time sewing, cooking—and even arguing; more than once Sor Juana was called upon to put down her quill and settle a dispute. As did other nuns who on occasion withdrew from daily routine for private "retreats," she would absent herself for weeks from her sisters to wrangle with intellectual pursuits. Sor Juana realized, however, that communal life would create conflicts between convent routines and her private "inclination," as she called her scholarly vocation. Taught from earliest childhood to expect criticism of her intellectual interests, she had nevertheless hoped for some miraculous change in either herself or the world that would finally let the two live together in peace. Until then, Sor Juana managed to steal hours from her religious obligations, and, by candlelight, while others slept, she kept up her habits from childhood and "read and read some more, studied and studied some more, with no other teacher than those very books."[3]

In the effort to satisfy this inner drive and at the same time fulfill her obligations, she scrupulously obeyed convent regulations. She tried to be patient and friendly to her sisters, and she accepted the routine duties of the convent stoically. When her studies were interrupted by voices from a neighboring cell or when she had to help with kitchen duties, Sor Juana generally controlled her impatience. Yet she longed for a more private life with no distractions and no interruptions, free from the restrictions that were often placed on her. Humble as she tried to be, there were times when her control snapped. A few years after she became a nun, the San Jerónimo convent elected a prioress who, whatever may have been her spiritual virtues, was uneducated and, in fact, quite ignorant. Once, after suffering her in silence for a while, Sor Juana burst out with "Be quiet, Mother, you're such a fool!" So offended was the mother superior that she wrote a formal complaint to Archbishop Payo. The archbishop, one of Sor Juana's admirers, merely scribbled in the margin of the letter, "If the Mother Superior can prove the contrary, justice will be done."

BY THE BOOK: FRIENDSHIPS AND POETIC LOVE

In 1673, the Marqués and Marquesa of Mancera were called back to Spain. The loss of such kind and interesting patrons must have been difficult for Sor Juana. For nine years the Manceras, and especially Doña Leonor, had been far more important to her than her own family. Then, only a few days after the Manceras' departure from Mexico City, Doña Leonor suddenly fell ill and died. On receiving word of her untimely death, Sor Juana wrote three sonnets later published under the title "On the Death of the Marquesa de Mancera."

No one can doubt that Sor Juana, then barely twenty-two years old, grieved over the death of Doña Leonor—"Laura," as she was called in the poems. Yet by the time Juana had put her feelings into verse, they became lost in the metaphors and difficult syntax that were the bread and butter of seventeenth-century poetry. No single voice of sorrow cuts through that elegant facade; instead, strangely impersonal images of loss dominate the poems:

> And love laments its bitter fate,
> For, if before, ambitious to enjoy your beauty,
> It searched for eyes to see you,
> Now those eyes serve only to weep.[4]

And:

> She was born where the red sails of the east
> Run swiftly as the rubicund star is born,
> And she died where, with ardent sighing,
> The deep seas give burial to its light;
> And it was fitting to her divine flight
> That like the sun, she traveled 'round the world.[5]

Sor Juana's poetry, even when her own feelings were most caught up in it, seemed restrained by the baroque style then popular. Such works emphasized wordplay, contrast, and, as above, a melancholy world-weariness. Far from being isolated from the tastes of Spain, she had ample access to the works of many Spanish poets and especially to the elaborate, technically dazzling works of Luis de Góngora. This influenced her own work. She was seduced by the colorful, unexpected verses of the great Castilian poet, and in her own favorite poem, "Primer sueño" ("First Dream"), she confessed openly to imitating Don Luis's famous poem "Soledades" ("Solitudes"). For the Mexican nun, writing in verse was as natural as writing in prose, and the rhymes that flowed from her pen lent themselves easily to the demands of baroque style. Intellectual and complicated plays on opposites—love and hate, beauty and death, fame and envy—abound in her poems. Delicate, but often impersonal, images and metaphors fill her sonnets, ballads, and romances with variety and color. Sor Juana was able to take these elements, so often abused by her contemporaries, and blend them into praiseworthy verse.

Of her seventy-five sonnets, twenty-two are about love—not as passion or emotion, but as a theme. This may have been in part due to the many requests she received for such work. Take, for example, these lines, translated with words as close as possible to the original Spanish:

> Who ungrateful leaves me I as lover seek;
> Who lovingly follows me I unthankful abandon;
> I adore him faithfully who mistreats my love;
> And I mistreat him who faithfully seeks my love.[6]

Or:

> Feliciano adores me and I despise him;

> Lizardo despises me and I adore him;
> I weep for him who ungratefully rejects me
> And him who cries tenderly for me I in turn reject.[7]

So many of Sor Juana's love poems follow this intellectual, rather than emotional, pattern, that scholars have debated whether she was writing about love at all. Yet there are other poems, written about a lover's absence or spoken directly to the beloved person, that seem as personal and as fragile as any love poem ever written. An example of these is the following one that Sor Juana entitled "In Which a Suspicion Is Satisfied with the Rhetoric of Tears":

> This afternoon, my love, when I spoke to you,
> When I saw in your face and in your manner
> That I could not persuade you with my words,
> Then my heart begged you to believe me.
>
> And Love, that helped me in my efforts,
> Overcame what seemed impossible;
> For among the tears that my pain spilled out,
> My heart, undone, was itself distilled.
>
> Enough of such severity, my love, enough;
> May despotic jealousy torment you no more,
> Nor low suspicion invade your quiet
> With silly shadows, with empty clues,
> For in that liquid humor you saw and touched
> My undone heart in your hands.[8]

It is tempting to think of Sor Juana, the lovely young nun, as a refugee from a sad love affair suffered while she lived at the viceregal court. Yet, despite the temptation of that theory, her temperament—even her own words written in later years—support the claim that her one true love was learning. That love proved to be the foundation of a friendship that lasted throughout Sor Juana's life. For the death of her beloved marquesa and departure of the Marqués of Mancera did not leave her entirely alone.

Sor Juana was often called away from her studies upon the arrival of notable figures seeking entertainment or scholarly discussion. Among the visitors who came regularly to talk with her in the locutory was a man about six years her senior who shared many of her problems and interests. Don Carlos Sigüenza y Góngora was highly unusual in tradition-bound New Spain because of his gruff independence of mind and love of the new scientific methods of observation. Unlike Sor Juana, Don Carlos had few elite connections, but he won the professorship of mathematics and astrology at the University of Mexico when he was in his twenties. He then launched himself into a lifelong effort to learn everything he could about the stars, Mexican history, geography, and scientific methods of investigation. As he pursued his studies, Sigüenza struggled to make ends meet. Unlike Sor Juana, who enjoyed financial security provided through the church, Don Carlos was forced to accept a broad variety of jobs over his lifetime, among them chaplain, mapmaker, official of the Inquisition, and professor. In addition, he found time to write poetry, motivated by the fact that poetry was the most common literary form of his time and by the fame of his well-known ancestor, Spanish poet Luis de Góngora.

Sor Juana and Don Carlos developed a fruitful friendship that each valued highly. Their frequent meetings in the San Jerónimo reception room were filled with discussions of new developments in science and with readings of their original compositions. Don Carlos was Sor Juana's contact with intellectual trends that were developing far off in Europe, and she was his superior in writing lyric verse. Sigüenza never failed to express his admiration for "Mother Juana Inés," who, he claimed, could equal or surpass any poet or scholar of the age. She, for her part, was enchanted to have so learned a friend, especially one who was a descendant of the great playwright Luis de Góngora.

Sigüenza y Góngora had an extensive influence on Sor Juana, as the new scientific methods that so fascinated Don Carlos came as an affirmation of the practices her own curiosity led her to follow. Toward the end of her life, she described an incident that clearly showed her belief in the power of observation as a guide to knowledge. In a later self-defense and explanation of her drive to study, she included a story of a mother superior who held that "study was a thing for the Inquisition to deal with," and who ordered her to abandon her books. Such an order could not be ignored, and Juana Inés was not permitted any contact with her studies for a full three months. Yet she continued to study by observing "all the things God created" and reflecting with equal concentration on a spinning top, a game played with pins, and an egg frying in oil. As she wrote, "Well, what could I tell you about the natural secrets I have discovered while cooking. . . . If Aristotle had ever done any cooking, how much more would he have written!" Ordinary observations such as these carry as much weight, she claimed, as all the church-approved knowledge contained in her library.[9]

The "natural secrets" she learned from the behavior of ordinary objects were sought out in accord with Descartes' command but in complete opposition to church teachings. Forget everything you learned, wrote Descartes, and through minute and painstaking observation rebuild your system of knowledge from the foundations up. This indeed was an idea "for the Inquisition

Figure 6.1 Portrait of Sor Juana Inés de la Cruz (1648–1695), by Miguel Cabrera, circa 1750. The famous painter never met Sor Juana in person and likely based his work on earlier renditions of the scholarly nun. (Universidad Nacional Autónoma de México)

to deal with." But Sor Juana could no more abandon her fascination with direct observation than she could quell the rhymes that came to her at every moment, even during her dreams.

Sor Juana filled her life with poetry, books, scientific observations, and friends who sought her company in the locutory. Among those who came to see her was Don Payo de Ribera, the archbishop who had defended her against the anger of her offended superior. The genial cleric became viceroy as well as church leader in 1673 and served in this dual capacity until 1680. During his reign as archbishop, Sor Juana wrote him a poem, friendly and familiar in tone, asking him to perform for her the long-delayed sacrament of Confirmation. The verses are full of wordplay and references to mythological characters, forms that might seem out of place—even disrespectful—had the request come from anyone but Sor Juana.

> Illustrious Don Payo,
> Beloved prelate of mine . . .
> I call you mine, so without risk
> That with the echo of your name
> I already have the convent
> Quite free of rats.[10]

The humor and confident familiarity of these lines written to a man who was the supreme civil and religious authority of New Spain show that Sor Juana knew how to enjoy her favored position. Within the convent itself her place was no less favored. Her sisters recognized her abilities by twice unanimously electing her prioress, a position she refused to take. For nine years, however, she served as bookkeeper of the convent and maintained its archive as well. In addition to these duties, Sor Juana studied music and created a system of musical notation that unfortunately has been lost. The musical instruments displayed in her cell did not lie idle but were put to good use performing original compositions for the pleasure of her friends and convent sisters. The convent choir publicly performed many of her carols written for Christmas, the Assumption, and other religious holidays; many of them were published the same year they were written.

San Jerónimo convent thus benefited from the presence of the famous nun. She, on the other hand, continued to suffer from the daily irritations and constant interruptions of convent life. But even these were minor irritations compared to the criticism she received because of her talent and erudition. "Who wouldn't believe," she wrote, "that I, so broadly praised, have not sailed, with the wind at my back and on a sea of milk over the palms of general acclaim?"[11] At about this time a visiting bishop chastised the nuns of St. Jerónimo for their frivolity and ornamentation of attire. He was especially scathing about the nun's oversized medallions, known as *escudos de monja*. Well-versed in the art of miniature painting, Sor Juana likely painted her own *escudo de monja*, seen in figure 6. In so doing she distinguished herself from her sisters by depicting the scene of the Annunciation, rather than that of Immaculate Conception, normally depicted on such medallions.[12]

Friendship with sophisticated persons of the nonreligious world, such as with Don Carlos, greatly enriched Sor Juana's daily life. Those friendships, however, were few. The vast majority of the 400,000 people who lived in Mexico City in the 1680s were poorly educated and painfully provincial. The most cosmopolitan element of the population was the 70,000 persons who were of pure Spanish descent or were from Spain itself; and of that total 30,000 were women. Within that relatively small population, the possibility of finding persons who could accept Sor Juana's gifts uncritically was extremely remote. Consequently, the extraordinary nun lived most of her days in isolation from kindred spirits. To most church people, among them her confessor, Father Núñez, her intellectual pursuits were mildly scandalous; to most men, except of course Sigüenza and a few others, Sor Juana was if not a threat to their own achievements, at least a peculiarity. To her sisters within the convent, she must have seemed incomprehensible. Trapped between the criticism of some and the awe of others, Sor Juana longed for some sympathetic woman to take the place left vacant when Doña Leonor, the kindly patroness of her adolescence, died.

In 1680, her place was suddenly filled. In that year the twenty-eighth viceroy of New Spain, the highborn count of Paredes, arrived to assume control of the government of New Spain. With him came his beautiful wife, the countess of Paredes, who quickly became Sor Juana's intimate friend.

Sor Juana's affection for the beautiful countess, "Lysi" as she called her, shows clearly in the many poems dedicated to her. From the first moment of her arrival, the countess praised and inspired Sor Juana's poetry, and it was she who asked Sor Juana to gather her poems together so that they could be published. Every act carried out between them, every event, was punctuated by a poem, and the gift of her collected poems was no different:

> The son that the slave-woman has borne,
> Belongs under law
> To the legitimate master, whom his mother obeys . . .
> . . . .
> Thus, Divine Lysi, these scribblings,
> Sons of my soul, born of my heart,
> Are rightly returned to thee.

And their imperfections cannot prevent it
For they are lawfully thine,
These, the thoughts of a soul that is thine alone.[13]

Poems mark the birth of Lysi's child, the birthdays of the count, the giving of a gift, and, above all, the beauty of the countess herself. "The heavens are the plate/ On which is engraved thy angelic form," wrote the nun in one of her ballads honoring the countess. The humility and courtliness of these poems, written by one woman to another, seem strange but not inexplicable given Sor Juana's almost complete emotional insulation. "Lysi" was the unique object of the nun's affections, and so it was to her that those emotions poured.

The year that the count and countess of Paredes arrived coincided with the appearance of the Great Comet of 1680, whose fiery path cut across the skies of Europe and the New World. Later named Halley's Comet, after the English astronomer who observed and recorded its passage, this heavenly apparition nonetheless caused widespread alarm among the people of the Old World and the New. Contemporary belief held that comets were a sign of disasters to come, a superstition rejected by the handful of scholarly people who were excited, rather than frightened, by the chance to observe the phenomenon. Among the few such coolheaded souls in New Spain were Carlos Sigüenza y Góngora and Juana Inés de la Cruz. Motivated by the desire to calm widespread fears, Don Carlos published a pamphlet in which he proclaimed both the innocence of comets and the virtues of scientific and mathematical methods in studying the heavens. The pamphlet immediately became the focus of a battle waged between those who believed in the ominous nature of comets (a noted German Jesuit in Mexico at the time, Father Eusebio Kino, described comets as being composed of perspiration and vapors that rise from corpses) and those who used mathematics to prove that comets behaved naturally, according to rational laws. Sor Juana participated in the debate indirectly, giving her support to Sigüenza.

Sor Juana was involved in this and other issues and events of her day. The limitations of convent life were balanced by her friendship with powerful people who visited her and brought her news of the secular world outside convent walls. Pirate raids, intrigues in the viceregal court, the latest sermon, gossip about love affairs, and scientific debates were all fair topics for conversation in the San Jerónimo locutory. Thus, there are among Sor Juana's poems a series of verses dedicated to pleading certain causes that came to her attention. In one of them she begs the countess to free an Englishman imprisoned in Mexico City; in another she asks that a widow be given protection from those who wanted to sell her house. At one point she wrote to the viceroy:

> Suffer my stubborn insistence
> That you listen every day
> To these continual petitions,
> Now that these my constant requests
> Have already become litanies.[14]

Her readiness to plead the cause of others reveals a sharp sense of justice, a sense of fairness, that was perhaps most offended by her society's treatment of women. From her earliest years, Sor Juana had suffered because she was born a woman. This fact bound her to her sisters who, although less gifted, were no less afflicted by prevalent social beliefs. Principal among them was the church's idea that women might study, but they should never teach. As a result, there were few schools for women and no women teachers in New Spain. Should a young girl's parents decide to give her some education, they were forced to hire a male tutor, who might take advantage of his student. "What is wrong," wrote Sor Juana, "with allowing a mature woman, learned in letters and wholesome in conversation and habits, to take charge of the education of young ladies?"[15] Sor Juana modestly denied being accomplished enough to teach. But there is little doubt that she would have supported the establishment of schools for girls run by women had such a radical idea been proposed to her.

The injustices suffered by women in the name of romance caused Sor Juana no less indignation than the lack of educational opportunities. The infamous double standard that has historically plagued male-female relations did not escape her notice, and she described it with deadly accuracy:

> Ignorant men who accuse
> Women wrongly,
> Without seeing that you cause
> The very thing you condemn,
>
> If with unequaled fervor
> You solicit their disdain,
> Why do you expect them to be virtuous
> When you encourage them to sin?
>
> You combat their resistance
> And then, gravely,
> You say it was their weakness
> That accomplished your end.
> . . . .
> Whose is the greater guilt,
> In a sinful passion,

> She who falls to his lure
> Or he who, fallen, lures her?
>
> Or which is more rightly to be reproached,
> Although both are guilty,
> She who sins for pay,
> Or he who pays to sin?[16]

In 1686 Sor Juana's friends the count and countess of Paredes returned to Spain, to be replaced in 1688 by the count of Galve, who reigned as thirtieth viceroy of New Spain during the remaining years of Sor Juana's life. The countess took many of Sor Juana's poems with her and had them published in Madrid in 1689. The title of this first book of verses, *The Castalian Flood*, or *Inundación castálida*, is an appealingly baroque reference to the Castalian spring that flowed from Greece's Mount Parnassus and was considered the source of poetic inspiration. In harmony with this metaphor, Sor Juana was called the "Mexican Phoenix" and the "Tenth Muse," the latter a not uncommon compliment paid to female poets of that elegant age.

As Sor Juana's fame spread to Madrid and praise began to flow back to New Spain, her own situation became more troubled. As the ninth decade of the century ended, the kind nun of San Jerónimo began to suffer acutely from loneliness and poor health. The departure of her beloved Lysi coincided with Don Carlos's travels away from Mexico City. Without the unfailing protection of the former and the intellectual support of the latter, Sor Juana bent before the critics who worried her with their advice. With no family or intimate friends to turn to, the lonely nun expressed her complaints in verse: "By persecuting me, world, what do you hope to gain?" Later she penned these poignant lines: "Let us pretend that I am happy, Sad thought, a while."[17] While in this frame of mind, she suffered the blow that finally broke her will.

CONTROVERSY AND CHALLENGE: SOR JUANA'S *LA RESPUESTA*

Early in 1689, the bishop of Puebla, Manuel Fernández de Santa Cruz, visited Sor Juana in her convent and learned she was familiar with a sermon written years before by the famous Portuguese Jesuit Antônio de Vieira. The conversation that followed was the kind that scholars of that era dearly loved. All the erudition, the finely trained memories and powers of subtle reasoning were brought to bear on Vieira's thesis: that none of the learned saints of the church—St. Augustine, St. Thomas Aquinas, and St. John Chrysostom—could name Christ's greatest work without he, Vieira, being able to mention an even greater one. Bishop Fernández persuaded Sor Juana to put pen to paper and elaborate on her thoughts. This she did by rebutting him in a piece entitled "Crisis of a Sermon." The bishop was so impressed by her clever reasoning that he published the argument using the pseudonym "Sor Filotea de la Cruz" and entitled "Athenagoric Letter of Mother Juana Inés de la Cruz." The title was laudatory, comparing its author to Athena, the goddess of wisdom and war. Had the bishop left their exchange at that, the lonely nun would have been pleased and quite encouraged. Instead, he chose to apply, in private, a heavy dose of criticism.

In a long letter that he signed "Sor Filotea de la Cruz," the bishop applauded her skills in scholastic debate but urged her to devote her talents to more spiritual pursuits than she had in the past. "Turn away from your scientific and worldly interests," he urged, "and devote yourself to holy activities as becomes a nun." "Don't forget," he continued, "that holy writings contain divine wisdom, which is far superior to all the books written by men." The letter, although critical, seemed to be composed by one who truly admired Sor Juana and wanted, in his own way, the best for her. The bishop concluded with these lines: "All this is wished for you by one who, since he first kissed your hand many years ago, has loved your soul, without distance or time proving able to cool that love, because spiritual love never suffers the shock of change nor does pure love admit any changes but those toward growth. May the Lord hear my pleas and make you most saintly and keep you in all prosperity."[18]

The letter left Sor Juana distraught. Although gentle in outward appearance, the criticism was harsh. For three months she brooded over her course of action. Should she remain silent and accept the bishop's advice without comment? This was the course recommended by Sigüenza, who warned her that the Inquisition might become involved if she protested. Should she ignore the letter and continue her life of study and verse? This was impossible; she was bound by vows of obedience to the church and had already created far too many problems through her independence of mind. Or should she answer his criticisms and, using all her powers of reason and debate, defend herself against them? At last, in 1691, she wrote her "Reply of the Poetess to Sor Filotea de la Cruz," now known as the famous "Respuesta" (Response), that has survived as one of the finest essays ever written in Spanish.

From the "Respuesta" comes much of what is known about Sor Juana's life and thoughts. Biographical details and lucid descriptions of her ideas and attitudes are woven around a central theme: that women no less than men have the right to intellectual freedom. By entering the convent, Sor Juana Inés wrote, "I thought I could escape from myself, but—woe is me—I brought myself with me and I brought my worst enemy in this inclination, that I cannot tell if heaven gave it to me as a gift or a punishment." Her drive to learn did not loosen its hold over her after she took religious vows. Even though she was but "a poor nun, the least important creature in the world," she had as much claim and right to her opinions as Father Vieira had to his. She defended her intelligence and thirst for study as divine gifts, "at least I see them celebrated as such in men," gifts that denial and penance could not destroy. Her verses, although not dedicated solely to spiritual themes, were innocent of any evil, she wrote, and they were written mainly at the behest of others. Even the Mother Church could not reproach her for her poetry, since the works of many saints, hymns, and the Bible itself all include verses. Drawing on everyday examples, subtle comparisons, and straightforward details, mixed together with reference to Greek mythology and quotes from Latin scholars, she bravely defended her position—but lost the battle.[19]

Following the exchange of letters, her confessor, Father Núñez, pressured her to change her way of life. Her involvement in secular affairs was unacceptable to him, and he convinced her that it put her very salvation in jeopardy. Suffering from poor health and the strain of mounting criticism, Sor Juana's spirit broke. It is ironic that as she was suffering her greatest personal crisis, her friend the countess of Paredes published a second volume of her poetry in Madrid. In an orgy of repentance for her "sins," Sor Juana sold her library of perhaps four thousand books, along with her musical and scientific instruments, and quietly gave the money to the poor. After days of confession in which every sin, real or imagined, was resurrected, she dedicated herself with feverish enthusiasm to penitence. Drawing blood from her own veins, she wrote in one of the great ledgers of the convent "I, the worst in the world, Juana Inés de la Cruz."

Scholars continue to contest the actual circumstances of Sor Juana's final years. She appeared to devote herself to the most severe forms of religious penance. Once renowned for her learning, beauty, and poetic talent, she now earned a new kind of fame for the mortification of her own flesh. Father Núñez tried to moderate her excesses, noting that "Juana Inés does not merely run toward virtue, but rather flies." Father Calleja, her earliest biographer, wrote that she gave away her books as though she were turning off artificial lights at sunrise. But in 1692, the same year she sold her scientific instruments and library, she continued to compose. At the request of a friend and patron, Sor Juana wrote "Riddles Offered to the House of Pleasure" (*Enigmas ofrecidos a la Casa del Placer*). These riddles, not included in complete works on the serious topics on which she often wrote, were instead a witty entertainment, revealing her natural penchant for amusement and fun.[20]

The year 1695 was one of plague and famine in Mexico, and hundreds of sick and dying jammed hospitals and places of charity. Against the advice of her friends, Sor Juana devoted herself to the care of nuns who suffered the highly infectious plague. In her weakened state, she herself soon contracted the disease and died. Her forty-four years of life had been remarkably productive, even within the limits of her time and position. Yet she died with little sense of her own lasting worth. Her friend the vicereine, now in Spain, had rallied a favorable response to Sor Juana's arguments against Vieira, but she could not fully appreciate the admiration of scholars across the Atlantic. Still, she was grateful and wrote an unfinished poem of thanks to those from faraway Europe who had praised her poetic work:

> I am not who you think,
> Rather from afar you have given me
> Another being with your pens,
> Another breath with your lips.
>
> And different from myself,
> Among your pens I wander
> Not as I am, but instead
> As you imagine me to be.[21]

EPILOGUE

Eighteen years after her death in 1695, Juan de Miranda painted the stunning full-length portrait of Sor Juana Inés de la Cruz, the one highlighting her unique adornment, her *escudo de monja*. In the painting the remarkable religious is shown in her library, a look of serious intent on her face—or perhaps simply of irritation at being interrupted from her work. In its exquisite detail the painting suggests the veneration with which Sor Juana was held decades after her death. However, a century later the celebrated nun had slipped from popular consciousness in a Mexico torn first by wars of national independence and then by political turmoil leading to civil war between liberal reformers and their conservative opponents. Sor Juana did not reemerge on the stage of Mexican history until the latter twentieth century, thanks to a number of works celebrating her life. Notable among them were those of historian Irving Leonard and philosopher and novelist Octavio Paz, as well as by Argentine filmmaker María Luisa Bemberg.

Today Sor Juana's remains repose in the small chapel of the San Jerónimo Order, repurposed as the University of the Cloister of Sor Juana (La Universidad del Claustro de Sor Juana). It is a much-visited tourist site in downtown Mexico City. Those who enter the chapel gaze upon Sor Juana's sarcophagus, set flush with the floor and oriented toward the altar. There they can reflect on the life and work of one of the most notable female figures of Latin American history.

NOTES

1. Octavio Paz, *Sor Juana Inés de la Cruz, o las trampas de la fe* (México: Fondo de la Cultura Económica, 1982), 98.
2. Sor Juana Inés de la Cruz, "Respuesta de la poetisa a la muy ilustre Sor Filotea de la Cruz," *Obras completas*, nineteenth edition (México: Editorial Porrúa, 1999), 831.
3. Sor Juana, "Respuesta," *Obras completas*, 831.
4. Sor Juana, "Mueran contigo, Laura, pues moriste," *Obras completas*, 155–56.
5. Sor Juana, "De la beldad de Laura enamorados," *Obras completas*, 155.
6. Sor Juana, "Al que ingrato me deja, busco amante," *Obras completas*, 145.
7. Sor Juana, "Feliciano me adora y le aborresco," *Obras completas*, 144.
8. Sor Juana, "Esta tarde, mi bien, cuando te hablaba," *Obras completas*, 143.
9. Sor Juana, "Respuesta," *Obras completas*, 838.
10. Sor Juana, "Ilustrísimo Don Payo," *Obras completas*, 16.
11. Sor Juana, "Respuesta," *Obras completas*, 834.
12. Elizabeth Perry, "Sor Juana Inés de la Cruz and the Art of Miniature Painting," *Early Modern Women* 7 (Fall 2012): 5–7.
13. Sor Juana, "El hijo que la esclava ha concebido," *Obras completas*, 158.
14. Sor Juana, "Juzgo, aunque os canse mi trato," *Obras completas*, 121.
15. Sor Juana, "Respuesta," *Obras completas*, 842.
16. Sor Juana, "Hombres necios que acusáis," *Obras completas*, 109.
17. Sor Juana, "En perseguirme, Mundo, qué interesas?" and "Finjamos que soy feliz," *Obras completas*, 134, 104.
18. Sor Juana Inés de la Cruz, *Respuesta a sor Filotea de la Cruz*, ed. E. Abreu Gómez (Mexico: La Voz Nueva, 1929), 46–48.
19. Sor Juana, "Respuesta," *Obras completas*, 827, 831, 839, 844–45.
20. Glenna Luschei, "Translating Sor Juana," *Prairie Schooner* 80, no. 4 (Winter 2006), 21.
21. Sor Juana, "Cuándo, Númenes divinos," *Obras completas*, 73.

REFERENCES

Altorre, Antonio. *Sor Juana a través de los siglos*. Mexico City: El Colegio de México, 2007.

Arenal, Electa, and Amanda Powell. "A Life Within and Without." *Women's Studies Quarterly* 21, no. 1/2 (Spring/Summer 1993), 67–80.

Bemburg, María Luisa. *I, the Worst of All*. 1990. A film based on the novel by Octavio Paz.

Cruz, Sor Juana Inés de la. *Obras completas*. Nineteenth edition. Mexico City: Editorial Porrúa, 1999.

Cruz, Sor Juana Inés de la. *The Answer (La respuesta)*. Second critical edition and translation by Electa Arenal and Amanda Powell. New York: The Feminist Press at CUNY, 2009.

Cruz, Sor Juana Inés de la, and Ermilio Abreu Gómez. *Respuesta a sor Filotea de la Cruz*. Mexico: La Voz nueva, 1929.

Leonard, Irving A. *Baroque Times in Old Mexico*. Ann Arbor: University of Michigan Press, 1966.

Luschei, Glenna. "Translating Sor Juana." *Prairie Schooner* 80, no. 4 (Winter 2006): 21–24.

Myers, Kathleen Ann. *Neither Saints nor Sinners: Writing the Lives of Women in Spanish America*. Oxford: Oxford University Press, 2003.

Paz, Octavio. *Sor Juana Inés de la Cruz, o las trampas de la fe*. Mexico City: Fondo de Cultura Económica, 1982.

Perry, Elizabeth. "Sor Juana Inés de la Cruz and the Art of Miniature Painting." *Early Modern Women* 7 (Fall 2012): 3–32.

Wallace, Elizabeth. *Sor Juana Inés de la Cruz: Poetisa de corte y convento*. Mexico City: Ediciones Xochitl, 1944.

Chapter 7

Chica da Silva, 1733?–1796

INTRODUCTION

On April 1, 1500, eight years after Christopher Columbus claimed the Caribbean islands and northern South America for Spain, Portuguese navigator Pedro Álvares Cabral made landfall at Porto Seguro, near the present-day city of Bahia (Salvador) in northeastern Brazil. The fleet had been sailing around Africa when a storm blew it off course. Scribe Pero Vaz de Caminha sent word to the Portuguese king Dom Manuel that Cabral had claimed the land for Portugal, naming it "The Island of Vera Cruz." Afterward the fleet continued on its way to the Indian Ocean in pursuit of lucrative spices.

The first settlers in Portugal's New World colony found no gold or silver there. But they did find brazilwood, a commodity valuable to the textile industry for the rich red and purple dyes it produces. That export gave Brazil its name. Other Europeans, notably the French and Dutch, soon challenged Portugal for possession of the vast and lush new territory. During the mid-1500s sugar production began in the northeastern captaincy of Pernambuco, leading to a brisk trade in the "white gold" so craved by European consumers. At first indigenous Tupinambá people were put to work on sugar plantations. But planters soon turned to African slave labor to help meet the burgeoning demand for sugar. By the end of the 1500s, sugar plantations flourished down the Atlantic coast from Pernambuco to Rio de Janeiro, turning Brazil into the world's greatest sugar producer. Competition soon followed, however, as other European countries began producing the commodity on their "sugar islands" in the Caribbean. That, as well as a prolonged Dutch challenge for Brazil's northeast, sent the industry into decline. By the late seventeenth century, Brazil's economy was in depression, albeit a short-lived one. In 1693 *bandeirantes*—explorers, fortune-seekers, and slave-hunters—discovered gold in the mountains north of Rio de Janeiro. A few decades later diamonds were discovered in the northern part of the new captaincy of Minas Gerais ("General Mines"). African slaves were an essential part of the dangerous work of mining both gold and diamonds. Slaves soon outnumbered free Brazilians in Minas Gerais.

The mining boom and the wealth it generated had a defining impact on Minas Gerais and, by extension, on Brazil at large. Monies generated by mining helped slaves buy their freedom more easily on Brazil's mining frontier than in any other part of the Americas. That easier path to manumission made it possible for significant numbers of Afro-Brazilians to enter society as free women and men.

The most spectacular example of social ascent through manumission was that of Francisca (Chica) da Silva, life partner of the crown's diamond contractor in Minas Gerais. Sensationalized accounts of her life depicted her as a slave who used her powers of seduction to dazzle the diamond contractor. That was in fact false. The real Chica da Silva was far more than the sex partner of João Fernandes de Oliveira Jr. Rather, she was his lifelong companion and the mother of his thirteen children, all of whom were freed at baptism and went on to live independent and productive lives. Chica da Silva's life partner granted her freedom more than a year prior to the birth of their first child. This most celebrated Afro-Brazilian woman broke through conventional social barriers and lived out her life as a respected member of Brazil's mining elite.

FROM GOLD COAST TO DIAMOND TOWN: THE "SLAVE TRAIL" TO MINAS GERAIS

Chica da Silva's mother was a *mina* from West Africa's Gold Coast. Born around the year 1720, she was sold into slavery as a child and sent to Rio de Janeiro. She was then sent northward to the region of the diamond fields. The slave girl reached Minas Gerais traveling by foot along the "slave trail," part of a coffle of adult slaves bound together by chains. The slave trail was dangerous, snaking up through mountains that rise above Brazil's narrow coastal plain. Travelers went well-armed against bandits and runaway slaves wielding firearms, swords, and spiked clubs. The road ran 250 miles due north from Rio to the mining camp of Vila Rica de Ouro Preto and Sabará, at length reaching Vila do Príncipe, the capital of Serro Frio district, at the northern edge of gold deposits. Thirty-five miles farther on lay the Arraial do Tejuco (from the Tupí "tyîuka" or "dirty water"), soon to be capital of Brazil's diamond district. It came to be called Diamantina.

The trip up through the mountains was not without its moments when slaves and captors alike paused to drink at a cascade of water, pausing to gaze out on the spectacular views greeting them as they climbed into the mountains. Travelers marveled at towering vine-covered trees, at flocks of brilliantly colored toucans, parakeets, and parrots, and at monkeys hooting in the trees. The little *mina* girl may have appreciated the butterflies that appeared to accompany the slave column, recognizing some of them as the same kind she had loved to watch back home. At length the coffle left the dense vegetation of coastal mountains, passing into the forbidding terrain of the *Serra das Vertentes* (Steep Mountains), and then the *Serra do Espinhaço* (Spiny Mountains), as seen in figure 7.1. Drained by the northward-flowing São Francisco and Jequitinhonha Rivers and the eastward-flowing Doce River, the Spiny Mountains were where Brazil's mineral wealth lay.

The child likely said little during the grueling trek, listening to what was being said in the strange language of her captors. Only a few of the adult slaves spoke her tribal language. This was by design. It was one of many ways slavers thwarted plans for escape. After a while the *mina* child understood many Portuguese words. She had noticed that her owner had dark skin like hers and that his name was Domingos da Costa. Soon afterward she understood that Senhor da Costa, as she was instructed to address him, had once been a slave but had bought his freedom. That, she reasoned, must have had to do with gold. In her own African village, her people had spoken of the shiny metal and had used it in trade among themselves and with the white men who came to their village. She may have glimpsed gold being exchanged at El Mina Castle, where she had been purchased. If Senhor da Costa had been a slave but now was not, he must have used gold to buy his freedom. Now he even owned a gold mine outside the village of Milho Verde (green corn), their destination.

Domingos da Costa's slaves learned much as they mastered the cadences and vocabulary of their new language. Around the campfire at night, they listened to their captors complain about the new rules and new taxes Portugal had imposed on miners just months earlier. They heard Senhor da Costa and his men speak of a tax revolt in Vila Rica and of miners who had shouted "Long live the people!" The uprising was not successful, but it did express the anger *mineiros* felt over Portuguese laws aimed at siphoning away their profits. The little girl heard her captors discuss Senhor da Costa's gold mine where many of his new male slaves would work. And she heard a word that she did not understand but heard repeated often in excited whispers: *diamantes*, diamonds.

At last, the coffle reached Milho Verde, in northeastern Minas Gerais. The village lay twenty miles south of Tejuco, soon to dominate the diamond district. Milho Verde was located on a small plateau rising above Fundo Creek, whose waters were shallow and flowed along an almost flat streambed filled with quartz pebbles that sparkled in the sun. The village plaza was dominated by the Our Lady of the Pleasures church. Village commerce was conducted

Figure 7.1 Slave Trail to Diamantina (Wikimedia Commons | Ricardo Moraleida)

in the plaza, located at a convenient stopping place for travelers passing on their way to and from Tejuco and Vila do Príncipe, the district capital. Our Lady of the Pleasures church was also the place where slaves of Domingos da Costa were baptized. One of them was the little *mina* girl, about seven years old in the latter 1720s. Having lived in Milho Verde for the better part of a year, she doubtless had little trouble answering questions the priest asked her about Christianity. By then she had a working knowledge of Portuguese. And Senhor da Costa and older slave women had coached her on how to answer the questions important to being accepted into the Catholic faith. At her baptism she was given the name Maria da Costa.

Slaves in Brazil began their working lives at about age seven, without thought of school—there were few schools of any sort in eighteenth-century Brazil. Talented sons of the elite were sent across the Atlantic Ocean to attend the University of Coimbra in Portugal. Non-elites were for the most part illiterate. Maria da Costa began work as soon as she reached Milho Verde. Within a few months she became proficient in helping the slave women prepare food for their master and for his male slaves as well. Slave fare usually consisted of boiled pumpkin or squash, cassava mush, and occasionally salted meat—and fruit when it was in season and could be had without cost. Maria da Costa was likely set to carrying water up from Fundo Creek and carrying laundry down to be washed and dried and carried back up to be ironed at the "big house," as it was called.

Female slaves in Minas Gerais served as a source of revenue for their owners, especially those living in towns along the Royal Road, as the "slave trail" was eventually renamed. That was particularly the case for slave women living within walking distance of mining camps. In Milho Verde the female slaves of Domingos da Costa sold sweet and salty snacks, water and fruit drinks, and cachaça, or white rum, to travelers and to men working in the mines as well. Such vendors, seen everywhere in Brazil, were known as *escravas de tabueiro* (food tray slaves). It is likely that one of the first things the slave women taught Maria da Costa was to balance her small wooden tray on her head and follow behind them with her own selection of snacks to sell. Male slaves who had managed to earn a few pennies usually bought a shot of cachaça to ease the pain of their work.

As they went about their daily tasks, the women of Milho Verde chatted about events taking place around them, especially those affecting the slave community. They may have gossiped about men who had died in mining accidents or who had been injured and crippled in mishaps. The average working life of a male slave was only twelve years. Because most gold was extracted through placer mining, extracting gold from riverbeds, slaves spent their days diverting streams by moving stones and boulders, all the while standing in icy water wearing little more than a loincloth. Slaves working underground faced the same conditions and worse. They soon became deaf from the incessant pounding at close quarters of steel hammers and chisels on cave walls. Another favorite topic of gossip was who among them was pregnant and by whom. There were few women in Minas Gerais, virtually none of them white.

Whether a woman was slave or free, *preta* (black) or *parda* (mixed-blood, or mulatta), she was sought after by men.

Religion was another topic of conversation. Slaves looked forward to frequent religious holidays that gave relief from their daily tasks. Prominent religious orders, such as the Jesuits and Franciscans, had been banned from the mining district due to the crown's well-founded suspicion they were involved in smuggling gold and gemstones. That meant the people of Minas Gerais were forced to form their own religious brotherhoods. These brotherhoods helped pay for the funerals of deceased members, maintained hospitals, cared for abandoned children, and performed numerous other social services. Whites and non-whites, and slaves too, had their particular brotherhoods. Membership in them signified that one merited respect in his or her social group. Leading white brotherhoods of northeastern Minas Gerais included Our Lady of the Holy Sacrament and Saint Quitéria. Slave brotherhoods included Our Lady of the Rosary and Our Lady of the Pleasures, commonly referred to as "slave churches." There enslaved Brazilians attended Mass on Christmas Day and numerous other significant dates on the Christian calendar.

One subject enslaved women discussed only obliquely was whom among them was currently sharing their master's bed. Male slave owners expected sex from their female slaves. That had been a feature of slavery throughout human history. In color-conscious Brazil, however, female slaves knew that when their child's father was white its skin would be lighter than that of its mother. That was important in negotiating social status. It was not uncommon for men to free their light-skinned offspring borne by slave women. For instance, Mathias Porto de Castro of Sabará, one of the wealthiest men in the captaincy, had numerous children by slave women in his household and had freed all of them at baptism. Because Porto de Castro was not married that meant his male mulatto children would someday inherit his estate. In this way the next generation would secure his family wealth.

Maria da Costa came of age during the region's most exciting years, when new diamond deposits were being discovered in most of the streams around Tejuco. Locals had known of the precious stones as early as 1714 but tried to keep the news secret, this because diamonds were legally property of the crown. Twenty years after their discovery Portugal had the region around Tejuco, now often called "Diamantina," surveyed and declared the Diamond District, a closed area. Access to the region was sharply restricted. A military post was established in the strategically located village of Milho Verde, where soldiers stationed at the post searched travelers for contraband diamonds, sometimes going so far as to examine their fecal matter.

In 1732 a relationship developed between Maria da Costa, then in her teens, and Antônio de Sá, a white captain of the cavalry posted at Milho Verde. At the end of 1733 she gave birth to his daughter. Early the following year the mixed-blood infant was baptized Francisca *parda* (mulatta), in the chapel of Our Lady of the Pleasures. Her sponsors were a freedwoman named Alexandre Rodrigues de Fontoura and Luis de Barros Nogueira, who was white.

FRANCISCA *PARDA* IN DIAMANTINA

Like her mother, Francisca *parda* was a slave and the property of Domingos da Costa, who had purchased her mother fresh off a slave ship some thirteen years earlier. At first it seemed that Francisca would live her life much as her mother had, working in the home of her owner, earning revenue for him as an *escrava de tabueiro*, and eventually giving birth to his child, or to the child of another. While in Milho Verde Francisca *parda* learned the routines of her owner's household, preparing meals for his family, cleaning house, doing laundry, and tending to the myriad other chores falling to a female slave in eighteenth-century Brazil. Yet Brazilian-born and half white, Francisca's status as *parda*, not *preta*, set her apart from her mother.

Although no likeness of Francisca exists, she must have blossomed into a striking adolescent.[1] She would have inherited her mother's *mina* poise and likely her soldier father's stature. This helps explain the chain of events that began changing her life in 1746. That year Domingos da Costa sold Francisca to a longtime resident of Tejuco, Dr. Manuel Pires Sardinha, born in northern Portugal in 1692. He immigrated to Minas Gerais about 1720, after earning a medical degree. He went on to amass considerable wealth over his years in the mining town. When Francisca *parda* entered his household, Pires Sardinha was one of the town's leading citizens. He was not only the town's physician, but he owned a gold mine and a stock of slaves so large that he rented them out to other mine owners. Known throughout Serro Frio district, he had recently been appointed to an important judicial post in Vila do Príncipe, an honor reserved for members of the white elite.

Despite his high standing in the community, Dr. Manuel Pires Sardinha, a bachelor, was criticized by whites for keeping two slaves as concubines. That was classified as a civil crime by both church and state. It was not bigamy, which was an extremely serious crime at the time. A white man could not marry one of his slaves because it was illegal to marry across racial lines. Living with multiple slave women was classified as a lesser civil crime known as "multiple concubinage." It did not matter that Pires Sardinha had fathered sons with his slaves and had freed them at baptism. He had even freed the mother of the elder boy, Cipriano, son of his slave Antônia *preta* (Black Antônia). Following the birth of Cipriano, his mother became known as Antônia Xavier. The doctor's second house slave, Francisca *preta*, or Black Francisca, was the mother of his second manumitted son, Plácido. And now Dr. Sardinha had bought a lovely slave to serve as his third concubine—Francisca *parda* of Milho Verde. That passed the boundaries of propriety, even in turbulent Tejuco.

Thirteen-year-old Francisca *parda* was probably oblivious to her new owner's violation of social norms when she moved into his house in 1746. However, it was no secret to the other house slaves why the doctor had purchased the young light-skinned woman. They nevertheless accepted her as one of their own and referred to her as "the young Francisca," or "Chica" Francisca.

Although now separated from her mother, Chica Francisca found herself in a place infinitely more interesting than Milho Verde. Tejuco, or Diamantina, was bustling and exciting, and Doctor Sardinha's house was finer than that of Domingos da Costa. The hut in Milho Verde where Chica had lived with her mother had grown crowded with the arrival of new half brothers and sisters. Her brother Anastácio, fathered by Domingos da Costa, was already six years old. Because Mr. da Costa had only a daughter with his wife, Ana, he had freed Anastácio at baptism, likely with the intention of making him his heir. Under Portuguese law male children of slave owners could inherit their father's property if they were manumitted. Their mothers could not.

In mid-1750 Chica *parda* became pregnant by Manuel Pires Sardinha. That set into motion another pivotal set of events in her life. Late that year, during the first week in December, Reverend Inquisitor Miguel de Carvalho Almeida e Matos arrived in Diamantina to investigate moral laxity among the citizenry. He posted notices throughout the town demanding that anyone having information on "public and scandalous" behavior of any town resident present himself along with a denunciation. During the stipulated twenty-four-hour period, a Portuguese gold miner named Manuel Vieira Couto came before the inquisitor and denounced Manuel Pires Sardinha for deviant behavior. But as no second person stepped forward to corroborate the complaint the investigation went no further. Not long after the inquisitor's departure, Francisca *parda* gave birth to her first child, a son. The doctor freed Simão Pires Sardinha at baptism.

Following their narrow escape from public humiliation, Chica, her infant son, and Dr. Sardinha settled into domestic routine. Little Simão was soon walking and before long charging around the house playing with his older half brothers Cipriano and Plácido. Meanwhile Chica seemingly got on well with the mothers of her son's playmates. To the best of anyone's knowledge, it was a happy if slightly unorthodox household within a society based on massive slaveholding. Two years passed uneventfully—until the day a new inquisitor arrived in Tejuco. The Reverend Vicar Manuel Ribeiro Taborda did not hesitate to call Manuel Pires Sardinha before him along with his slaves, Antônia *preta*, Francisca *preta*, and Francisca *parda*. As the three women probably appeared before Vicar Taborda along with their mulatto children, there could be no doubt that the doctor had had sexual congress with each of them. The verdict of the inquisitor was as speedy as it was damning: Manuel Pires Sardinha and his slaves were guilty of concubinage in the first instance. They were all ordered to cease their illicit behavior and to sign a confession of their immorality. Pires Sardinha signed with his full name and each slave woman with an "X."[2]

If a mulatta slave girl sold for sexual purposes can be said to have had good luck when she bore her owner's son, then Francisca *parda* had indeed been lucky. Freed at baptism, Simão Pires Sardinha stood in line to inherit a portion of the bachelor doctor's considerable estate. Meanwhile, Chica's luck was about to become even better. She was on the verge of becoming co-administrator of one of the great fortunes of the Portuguese empire.

FAMILY FORTUNES: CHICA DA SILVA AND THE DIAMOND CONTRACTOR

Chica's approaching improvement in fortune was bound up with five interconnected factors. The first involved the crown's manner of managing diamond extraction and export. Second was that she lived in Diamantina at the height of her youthful beauty. Third was that her owner, Manuel Pires Sardinha, was condemned for immoral acts and ordered to divest himself of his slave Chica *parda*. Fourth was the fact that when that happened, João Fernandes de Oliveira Jr., the crown-appointed contractor of the Diamond District and the captaincy's most eligible bachelor, was fast approaching town. Fifth, the new diamond contractor and Francisca "Chica" *parda* were native-born Brazilians raised in Minas Gerais and steeped in the slave-based culture of the captaincy.

João Fernandes de Oliveira Jr. was the legitimate son of businessman João Fernandes de Oliveira Sr. and Maria de São José, the daughter of a merchant living in Rio de Janeiro. He had led a charmed life. His Portuguese-born father had immigrated to Minas Gerais early in the 1720s, holding the military rank of Sergeant Major, along with a royal appointment as tax collector. A diligent cultivator of friendships at high administrative levels, the elder Fernandes de Oliveira soon became well off. After 1740 he grew wealthier still as the crown's first diamond contractor. His firstborn son and namesake was born in 1727 on a family property called the Vargem farm, located twenty miles east of Vila Rica. João Fernandes the younger lived happily on the farm until age thirteen, when his father sent him to study in Rio for two years, and then on to Portugal to complete his education. João Fernandes junior was a devout young man whose five sisters eventually took the veil. He left Brazil for Portugal in 1742, resolved to become a priest. He started his formal education at Lisbon's San Patricio Seminary, run by Irish Jesuits. Two years after that he requested permission to enter the Lower Orders. Two years later, at age sixteen, he departed the seminary and enrolled at the University of Coimbra. Five years later, in 1749, he was awarded a law degree. One year after that he was awarded the title of Knight of the Order of Christ, the most prestigious honor for men not born to the nobility. He was admitted to the bar in 1752 and appointed chief judge of the Porto court of appeals. His meteoric rise was owed in large part to his father's guidance and political connections, and to his family's immense wealth derived from his father's post as the crown's diamond contractor.

In August 1751, just months before the younger João Fernandes de Oliveira completed his study of law and took up his duties as chief judge, his father and stepmother arrived in Lisbon. João Fernandes Sr. had run into problems with his partner on the third diamond contract. The man had proved unwilling to follow rules stipulated by the crown and had promiscuously awarded mining contracts. He was also rumored to be a smuggler of the king's diamonds. The elder de Oliveira traveled to Lisbon to negotiate a fourth contract in his name only, something he achieved in late 1751. His path was smoothed thanks to his friendship with a royal counselor named Sebastião de Carvalho Melo, the future Marquis of Pombal. Taking effect on January 1, 1752, the fourth diamond contract would be administered over the calendar year by business associates living in Diamantina. Oliveira Sr. would take up the task upon his return home. But he did not return home. João Fernandes de Oliveira Sr. had traveled from Brazil to Portugal with his second wife, Isabel Pires Monteiro. The couple's wealth and lavish spending permitted them to hobnob with Lisbon aristocracy and participate in court life. The upshot was that the first diamond contractor decided to send his son to serve in his stead. His dutiful son resigned his judgeship, packed his bags, and returned to Brazil. Without a murmur he sacrificed both his legal career and any hope that he could ever become a priest. He departed Portugal on June 7, 1753, reaching Rio in early August.[3]

João Fernandes de Oliveira Jr. was in no hurry to take up his duties in Diamantina, a town located in far northern Minas Gerais that he had never visited. While in Rio he spent several days with his maternal grandparents learning the details of his mother's death, and then he took the Royal Road northward through Minas Gerais. The road was much improved, and safer, than it had been in 1720, when both his father and young slave girl Maria da Costa had struggled over it. When Oliveira Jr. reached Vila Rica, he visited relatives and met with the governor of the captaincy and with other political officials. In early September he reached Vila do Príncipe. There he introduced himself to new diamond intendant Tomás Robi de Barros Barreto and to political officials of Serro Frio district. They briefed him on problems plaguing the Diamond District in his father's absence. Over the course of their conversations the new diamond contractor and the diamond intendant learned that both he and Tomás Robi de Barros Barreto had personal ties with Gomes Freire de Andrade, the powerful and influential governor of Minas Gerais. Freire de Andrade was highly respected in Lisbon and the man selected by the crown to establish Brazil's southern boundary with Spanish Rio de la Plata, as stipulated in the 1750 Treaty of Madrid. Being part of the governor's circle would serve both men well in the future.

While in Vila do Príncipe, the chief judge, as most called him, received an urgent visit from his father's old friend and business associate, Manuel Pires Sardinha. The younger man knew of Sardinha, who had been his father's guarantor on the second diamond contract and had served as his personal attorney as well. Pires Sardinha and Fernandes de Oliveira Sr. were both from northern Portugal, had mutual acquaintances there, were members of several of the same religious brotherhoods, and were leading lights among Diamantina's white elite. For all these reasons João Fernandes de Oliveira Jr. listened intently and sympathetically as Pires Sardinha poured out his tale of woe involving inquisitor Ribeiro Taborda and the condemnation he had recently suffered for double concubinage.

The younger man heard his father's friend explain his pressing and immediate need to find homes for the two female slaves in question, each of whom was mother to a manumitted son bearing his name. Would he, the physician implored, purchase one of them—a twenty-year-old mulatta called Chica? The diamond contractor could hardly refuse the request. Bonds of family friendship and of clientage determined his answer. The transaction was soon completed. Chief judge and bachelor João Fernandes de Oliveira Jr. thus suddenly found himself in possession of an instant and extended family consisting of a free and light-skinned mulatto three-year-old named Simão Pires Sardinha and his slave mother. Little Simão's half brother Plácido would be living just a few houses away with his mother, the freedwoman Antônia Xavier, in the home of Doctor Pires Sardinha. Simão's other half brother, Cipriano, would be living nearby too, in a household that the physician would soon be establishing for his slave mother Francisca *preta*. It was a complicated arrangement peculiar to the complicated culture of eighteenth-century slave-holding Minas Gerais.

There were other complexities surrounding the sale of Chica *parda* to João Fernandes de Oliveira Jr. Manuel Pires Sardinha was sixty-one years of age, old by the standards of the time. Both the doctor and the chief judge were aware that when Pires Sardinha died, something that occurred seven years later, João Fernandes de Oliveira Jr. would be thrust into the role of helping settle the affairs of the bachelor physician. Having agreed to take the doctor's son Simão under his roof meant that at Doctor Pires Sardinha's death the chief judge would have fiduciary duties involving not just Simão, but the physician's other two sons as well, both of whom were free and destined to inherit portions of their father's estate. That moral responsibility extended to the boys' mothers as well. All three of the women were illiterate and would require his protection. In short, the well-being of Doctor Pires Sardinha's dependents, not to mention his gold mine, houses, farms, and slaves, would also be under the administrative control of the crown's diamond contractor.

Perhaps neither man mentioned these things as they worked out details of the sale of Chica *parda*. But both surely understood the implications of the transaction. That helps explain to an extent the princely 800,000 réis paid for the young slave woman. Two years later, in 1755, when Manuel Pires Sardinha drew up his will, he made clear that his three freed mulatto sons were to inherit his estate. After having his will notarized, Manuel Pires Sardinha could rest easy in the knowledge that upright chief judge João Fernandes de Oliveira Jr. would not allow his sons to be cheated out of their inheritance.

The new diamond contractor had much to think about as he departed Vila do Príncipe for Diamantina in mid-September of 1753. Things had gone very wrong in the Diamond District during 1748–1753, the period when the third contract was in force. Felisberto Caldeira Brant, his father's former partner, had disregarded crown rules governing diamond mining. Among other things, he had allowed as many as five thousand slaves to work individual mines. Settings things right would require an immense amount of work. Then there was the matter of his personal life. The new diamond contractor was under pressure from well-meaning friends anxious to introduce him to marriageable young women of his own social class. But the young chief judge did not want to rush into marriage. He had planned for a life in the church after all, and the sour relationship between his father and stepmother made him suspicious of the deeper motives lurking behind matrimony. It was well-known that his father had married Isabel Pires Monteiro for her money and that the widow, repulsed by the Sergeant Major, had married him only because her family pressured her to do so. Their marriage was an unhappy one that hardly cast the legally sanctioned union of husband and wife in a good light.

All Diamantina awaited the arrival of the new diamond contractor. Nearly everyone in town knew the Sergeant Major but almost none of them had met his son, who had departed the Vargem farm en route to Portugal in 1740, the same year his father arrived in the village at the time called Tejuco, to administer the first diamond contract. Still, they had followed the young man's remarkable progress through his father's proud updates. When at last João

Fernandes Oliveira Jr. reached his family's substantial two-story house on Opera Street, all the family retainers, most of them slaves, were lined up to meet him. They had cleaned the two-story dwelling, a mansion by local standards, polishing its glass windows, imported from Europe at great expense, as well as the home's interior. The chief judge greeted the house slaves, asking the name of each, going on to inspect his new home. His mind surely drifted to Manuel Pires Sardinha, to young Simão Pires Sardinha, and to the boy's mother, Chica *parda*, now his possession. As soon as he could manage, he made his way to the nearby home of Dr. Pires Sardinha.

The first meeting of Chica da Silva and the diamond contractor can only be imagined. Chica *parda* seemed to be living the story she had heard so many times from the women of Milho Verde, about a slave woman who went to live in the house of a rich white man. That of course had already happened to her in the case of Dr. Pires Sardinha. But he was old, and her new owner was young. She likely knew that he possessed great wealth. For his part, João Fernandes de Oliveira knew little about Francisca *parda* other than that her nickname was "Chica," that she had a young son by his father's friend—and that both mother and child were now his responsibility.

The two young Brazilians were doubtless pleased with what they beheld at their first meeting. She saw a serious, well-dressed, and attractive man who arrived mounted on a respectable horse. He perceived an attractive young woman simply but neatly dressed, barefoot, as slaves were required to be, and holding her child in her arms. It surely occurred to both at their first meeting that they were living a drama not of their own choosing. That was certainly the case for Francisca *parda*. She, a slave, was being passed from the household of one white man to that of another. João Fernandes de Oliveira was likewise a victim of circumstances in the sense that he had not sought the young slave woman standing before him. Instead, a complex series of events rooted in honor and family obligation had led him to purchase her. Both may have pondered these things as they made their way through the streets of Diamantina to the grand house that would become their home.

Over the weeks that followed, João Fernandes de Oliveira found himself besieged by visitors from near and far. Most were men of varied social classes, anxious for contracts allowing them to mine rivers and streams of the Diamond District. All of the town notables called to pay their respects. A few perhaps came with white wives and children in tow. One or two others were likely accompanied by darker-skinned companions with their mixed-blood children. Technically, mixed-blood companions of white men were defined as their concubines, as neither church nor state permitted interracial marriages involving whites. On the other hand, the term "concubine" was deceptive in that a significant number of such relationships between white men and mixed-blood women were of a long-term committed character. Meanwhile, Chica *parda* quickly became mistress of the mansion on Opera Street. Senior house slaves willingly if grudgingly followed her orders because they assumed their new master had chosen her as his concubine, as had her previous owner. They and the other residents of Diamantina were certainly unaware of the complexities surrounding Chica's purchase by João Fernandes.

History and historians initially assumed the diamond contractor had acquired Chica da Silva for sexual purposes. The facts do not bear this out. Their first child, Francisca de Paula, was not born until eighteen months after her parents started living under the same roof. Over her lifetime Chica da Silva gave birth to fourteen children, thirteen of them fathered by João Fernandes Oliveira. The frequency and regularity of Chica da Silva's pregnancies (a new child was born to her on average every thirteen months after the birth of Francisca da Paula) argues that the couple did not consummate their relationship until many months after their first meeting. Chica and João Fernandes became model parents, shepherding their large brood through to adulthood. How, one wonders, did this seemingly mismatched pair become eighteenth-century Brazil's wealthiest and perhaps most exemplary couple? For an answer it is well to understand the background and mentalities of João Fernandes de Oliveira Jr. and Chica da Silva.

As a native-born Brazilian and the son of the crown's first diamond contractor, João Fernandes was entirely comfortable living in the slave-labor-based culture of his time. He had grown up on the Vargem farm surrounded by people of every hue, their skin color running from the white of his own family members to the black of the *mina*, Congo, and Angola slaves who served them. One of his earliest playmates was his older mulatto half-brother Teodósio, the son of his father and slave Lourença Batista. The father of the chief judge had manumitted Teodósio at baptism, later sending him to France to study medicine. Young João had been on hand when Teodósio departed for Europe. The two may well have been reunited during the years the younger João Fernandes studied in Lisbon. By the time the chief judge took up residence in Diamantina, the cohabitation of white men and mixed-blood women was accepted by him as a normal facet of life in Minas Gerais.

Up to the moment João Fernandes de Oliveira and Chica da Silva started living under the same roof, the chief judge had done everything that others asked of him. He had been a good son to his father. He had given up a promising career in Portugal and sailed away to distant Minas Gerais so that his father and stepmother could enjoy the high life in Lisbon. He had agreed to become the crown's diamond contractor even though his expertise and his interests lay in the areas of law and theology. But now, as of September of 1753, he was determined to make his own decisions and to live his life as he

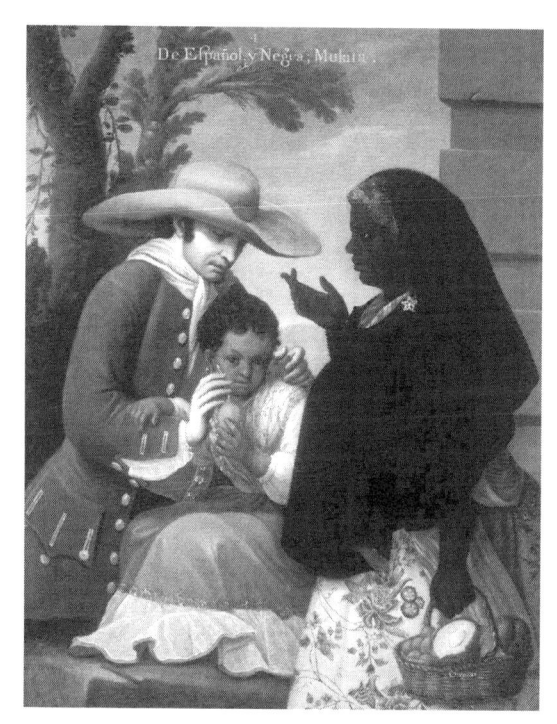

Figure 7.2 Casta painting, no. 4. "From male Spaniard and Black female, mulata." By Miguel Cabrera, circa 1763. Castas paintings depicting different racial, ethnic, and class groups to signal economic and class divisions became popular in Spanish America during the lifetime of Chica da Silva. These taxonomies paralleled social hierarchies in Brazil. Born of a Portuguese father and an enslaved black woman from Costa da Mina, Chica da Silva was classified as a "mulatta" in Brazil. Given the social rules against ethnic intermarriage, she was not permitted to marry the diamond contractor with whom she had an enduring relationship. While there exists no contemporary image of Chica da Silva, she did, however, gain her freedom and became a wealthy, propertied woman in her own right—and a fixture of social and cultural life in the diamond society of Minas Gerais. (Galería de Castas Mexicanas)

chose. It was in that light that João Fernandes de Oliveira contemplated Chica da Silva (see figure 7.2).

During his first months in Diamantina, the chief judge had been impressed with the smooth way the young woman had taken charge of his household. She had of course just completed a seven-year apprenticeship in the management of the well-appointed house of Manuel Pires Sardinha. Also impressing João Fernandes was the competent way Chica handled her son, Simão. He liked coming home from work at his office on Contract Street and seeing Simão and his half brothers playing happily together. By late 1753 João Fernandes de Oliveira had become quite comfortable living in his new house alongside his *parda* slave and her son.

By December of 1753 the diamond contractor had made a series of decisions regarding his career and personal life. He would remain in Diamantina for as long as the crown wanted him to remain there. He would not marry a woman of his own rank because he had not met any marriageable young woman remotely as competent or as attractive as Chica da Silva. For those reasons he would make Chica da Silva his lifelong companion and the mother of what he hoped would be an abundant progeny. While he could not marry her, he at least had the power to do everything short of that to let everyone in town, province, and captaincy know that he, chief judge and diamond contractor for the crown, intended to keep her by his side. To put his plan into motion João Fernandes de Oliveira Jr. took the unprecedented step of not simply manumitting Chica *parda* before the two became intimate, but freeing her in such a way that his honorable intentions toward her were clear to all. He would formalize the bestowing of her freedom on the Christian world's most auspicious day for new beginnings, December 25.

Chica da Silva was certainly happy if not entirely surprised when João Fernandes confessed his feelings for her late in 1753, going on to explain the elaborate way he planned to give her her freedom. The entire household likely passed November 1753 in perplexed confusion over what was going on in the mind of the chief judge, who obviously wanted to deepen his relationship with his handsome mulatta slave but had taken no concrete steps in that direction. Finally, in early December 1753, the plan of João Fernandes de Oliveira Jr. started unfolding before the eyes of everyone in town. Early in the month he drew up a document of manumission for Chica *parda* and had it notarized. Over the following days he was seen increasingly with Chica at his side. It was about then that she had begun using the surname da Silva. As Christmas approached and the diamond contractor was asked to lead in the processions of his several religious brotherhoods, Chica was prominent among the spectators. By then she was dressing not as a slave but as a lady, showing off full skirts and bonnets made from the finest materials. She wore exquisite shoes, the most visible sign of her new status as a freedwoman and, no doubt shockingly, a member of the town's upper class. When Diamantina's elite processed to church on each of the seven days leading up to Christmas, the diamond contractor had Chica da Silva at his side. And once they entered church, she did not stand with other slaves at the rear of the sanctuary as she had before; she sat in the first rank of pews with the wives, mothers, and daughters of the town's white leadership.

When Christmas Eve arrived everyone in Diamantina understood that the diamond contractor intended to formalize his relationship with his slave in a highly symbolic way. This account of events leading up to the symbolic uniting of the chief judge and his former slave are based in documents relating to the manumission of Chica da Silva and to accounts of the Christmas

Day receipt of her freedom. As no narrative record of these events exists, the following must be surmised: The diamond contractor and Francisca "Chica" da Silva attended midnight Mass at San Antônio church and then returned to their house on Opera Street. There in the presence of family and friends, with beaming house slaves looking on, the chief judge handed his former slave the prized document proving that she had risen to the category of "freedwoman." Later that evening they retired together. Everyone in Diamantina certainly understood that a singular event had taken place in their midst.

Sixteen months later, on April 7, 1755, Francisca da Silva de Oliveira, as her name now appeared on official documents, gave birth to her first child with João Fernandes de Oliveira. As Chica and the diamond contractor were not in fact married, customs of the day dictated that the birth certificate of Francisca de Paula Oliveira contain the phrase "father unknown." Another feature illustrative of the complexities of *Mineiro* society had to do with the infant's godfather. He was none other than Chica's second owner and the father of her first child, Doctor Manuel Pires Sardinha. There was a legal and practical aspect of this arrangement. A 1719 decree of Minas Gerais governor Pedro de Almeida had required that white men stand as godparents of black and mixed-blood children. De Almeida issued his decree to prohibit slaves from standing as godfathers, which he viewed as a threat to the social order. He found it distasteful that slave women could be manumitted by their owners after bearing them sons. It also irritated him that slave women could purchase their freedom with money earned through prostitution. De Almeida especially disliked the sight of dark-skinned women who had achieved liberty through such means dressing and behaving "above their station."[4]

Over the ten years following the birth of Francisca de Paula, Chica and João Fernandes had seven more children, three sons and four daughters. They were, in order of birth, João, Rita, Joaquim, Antônio Caetano, Ana Quitéria, Helena, and Luisa. With each birth their mother handed the infant over to a slave wet nurse purchased specifically for that task. With the birth of each child, Chica bought additional house slaves to help her keep up with the growing demands of her burgeoning household. True to the slave-labor-based society of which she was a part, Francisca da Silva de Oliveira purchased 104 slaves over her lifetime, most born in Africa, particularly in Angola and the Congo.

HIGH SOCIETY AT PALHA

Following the dramatic events of December 1753, Chica da Silva and João Fernandes de Oliveira settled into what can be described as flamboyant domesticity. The couple became mainstays of Diamantina's society over the sixteen years they lived together in the bustling mining town. The seemingly limitless wealth of the diamond contractor permitted him to make lavish gifts to the church, raise children abandoned on his doorstep, and host both members of the local elite and visitors from near and far. Part of the hospitality offered by João Fernandes and Chica involved two luxurious houses they had constructed on their Palha and Buriti farms, located not far from Diamantina. The Palha farmhouse was a veritable paradise, complete with formal gardens and ponds fed by cascades of water flowing over quartz and amethyst crystals gathered from the mines of Minas Gerais. The farm's grounds featured fruit trees, flowers, and flowering shrubs of the captaincy, mango, banana, and jaboticaba. Other plants were imported from Europe. Among them were fruit trees bearing peaches, plums, pears, and apples. Oranges and lemons, introduced by European settlers in the early sixteenth century, grew everywhere.

The Palha farmhouse also included on its grounds a chapel that was a favorite place for marriages. Several daughters of Chica and João Fernandes were married there, as were the sons and daughters of family friends. Slaves owned by the couple were also married in its chapel. Elegant dinner parties were hosted both at the Palha farmhouse and at its equally posh counterpart, the Buriti farmhouse. The dining room of the Buriti farmhouse was finely appointed, some of its cutlery made of solid gold. Its soup tureens, serving platters, and other fine tableware were imported from China. The Palha farmhouse included a theater/concert hall where Chica and João Fernandes and their guests gathered to enjoy musical soirées, balls, and theatrical productions. They hired noted directors to stage plays popular in Rio, Olinda, and Lisbon. Among them were *Persistin Love*, an elaborate production paid for by local merchants through subscription. Another was the comedic *Xiquinha for the Love of God*. Most of the Palha farm entertainments were comedic in nature. One of the favorites was *Enchantments of Medea*, written by Rio-born Antônio José da Silva, nicknamed "the Jew." Its performance was all the more piquant because everyone knew da Silva had been accused of "Judaic heresy" and burned at the stake in Lisbon in 1739.[5]

The days sped by pleasantly for João Fernandes de Oliveira and Chica da Silva. Chica now possessed a proper surname and the ability to sign it on legal documents. During most weekdays João Fernandes worked in his office on Contract Street while Chica administered their boisterous home. Inside the house on Opera Street, a phalanx of slaves incessantly cleaned, cooked, and did laundry, while others scoured the town and countryside for the food needed to feed the throng. Chica's mother had been manumitted and installed in her own house in Tejuco. There she raised Chica's half brothers and sisters, all of whom had been manumitted or sold by their former owner, Domingos da Costa. At least one of them, her son Anastácio, had been fathered by da Costa. Maria da Costa and her children spent considerable time at Chica's mansion helping her take care of her children. Their help was vital because Chica was constantly out and about, visiting friends, shopping, attending the meetings of her several religious brotherhoods, and of course attending Mass.

Chica spent a great deal of her time in religious activities. Deeply involved in several religious brotherhoods, she attended baptisms, weddings, and funerals and made endless charitable donations. These were dispersed to needy brotherhood members, many of whom were slaves. Chica made sure slaves who joined brotherhoods were baptized and given Christian names, symbolizing the beginning of their new lives. Additionally, as in other conventional Brazilian households, the mistress of the mansion on Opera Street ensured that all living within its walls, including adult slaves, were active in church and, where possible, brotherhoods. An assiduous churchgoer, Chica often made her way to Mass through the streets of Diamantina in a palanquin draped in heavy damask cloth and carried by four slaves. During the decade of the 1760s, she increasingly attended services at the church Our Lady of the Carmão, built by João Fernandes across the street from his office.

In the mid-1760s education of the couple's children became a growing concern. Educating the young was difficult in eighteenth-century Minas Gerais. The captaincy had only one secondary school at mid-century, and illiteracy rates there approached 100 percent. The crown sent well-educated nobles to administer its American colony and at the same time found it advantageous to keep the locals ignorant. Brazilian-born elites interested in educating their children were left to their own devices.

As had ever been the case in Brazil's patriarchal society, the education of sons took precedence over that of daughters. As of 1767 João Fernandes and Chica had been supervising the education of their sons for several years. The first to begin these studies was Chica's son Simão. With the death of Manuel Pires Sardinha in 1760, the education of Simão's half brothers Cipriano and Plácido also fell to the couple. Before long Simão, Cipriano, and Plácido were joined by their own sons João and Joaquim. In the Brazil of that day sons of the elite were educated by tutors. The diamond contractor and his partner found themselves scouring Diamantina for men capable of teaching the five boys. It was understood that when the time was right, they would all be sent to Portugal to complete their educations.

Educating the couple's daughters posed special problems. The tradition in colonial Brazil was not to educate females. Save for a few finishing schools located in major cities, there were no secular institutions offering even primary education for girls. In the mining town of Diamantina there were no women capable of tutoring the daughters of Chica and João Fernandes. By 1767 the situation had grown critical. The eldest girls, Francisca de Paula and Rita, were twelve and ten respectively. Soon Ana Quitéria, Helena, and Luisa would be of school age. No longer was it possible to continue educating them at home. Up to that time the chore had fallen to their father, to their teenaged half brother Simão, and to Simão's older half brother Plácido.

João Fernandes and Chica decided to send their eldest daughters to the celebrated religious retreat of Macaúbas, located fifty miles down the Royal Road in the direction of Vila Rica. Dedicated to Our Lady of the Conception, the Macaúbas convent also offered education to daughters of the better-off citizens of the captaincy. By the mid-eighteenth century, it housed approximately seventy students. Because Chica and João Fernandes intended to send their six—soon to be eight—daughters there, each accompanied by a servant, Macaúbas needed to expand. In addition to adding space for their daughters and their belongings and servants, a dwelling would have to be built outside the school's gates to house the married slave couple sent to help in time of need and to carry messages back home when required. In this way João Fernandes de Oliveira became the major benefactor of Macaúbas. When he enrolled his first three daughters there, the diamond contractor placed the mother superior in charge of their 60,000 réis allowance. He also prepaid 900,000 réis to cover their tuition and maintenance up through the time that they took their first vows. It was clearly the intention of the diamond contractor that all of his daughters should become nuns, as had his five sisters. While all eight daughters of Chica and João Fernandes studied at Macaúbas, only three of them took the veil, two of them going on to live out their lives at the convent.

When Chica and João Fernandes began sending their daughters away to study at Macaúbas, the diamond contractor had a new dormitory wing added to the institution. He paid for the construction of a trellised belvedere from which students and nuns could enjoy viewing the surrounding mountain landscape. He also had a new chapel built for the school, its altar painted in the same sky blue and decorated with the colorful spring flowers that he remembered from the chapel at Vargem farm where he grew up. By the end of the 1760s, with five of the couple's eight daughters in residence at Macaúbas, João Fernandes de Oliveira and Chica da Silva de Oliveira had revealed themselves to be loving parents of their sons and daughters alike. All of their children would become well educated and capable of defending their interests in a Brazil on the cusp of change.[6]

In 1770 João Fernandes de Oliveira received three pieces of life-changing news. First came word that the crown had abolished the diamond contract system, effective at the end of that year. Portugal's government would henceforth put the mining and sale of Brazilian diamonds under direct state control. Then, in October 1770, word arrived that the father of João Fernandes had died and that his stepmother had arranged a deathbed revision of his will by which a major part of his estate would be given to a religious order in the north of Portugal. Finally, the chief judge learned that his father's friend and business associate the Marquis de Pombal had delayed the reading of the will until such time that he could travel to Lisbon to contest it. For these reasons December 1770 found João Fernandes de Oliveira Jr. on his way to Portugal accompanied by his three eldest sons, João, Joaquim, and Antônio Caetano, his stepson Simão, and Simão's half brother Plácido. The young men would continue their education in Lisbon while the chief judge fought to nullify the amended will concerning his father's estate. His campaign to do this was ultimately successful. Simão and Plácido enrolled at the University of Coimbra, going on to take degrees in the arts. The younger boys attended primary and secondary school in Lisbon and later enrolled at the University of Coimbra. During the decade of the 1770s all lived in the outskirts of Lisbon at the family's Lapa mansion, constructed there following the 1755 earthquake that destroyed Lisbon's city center.

Chica da Silva and João Fernandes de Oliveira bade farewell in late 1770, she holding their last child, Agostinho, in her arms; the two never saw each other again. Despite that, João Fernandes and Chica remained in contact during the 1770s by letter and through messages delivered by family members, business associates, and friends traveling between Lisbon and Diamantina. One of Chica's daughters was always close at hand to read her father's letters and write out her mother's responses. Prior to his departure the chief judge had charged one of his associates to look after the legal affairs of Chica and members of his extended family.

Early in 1780, Chica da Silva received word of the death of João Fernandes de Oliveira, in Lisbon on December 21, 1779. The news was delivered by the couple's eldest son and heir, João Fernandes de Oliveira Grijó. The diamond contractor's passing was almost precisely twenty-six years from that memorable Christmas Day in 1753 when the wealthiest man in the Diamond District had dramatically handed his mulatta slave Chica da Silva her document of manumission.

As soon as she received word of the death of João Fernandes, Chica withdrew seven of her eight daughters from Macaúbas and gathered them around her in Diamantina. The eighth and youngest of her daughters, twelve-year-old Antônia, had declared her intention to become a nun. She remained at Macaúbas for the remainder of her life. The sons of Chica and João Fernandes completed their education in Portugal. Several of them remained in the realm while others returned to Brazil. Of all her five sons, Simão, the eldest, lived the most notable life. Like his stepfather he became a Knight of the Order of Christ. Legitimized in 1779 by Queen Maria I of Portugal, he obtained the rank of Sergeant Major in the armed forces of Minas Gerais. That was the same rank awarded to his step-grandfather some six decades earlier. In 1784 Simão returned to Brazil in the entourage of the new governor of Minas Gerais, Luís da Cunha Meneses. Educated in the arts, Simão Pires

Sardinha became a self-taught scientist of some note, unearthing a mastodon whose remains were studied by Enlightenment-era naturalists in both Brazil and Portugal. An acquaintance of conspirator for national independence Tiradentes (Joaquim José da Silva Xavier), the eldest son of Chica da Silva was questioned about the advocate for Brazil's independence following the Inconfidência Minera of 1788–1789. According to his testimony the two men had met at the Literary Society of Rio de Janeiro.

EPILOGUE

Later-day Brazilians fictionalized Chica da Silva, depicting her both as a lusty mulatta known for her mysterious sexual abilities and as an enemy of slavery. The real Chica da Silva was neither of these. Born a slave on the Brazilian frontier, where women of any race and social condition were few, she became the slave and sexual partner of one wealthy white man and the life partner of another. She gave sons to each of them. Those sons were freed at baptism and ended up inheriting their fathers' property. Similar though less spectacular family arrangements were repeated elsewhere on Brazil's eighteenth-century mining frontier. But Chica *parda*'s social ascent, eventually to becoming Dona Francisca da Silva de Oliveira, was unique among them.

Francisca "Chica" da Silva de Oliveira died on February 16, 1796, surrounded by her children at her home in Diamantina: The mother of fourteen children, wealthy, devout, and a pillar of the community, she was respected for her piety and charitable acts and admired by those who knew her. She was mourned throughout the Diamond District and laid to rest in the church of St. Francis of Assisi, up to that time restricted to the town's white elite.[7] Because her last will and testament has been lost, it is impossible to know the entirety of her estate. Some Brazilians point to Chica's story as an example of their country's "racial democracy"—though the extent to which this is true continues to be debated. What is undeniable is that Chica da Silva was a maker of Brazilian history.

NOTES

1. On Chica's complexion, beauty, and physique, as well as general labels regarding classification by skin tone, see Júnia Ferreira Furtado, *Chica da Silva: A Brazilian Slave of the Eighteenth Century* (New York: Cambridge University Press, 2009), 43, 114.

2. Furtado, *Chica da Silva,* 47.

3. For further reading on João Fernandes de Oliveira Jr.'s upbringing, schooling in Brazil and Portugal, and route to a position as diamond contractor, see Furtado, *Chica da Silva*, 85–100.

4. Kathleen J. Higgins, *"Licentious Liberty" in a Brazilian Gold-mining Region* (University Park: Pennsylvania State University Press, 1999), 150. See pages 145–74 for the author's discussion of sex as a determining factor in the manumission of female slaves in Minas Gerais.

5. Furtado, *Chica da Silva*, 194–98.

6. Furtado, *Chica da Silva*, 261–83.

7. Furtado, *Chica da Silva*, 260.

REFERENCES

Cheney, Glenn Alan. *Journey on the Estrada Real: Encounters in the Mountains of Brazil*. Chicago: Academy Chicago Publishers, 2004.

"Chica da Silva without an X." *Pesquisa Fapesp* 93 (November 2003). https://revistapesquisa.fapesp.br/en/chica-da-silva-without-an-x/.

Freyre, Gilberto. *The Masters and the Slaves: A Study in the Development of Brazilian Civilization*. New York: Knopf, 1964.

Furtado, Júnia Ferreira. *Chica da Silva: A Brazilian Slave of the Eighteenth Century*. New York: Cambridge University Press, 2009.

Higgins, Kathleen J. *"Licentious Liberty" in a Brazilian Gold-mining Region*. University Park: Pennsylvania State University Press, 1999.

Kiddy, Elizabeth W. *Blacks of the Rosary: Memory and History in Minas Gerais, Brazil*. University Park: Pennsylvania State University Press, 2005.

Pereira, Maria Angélica Alves, Vânia Gico, and Nelly P. Stromquist. "Chica da Silva: Myth and Reality in an Extreme Case of Social Mobility." *Iberoamericana* 5, no. 17 (Marzo de 2005): 7–28.

Pestana Ramo, Fabio, and Marcus Vinícius de Morais. *Eles Formaram o Brasil*. São Paulo: Editora Contexto, 2012.

Xica da Silva. 1978. Directed by Carlos Diegues (US release 1982, New Yorker Films; English subtitles).

Chapter 8

Micaela Bastidas, 1745–1781

INTRODUCTION

Through the seventeenth and eighteenth centuries, Spain consolidated its hold on its American possessions. In the Viceroyalties of Peru and New Spain, the discovery of silver at Potosí and Zacatecas, and mercury at Huancavelica, in Peru, helped fund a sprawling global empire. Buoyed by this flood of silver, Spain emerged as Europe's wealthiest and most powerful state in the sixteenth century.

In the eighteenth century, however, Spain fought challenges to its far-flung empire. In the first decade of the 1700s, it weathered a succession crisis, with the House of Bourbon replacing that of the Habsburgs. The war won by the Bourbons led to further erosion of Spain's empire. Later in the century, Spain experienced economic decline extending through the entire century. Still, it continued to extract a steady income from its American colonies. This flowed both from its silver mines and from its subjects, who paid a wide range of taxes to the crown. Spanish taxes were so numerous that colonists did their best to evade paying them, a situation Spain tolerated, or simply failed to police, during its first two centuries of rule. This lax control, with its negative impact on the royal treasury, eventually forced a more rigorous approach to revenue collection. After mid-century, modernizing ministers of King Charles III introduced an array of policies known as the Bourbon Reforms. They were aimed principally at increasing tax revenues.

Collection of colonial taxes, many of them sharply increased, fell to *visitadores*, men sent directly from Spain to Spanish America. They were invariably arrogant, overbearing, and corrupt as a group, and they were roundly hated by locals. This was evidenced by numerous popular uprisings. Peru alone witnessed fifty-six such incidents between 1740 and 1780, most of them in the viceroyalty's heavily indigenous Andean highlands. Protests against the Bourbon Reforms reached fever pitch late in the 1770s, when Spain and its ally France declared war on England in support of American revolutionaries fighting to achieve independence from Britain. While monies raised by Spain in support of the North American cause helped defeat England, Spain's zeal in collecting revenues on the backs of its own colonists drove them to revolt. The two most important of these occurred in the Viceroyalties of New Granada and Peru. The Peruvian revolt was the longer and bloodier of the two. Its leader was José Gabriel Condorcanqui, widely known as Tupac Amaru II.

The Tupac Amaru Revolt (1780–1782) was notable in three respects. First, it took place in the part of Spanish America where indigenous peoples had historically suffered most intensely from Spanish rule. Second, the Tupac Amaru Revolt stood out for its duration and extreme brutality with which the Spanish suppressed it. Third, women figured in it more prominently than in any other popular uprising of the time. The revolt's most prominent female was Micaela Bastidas, the wife of Tupac Amaru II.

[handwritten annotation: The woman is described only in relation to the man.]

BEGINNINGS: THE EARLY YEARS OF MICAELA BASTIDAS

Although the Inca Empire had fallen to Spanish invaders two centuries before, eighteenth-century residents of highland Peru still saw evidence of the Inca all around them. The stone-paved Inca highway linking Cusco to the Lake Titicaca region remained in use by travelers who threaded mountain ranges comprising hundreds of towering peaks reaching 14,000, 16,000, even 20,000 feet into the cold Andean air. Massive granite blocks pieced together by Inca stonemasons centuries before formed arable terraces on mountain slopes and supported Spanish buildings constructed atop destroyed Inca palaces, fortresses, and temples. Although the Inca were decimated by war and disease during the centuries following conquest, most residents of Andean Peru were their descendants. They, along with mestizos and creoles, spoke Quechua, although the more Hispanicized among them spoke Spanish as well. Local *kurakas*, or chiefs, were usually of indigenous or mixed descent, whose families had held these positions since Inca times. The substrate of indigenous customs, along with family relationships and traditional ways of life at forbidding altitudes, coexisted uneasily with Hispanic culture.

Micaela Bastidas Puyucahua was born into this mix of cultures and races. Although her birth certificate has never been found and details of her early life are hazy, she is thought to have been born in 1745 in either Abancay, Apurímac district, or in Pampamarca, in the Cusco region. Micaela spoke Quechua before she learned Spanish and was likely mestiza, although some observers add Afro-Peruvian to the racial mix. Like most women of her time and place, she received little formal education. Her place of birth, whether she could read and write, and her degree of fluency in Spanish have been debated over the years. Little is known of her father, Manuel Bastidas, though there is speculation that he may have been a Roman Catholic priest or an immigrant from Chile. Micaela's father and mother, Josepha Puyucahua Sisa, never married. Manuel died in 1746, soon after her birth, leaving Josepha to raise Micaela and her brothers, Antonio and Miguel, in Pampamarca. The family was nevertheless prominent in their community, and beautiful Micaela soon caught the eye of a well-to-do young mestizo of Surimana named José Gabriel Condorcanqui Noguera. He was heir to a *kurakazgo*, an age-old kinship-based group organized for the purpose of tribute and labor mobilization. The members under his jurisdiction included Surimana, Pampamarca, Tungasuca, and surroundings, located at an altitude of twelve thousand feet in mountains south of Cusco.

José Gabriel's family, the Condorcanquis, claimed direct descent from the last Inca ruler, Felipe Tupac Amaru, who had rebelled against the Spanish and was executed in Cusco's Plaza de Armas in 1572. The family often emphasized their connection to the celebrated Inca ruler by using the royal name Tupac Amaru. Like Micaela, José Gabriel spoke Quechua. But unlike his future bride, he was well educated. In his early years the local priest, Father Antonio López de Sosa, had taught him to read and write and had given him religious instruction. When José Gabriel was old enough, he was sent to Cusco to attend the Colegio de San Francisco de Borja, a Jesuit school for sons of noble *kurakas*. There he polished his Spanish, learned about indigenous and Spanish history, and studied Latin. In 1758 he returned to Surimana and took on the responsibilities of businessman and local leader.

At the time of their wedding in Surimana on May 25, 1760, Micaela was about fifteen years old and José Gabriel was probably nineteen. Father López de Sosa prepared the marriage license, reading in part, "I, Doctor Don Antonio López de Sosa . . . married and blessed . . . José Tupac Amaru, single, legitimate son of Don Miguel Tupac Amaru and Rosa Noguera, and Micaela Bastidas, single, illegitimate daughter of Don Manuel Bastidas and Josepha Puyucahua, Spaniards of said town."[1] Parents of the young couple were described as "Spaniards" despite their mixed ancestry. In the complicated racial calculus of that time, mestizos who spoke Spanish and were integrated into the predominant social system were routinely viewed as Spaniards. Although José Gabriel had the advantages of education and wealth, Micaela brought beauty, intelligence, loyalty, and strength of character to the marriage—as later events revealed.

Soon after the wedding, the couple made their home in Tungasuca, one of the three towns in the Tupac Amaru's *kurakazgo* governmental district. The family owned two houses in Tungasuca, property in Surimana, Pampamarca, and Cusco, a small farm in Tinta, and several fields given over to agriculture. They settled into one of Tungasuca's unique two-story houses. It opened to the street on the first floor and likely had a basement serving as a jail for minor lawbreakers. Micaela joined the *ayllu*, or kinship group, of the Tupac Amarus and assumed the duties of running a large household full of extended family members and meeting the challenges of domestic life at extreme altitudes. This included overseeing the production of goods. While some necessities could be purchased and brought in by mule trains, most were made locally. Since Inca times, textiles were produced in workshops, or *obrajes*, as the Quechua term was translated by the Spanish. In these workshops indigenous textiles were made into skirts, ponchos, wool overshirts, and the all-important head coverings providing protection from intense rays of the sun during the day and freezing temperatures at night. Food came from agricultural products and livestock, the llamas, vicuñas, and sheep that thrived in the mountains, and guinea pigs, sociable creatures that were raised in the kitchen. Micaela made sure meat was salted and dried and turned into *ch'arki*, or jerky, one of the few Quechua words adopted into English. Countless varieties of potatoes were harvested after the November-to-April rainy season, and they were often preserved by a process of freeze-drying: frozen at night and dried in the sun during the day. Cooking could take hours, often over hot rocks buried underground. *Pachamanca*, a roasted meat and potatoes dish, was prepared in this way.

LOVE, MARRIAGE, AND LABOR

The marriage of José Gabriel and Micaela produced three sons, and, as was the custom in Spanish America, all were raised in the Catholic tradition. Hipólito was born in 1761, Mariano in 1762 in Tungasuca, and Fernando in 1768 in Pampamarca. All were baptized by Father López de Sosa. They grew up in a society comprising the three main groups of highland Peru—indigenous, mestizo, and creole—and led a lifestyle punctuated by religious festivals and observances. Both José Gabriel and Micaela were devout Roman Catholics and maintained close contact with their local priests, especially Father López de Sosa. As the most important family in the region, they were prepared to shoulder the costs of supporting the church with tithes and fees that priests commonly charged for baptisms and funerals and for masses said for the dead.

As heir to his father's *kurakazgo*, property, and business interests, José Gabriel occupied an intermediate level of authority in colonial government, between the local district administrators, or *corregidores*, who answered to

Spanish authorities in Lima, and the people of highland Peru. He assumed the position of *kuraka* in 1766, at the age of twenty-five. The position brought special privileges: exemption from the *tributo* (the head tax) and from the *mita* (forced labor); ability to ride horseback, use a saddle, carry arms, and wear Spanish-style clothing; and the right to be addressed with the honorific "Don." In exchange, however, he was responsible for collecting taxes and enforcing the *mita*, an Inca system of forced servitude that the Spanish had adapted to their own purposes; he periodically "recruited" men who traveled from their homes to work in the silver mines of Potosí, some seven hundred miles south of Cusco. In his role as businessman, he managed the property he had inherited from his father, particularly the 350 pack mules that carried goods between Cusco and the region around Lake Titicaca. This took him over the *camino real*, or royal highway, a route following ancient Inca highways that wound through the high mountain cordilleras. The business of *arriero*, or muleteer, was important in the region and provided José Gabriel many contacts between Cusco and Upper Peru and familiarity with the challenging terrain.

In these endeavors, *kuraka* Tupac Amaru worked hand in glove with his wife, Micaela. In accord with Inca social norms that still held sway in Andean Peru, women like Micaela were considered full partners with their husbands. The household was widely recognized as having two heads, one male and one female, with joint responsibilities and shared authority. Wives' authority derived from their husband's, but it was no less valid for that. In the region around Cusco, it was common for a woman to act as *kuraka* in her own right or when her husband was away. This was the case with Tomasa Tito Condemayta, a female *kuraka* in neighboring Acos. The wife of a Spaniard and mother of several children, Tomasa inherited the position from her parents.

As the wife of a *kuraka*, Micaela understood her place in this system and did not hesitate to demand obedience and exact punishment when necessary. When José Gabriel was away, she supervised the household and the family's business affairs, paid workers, collected payments, oversaw the crops and livestock, and managed the family's properties. She handled the duties of *kuraka*, settling minor disputes, collecting taxes, enforcing the *mita*, and seeing to the welfare of the indigenous population. When necessary she jailed lawbreakers in the basement of her house.

At first Micaela may have had some difficulty in establishing her authority. Young, attractive, and slender, her dark hair in long braids, she had to ensure that people of the region understood that her word must be taken with the same seriousness as that of her husband. *Kuraka* Tomasa made this point when she said that as a woman, she had to work hard to maintain her authority. Doing so required a willingness to speak forcefully and sometimes impose harsh punishment for disobedience. Micaela was up to the task, judging from a complaint lodged against her by a tax collector: Micaela, he said, had threatened to punch him during an argument over taxes.

Given their responsibilities under the *kuraka* system, both Micaela and José Gabriel witnessed many abuses inflicted on the indigenous population. They saw that the *mita* system forced families to sell their few possessions, leave ancestral homes, and trudge hundreds of miles on foot to the mines of Potosí, often never to return. Although under Spanish law the *mita* required indigenous men to work once every seven years, local authorities often called them back more than the law stipulated. Meanwhile, *kurakas* who were unable to provide laborers for the *mita* were forced to pay fines out of their own pockets. José Gabriel's uncle went bankrupt for this reason. Labor conditions in *obrajes*, or textile workshops, worsened as well. By promising up to a year's worth of advance wages, this work usually led to debt peonage—or worse. Often, workers were locked inside their workshops. More than a few workers were condemned to the *obrajes* as punishment. When that happened, *obrajes* served the dual purpose of town factory and prison.[2]

Corruption led to another abuse in the form of the hated *reparto*. The *reparto* was originally designed to sell mules, clothing, and tools needed by indigenous laborers working under supervision of c*orregidores.* But by the mid-1700s, *corregidores* routinely abused the system to enrich themselves by forcing indigenous workers to buy unwanted goods at inflated prices. Micaela and José Gabriel saw the negative effects of this scam on their beleaguered people. José Gabriel and Micaela also suffered from both the *reparto* and unfair taxes. In 1768, for example, José Gabriel took Gerónimo Cano, a tax collector of Tungasuca, to court. Cano had collected payment for goods that he then failed to deliver. The tax collector had also harvested crops from the *kuraka*'s property without paying for them.

RESISTANCE AND REACTION: *KURAKA* VS. *CORREGIDOR*

When José Gabriel had assumed the duties of *kuraka* in 1766, his claim was approved by the local *corregidor* of the district south of Cusco. For some reason—perhaps owing to bad advice or a failure to recognize the seriousness of threats to the old system of inherited *kurakazgos*—José Gabriel failed to petition the Audiencia of Lima for confirmation of his claim. This lapse soon caused him problems. In 1769, possibly due to the dispute with the local tax collector, José Gabriel was arrested and held in a local jail for twelve days; the *corregidor*, exercising his authority as principal administrator of the region, went on to strip him of his *kurakazgo*, an action overturned in 1771.

José Gabriel began to understand that his position as *kuraka* was no longer secure. More and more *kuraka* positions were being handed out to creoles and mestizos, leaving members of the old Inca nobility, himself included, without recourse. In an effort to secure his position, José Gabriel turned to the judicial system and initiated a long legal process that he hoped would establish his right to the fertile land to the north of his *kurakazgo*, the marquisate of Oropesa. His claim rested on the fact that he was the direct descendant of the last Inca ruler. This claim would provide a strong defense against challenges and establish him as a direct descendent of the first Tupac Amaru. But as the petition wound its way through the Cusco legal system, it became clear that there would be no easy solution. A counterclaim on behalf of a well-placed Cusco businessman caused progress to slow and then stop. Accusations of fraud, unfair influence, and stolen documents complicated the process. Despairing of finding resolution in Cusco, José Gabriel prepared hundreds of pages in support of his claim and submitted them to the Audiencia. In early 1777 he was called to appear before officials in Lima, leaving Micaela in charge at home.

Even with these threats hanging over their heads, José Gabriel and Micaela could see other ominous changes overtaking Spanish America, stemming largely from the directives of José de Galvez, first *visitador* to the Americas and now minister to King Charles III. One of the first of these was the expulsion of the Jesuits from Spanish possessions in 1767, along with the seizure of their lands and buildings, one way to extract wealth for the crown. In Cusco this meant that the Jesuit complex on the Plaza de Armas, called *La Compañía*, became property of the king. Then, in 1776 the crown established a new viceroyalty in Rio de la Plata. The measure caused consternation throughout the Viceroyalty of Peru as wealth from the Potosí silver mines began flowing southeast to the port of Buenos Aires. This brought economic hardship to Peru. In the Andean highlands, muleteers, landowners, *kurakas*, indigenous peoples, traders, and officials witnessed a sharp decline in their incomes. Meanwhile, the king's urgent need for money led to new taxes and harsher collection measures. Heavy-handed royal tax collectors replaced Peruvian-born creoles who had historically been lax in collections. Tax exemptions for *kurakas* and other indigenous leaders were abolished. Products such as *aguardiente* and coca leaves were suddenly subject to excise taxes. The *alcabala*, or sales tax, rose from 2 to 4 percent in 1772, and to 6 percent barely four years later. Also, José Gabriel and his cousin Diego Cristóbal were among the first members of the indigenous elite required to pay the *alcabala*. Internal customs duties increased and were imposed on such agricultural products as corn, wheat, and even bread, all previously exempt. This hurt business generally and caused delays in the movement of goods. Suffering intensified at all levels of society.

Burdened with worry, José Gabriel departed for Lima in early 1777. He feared he would be gone for many months. By this time, he was in his mid-thirties, taller than average, well dressed in the Spanish style, with distinguished features and long dark hair that hung below his shoulders. He moved confidently among all groups in society, from well-to-do creoles and indigenous aristocrats, to mid-level creoles, mestizos, and indigenous groups living throughout the high Andes around Cusco. Like Micaela he listened sympathetically to the problems of the indigenous people who lived and worked in the *kurakazgo* and beyond. Heavy-handed changes ordered by the Spanish crown warranted his presence, his best chance of alleviating the increasing tax burden.

At about the same time José Gabriel arrived in Lima, so too did the *visitador* José Antonio de Areche. Invested with the power to speak for and report back to the king, Areche had been sent to enforce the new revenue-raising measures throughout the Viceroyalties of Peru and Rio de la Plata. He had little understanding of or sympathy for the residents of either jurisdiction. Within this setting José Gabriel presented his case to the Audiencia and asked to be recognized as the direct descendent of the last Inca ruler and rightful holder of the marquisate of Oropesa. He knew full well that should he lose the case he would lose the right to both the marquisate and the title of Inca, to his inherited *kurakazgo*, and perhaps even to the family name Tupac Amaru. While the petition languished in the courts, he also pursued a separate case in defense of the indigenous people of the provinces south of Cusco, seeking relief on their behalf from the hardships they suffered under the *mita*. In a strongly worded petition he presented in December 1777, José Gabriel listed the terrible impact of the *mita*, the failure to reimburse costs of travel to Potosí as required by the king's law, the depopulation of small towns across the region, and time lost when *corregidores* illegally extended the time of forced labor. The viceroy sent the case to *visitador* Areche, who blocked further action on the legal cases. In January 1778 José Gabriel returned home having achieved no resolution of his case or that of the indigenous peoples.

After his return, Micaela remarked that her husband's eyes had been opened by his experience in Lima. José Gabriel agreed with her, telling her that he sensed rebellion in the air. More than two centuries before, Inca Garcilaso de la Vega had stated, in his *Royal Commentaries of the Incas*, that Peru had been ably ruled before the conquest and that it had been brought low by the Spanish. In 1777 José Gabriel Tupac Amaru had come to perceive the same thing, that Spanish rule had brought disaster to Peru. He decided that direct action must be taken against its uncaring viceroy and his venal government.

When José Gabriel at last reached Cusco in early 1778, he learned that Quechua speakers of the region viewed him as a potential savior. They greeted him with reverence, some addressing him as Inca. For his part, the *kuraka* of Tungasuca understood that legal redress for their suffering would never be forthcoming. So it was that the man descended from Peru's last Inca ruler began plotting rebellion. In two years' time he was prepared to act.

On November 4, 1780, José Gabriel Tupac Amaru went to the home of an old friend, the priest of Yanaoca. He did so because he knew the *corregidor* of Tinta, Antonio de Arriaga, a Spaniard known for his ruthlessness toward the native population, would be there. Arriaga and José Gabriel Tupac Amaru knew each other well. Tupac had borrowed money from Arriaga and had learned only the day before that if he did not repay the loan within twenty-four hours' time, the *corregidor* would have him hanged. Their meeting was a luncheon at the priest's house. The meal passed without incident. After Arriaga departed for home, Tupac and several of his men lay in wait and seized the official, who was traveling with his scribe and two servants. The ambushers bound the astonished men in chains, took them to Tungasuca, and locked them in the basement of Tupac Amaru's house.

The following day Tupac Amaru ordered the *corregidor* to hand over 22,000 pesos, mules, several pounds of gold, and weapons. Next, he ordered Arriaga to summon citizens of the region to Tungasuca, without explaining why. During the next few days, businessmen, local officials, mestizos, Spaniards, and thousands of indigenous people flocked to the town. Men armed by Micaela guarded roads leading to Cusco so news of events taking place would be slowed. Two days later, Arriaga was brought from his cell to an open area where a gibbet had been erected. Thousands watched in shocked anticipation. A proclamation was read in Spanish, then in Quechua, stating that José Gabriel Tupac Amaru had received orders from highest authority to punish anyone who collected the hated new taxes and who abused the *reparto* and the *mita*. The proclamation contained assurances that acts to follow implied no disloyalty to either the king or the church, but, rather, were to punish the venal *corregidor* of Tinta. Arriaga was then led to the gallows, where one of his own servants placed the noose around his neck. But when the rope tightened, lifting him from his feet, it snapped and the man fell to the ground. A second rope did not break. With the execution of the *corregidor* of Tinta there was no turning back.

RAISING REVOLUTION

In the days following Arriaga's execution, Tupac Amaru and Micaela Bastidas brimmed with optimism (see figure 8). The two were determined to end government abuses. Confronted with the question of what to do with royalist Spaniards, creoles, and mestizos imprisoned in Tungasuca, most of them associates of Arriaga, Tupac insisted they should all be hanged. Micaela argued they would be more useful alive. Her position prevailed, and a number of the prisoners agreed to serve Tupac Amaru as scribes, munitions experts, and clerks. At the same time, Tupac and Micaela built their rebellion with trusted members of their extended families.

Nonelite men and women continued to stream into Tungasuca. Meanwhile, Tupac Amaru led the rebels from town to town, seizing money, livestock, and supplies and closing the hated government-run *obrajes*, releasing workers who toiled in slave-like conditions. He gave speeches, in Quechua, from church steps, always ending with the same message. The uprising would bring an end to the abuses of the *corregidores* while posing no threat to the political order. His final ringing words were "Death to bad government, long live the king!" A column seven miles long followed Tupac Amaru as he passed through the province delivering this message.

By mid-November 1780, Tupac Amaru was back in Tungasuca, where he and Micaela worked to bring order to a chaotic but exhilarating scene. As news of the rebellion spread, Tupac issued edicts and orders, sending them

Figure 8.1 Statue of Micaela Bastidas in Abancay, Peru (Wikimedia Commons | Thayne Tuason)

to leaders throughout the Cusco region and southeast to the region of Lake Titicaca. One of his emissaries called on residents of Cusco to turn against the "*chapetones,*" a pejorative term for abusive Spaniards. Tupac promised freedom to African slaves who rose up against their masters. Violence soon followed. In the nearby town of Sangarará, royalists died in the town's church when it caught fire as rebels fought royalist troops outside. In the end Tupac claimed victory in the Battle of Sangarará. He lost only thirty men, while royalist dead numbered in the hundreds.

The Battle of Sangarará, on November 18, 1780, showed that Tupac Amaru's rebels were capable of defeating royalist troops. Tupac and Micaela celebrated the fact by commissioning a portrait depicting them as Inca royalty. But they could not control the narrative emerging from royalist accounts of the battle. Their enemies portrayed Tupac and his followers as traitorous barbarians bent on burning those loyal to the king inside churches. Such stories sent many into the royalist camp. One such was Bishop Moscoso of Cusco. Within a week of the church burning in Sangarará, he excommunicated Tupac Amaru and his supporters. That was a serious blow to the rebels, all of whom were devout Roman Catholics.

Word of Arriaga's execution reached Lima in November. While authorities in Cusco dithered, and some royalists planned to flee the viceroyalty, authorities in the capital dispatched two hundred soldiers to the zone of conflict. An additional four hundred troops soon followed. Royal officials fought the rebellion in other ways as well. In early December, the viceroy announced the abolition of the *reparto*. He further reined in abuses of *corregidores* by placing them on salary. In Cusco, persons of indigenous and mixed descent were ordered freed from internal customs duties and certain taxes. The *mita*, however, was left in place. It would only be eliminated decades later during the Wars for Independence.

Back in Tungasuca, and as yet unaware that royalist troops were on their way, Tupac Amaru and some three thousand fighters departed on November 22 for the southeastern region of Lake Titicaca. Micaela remained in Tungasuca, where she was in charge of headquarters. During Tupac's absence the couple communicated through letters delivered by couriers. Many of these communications were intercepted by royalists, and they constituted prima facie evidence against leaders of the rebellion. The letters provide a remarkable account of two people working together to achieve victory amid chaotic conditions. They invariably began with endearing salutations such as My Chepe, My daughter Mica, Daughter of my heart—and ended with Your Chepe, Your Micaco, Your loving wife. The couple's mutual affection and trust came through clearly in discussions running from the mundane to tactical and strategic questions of war—and to the grave danger each faced. Be careful to eat food only from people you trust, Micaela warned her husband.

She shared her fears that the rebel forces were surrounded by enemies and suffered imminent betrayal. For his part Tupac Amaru reassured his wife that he was safe and urged her to take precautions.[3]

Ever the strategist, Micaela knew success of the rebellion depended on provisioning the troops. That led her to order that fighting should not begin until the crops were planted, prior to onset of the rainy season, which began in November. She understood that soldiers must be fed and paid, not just in currency but also in *aguardiente* and in coca leaves. Meanwhile she was deluged with requests for supplies, money, arms, and ammunition. While Tupac's troops seized crops, livestock, arms, and silver as they moved south, Micaela worked to keep supply lines open and the Tungasuca troops fed and paid, or the men would simply leave and return to their homes. Despite her best efforts many troops deserted after payday or when it rained.

Micaela's principal concern was that her husband's continued absence placed them all in danger. Meanwhile, she did her best to protect the uprising and its gains. She placed sentries at key points around rebel territory and sent soldiers to block bridges and roads. She maintained a network of informants who kept her abreast of royalists' actions. In letters to neighboring *kurakas*, she ordered the destruction of bridges between Tungasuca and Cusco and urged her husband to destroy a key bridge west of Cusco, adding that she would take care of the task if necessary. Those traveling through the area came to Micaela for passports and safe-conduct passes. She issued warnings that she would punish anyone who disobeyed her orders. That led one observer to note that her orders "were stronger than her husband's."[4]

Working with her scribes, Micaela answered the letters that came for Tupac during his absence. She composed letters to other *kurakas* and local leaders in which she laid out the causes of the rebellion and made the case for winning their support. It was the same message Tupac carried into the southern provinces: that the Europeans and the "thieving *corregidores*" had humiliated and burdened the people with the *mita* and taxes and had treated them like dogs, all the while stealing their property and possessions. She promised that Tupac Amaru would soon move on Cusco with tens of thousands of troops. Micaela ended by asking regional leaders to send troops. They were to wear crosses on their hats to show they were good Christians.

Micaela's efforts at recruitment extended to forays into neighboring towns. In private she worried about Tupac's failure to return to Tungasuca, concerns shared by *kuraka* Tomasa Tito Condemayta, in the neighboring town of Acos. Tomasa wrote Micaela in early December begging for help in fending off growing disorder in Acos district, adding "I have been upset with Don José's delay." In early December Micaela received word that Tupac had been attacked by royalists on the southern route. She left hurriedly on foot and then on horseback, along with one thousand armed men, stating she was prepared to "die where her husband died."[5]

While Tupac's letters home brought news of his whereabouts and plans, as well as requests for money, arms and ammunition, he did not say when he would return to Tungasuca. At the end of November, he wrote: "I know you are distressed, and your companions also, but don't be discouraged. If it is God's will that we must die, his will be done; so resign yourself to it."[6] On receiving this message Micaela wrote two remarkable letters dated December 6 and 7, 1780. Reproduced in F. A. Loayza's documentary collection, and translated by the authors, they read in part,

> Chepe mío, You're killing me with sorrow, as you move slowly from town to town . . . carelessly [until] the soldiers get fed up and leave for their villages . . . this situation endangers everyone's lives. We're in the midst of our enemies; our lives are no longer secure, and because of you they're about to endanger my sons and everyone on our side. I've begged you not to delay in these towns where there's nothing to be done. But you've spent your time going about without recognizing that the soldiers lack food and supplies. And even though they get their pay, this will run out soon. Then they will all go away, leaving us defenseless. . . . I warned you many times to return to Cusco right away, but you've brushed off my warnings, giving [our enemies] time to prepare, as they have done [by] placing cannons and other dangerous weapons on Piccho Hill so that you've lost the advantage.[7]

On December 7, she wrote:

> Hijo Chepe, I'm getting ready to march to Paruro on Monday, December 11; for this purpose, I'm calling on the people of all the towns, because there's a lot of suffering among the wretched residents of Acos and Acomayo who are afraid now that the soldiers have left town. In addition, they're going into the hills to stop the theft of their livestock. My goal is to recruit troops . . . to begin gradually surrounding Cusco. . . . As I warned you in my previous letter, if we proceed with leaden feet the trap will fail.[8]

She went on to list all the defensive measures taken by defenders of Cusco, ending with an indictment and desperate plea: "You've paid little attention to my letters, leaving me in a very bad situation; don't let them kill me, as your absence has led to all this." At last Micaela's letters had the desired effect. On December 16, as her husband approached Tungasuca, an elated Micaela wrote: "I am celebrating your safe arrival."[9] Tupac Amaru had returned and had Cusco in his sights.

During the rebel leader's monthlong absence in the south, Cusco prepared for the rebel attack that residents of the city expected and feared. An overriding worry was that Tupac's call to rebellion would cause an uprising of the substantial indigenous population of Cusco. Royalist leaders used that fear to energize residents—mestizos, creoles, and even priests—to defend themselves. They persuaded *kurakas* of the indigenous elite surrounding Cusco to oppose the uprising, leading the formidable *kuraka* Mateo Pumacahua to reject Tupac's claims to Inca nobility and to arm a force against the rebels. In several actions before Christmas, Pumacahua's indigenous fighters drove the rebels back as they tried to encircle Cusco to the east and north. The rebels consequently failed to destroy the bridge to the north of Cusco, across which royalist forces from Lima would soon march. By the time Tupac Amaru laid siege to Cusco, the city's royalist population was well prepared to resist him.

Just after Christmas 1780, Tupac Amaru and Micaela placed their forty thousand poorly armed troops in three divisions, commanded by Diego Cristóbal Tupac Amaru, Andrés Castelo, and Tupac Amaru himself. Theirs was a classic military plan hammered out by Tupac, Micaela, and their staff. It involved a three-pronged assault on Cusco, the old Inca capital. Diego Cristóbal's forces would move along the eastern bank of the Urubamba River to attack from the north, while Andrés Castelo would lead his troops through the rich agricultural region of the Sacred Valley northeast of Cusco. Tupac Amaru would seize the hills Picchu and Puquín, lying just to the west of Cusco, and within sight of the city's Plaza de Armas.

By the last days of December, the rebels were on the move. Tupac Amaru and Micaela Bastidas left Tungasuca on December 28 with a large force of indigenous fighters and the expectation that they could enlist additional forces as they approached the city. By framing the rebellion as an uprising against bad government, they hoped to persuade the city's residents to abandon the royalists with little or no violence. But they failed to appreciate the fear gripping Cusco's residents. The sight of thousands of indigenous fighters camped on the hills to the west strengthened their determination to resist the rebels. As it turned out, the siege ended quickly. Both Diego Cristóbal's forces to the north and Andrés Castelo's in the Sacred Valley were defeated in battles on January 2, 1781. Tupac Amaru's column held out for a week. But with supplies running out, no hope of reinforcements, terrible weather, and weapons that malfunctioned, probably owing to sabotage, he left the field in chaotic retreat on January 10. In his haste Tupac left behind a gilt bed that two months earlier had belonged to *Corregidor* Arriaga.

Trial and Punishment

Following the retreat from Cusco the rebels headed to Tinta, where Tupac and Micaela established their headquarters. Still in command of the region south of Cusco, Tupac claimed his retreat was owed to his reluctance to fight against his own people who had remained loyal to the royalists. He added that as a Christian he feared churches and monasteries would be destroyed in a sack of the city. Still, he understood the demoralizing effect of the loss and made every effort to keep word of it from reaching forces in the area of Lake Titicaca. A royalist defender suggested that had Tupac attacked Cusco early in the rebellion the city would have fallen. Had the rebels controlled the city, it would have been nearly impossible to dislodge them. As Micaela had repeatedly warned, by dragging his feet her husband had doomed the uprising to failure.

Over the succeeding weeks, the rebellion was soon reduced to a series of small battles fought in towns south of Cusco. Tupac and Micaela struggled to control their troops and to prevent looting and random violence. Micaela continued to gather intelligence and send supplies and ammunition to rebel leaders. Among them was her brother Antonio Bastidas, a field commander who spent most of his time moving from town to town in the highlands south of Cusco. "Send me coca and *aguardiente*," he begged his sister, "because these two items give encouragement to our Army. . . . Order them to provide us with jerky or wheat so we can pay our people, because there's nothing left and I haven't paid anyone for three days." In another letter he wrote, "I'll carry out the orders of my brother-in-law . . . even though by pleasing your Graces I may lose my life."[10]

During the first two months of 1781, trained and well-provisioned royalist militias began reaching Cusco from Lima, and by late February, battle-ready royalist forces totaled more than seventeen thousand troops formed in six columns. In comparison, the rebels lacked weapons and training, if not numbers. Indigenous fighters supporting the rebellion were skilled at operating at unforgiving altitudes, but they fought on both sides of the conflict. Early in March *visitador* José Antonio de Areche offered a pardon to all but thirty-five rebel leaders of the rebellion, for whom he offered a twenty-thousand-peso reward for their capture. The new measures further damaged rebel morale.

Around the same time, royalist forces moved south into rebel territory. Panic spread through rebel ranks and reached into the Tupac Amaru household. Diego Cristóbal reportedly fell into depression, and rumor had it that Micaela herself was often in tears. Reports from the battlefield—where the conflict grew increasingly violent—did not improve matters. In mid to late March two rebel commanders were killed in battle, their heads carried into Cusco on pikes.

On March 20, Tupac and his forces planned a surprise attack on royalist forces under Commander del Valle at Pucacasa. An informant betrayed the rebels and the element of surprise was lost. Yet the royalists barely beat back the rebels before being forced to retreat to lower ground. Tupac took heart from his near victory, but conditions continued to deteriorate. Letters exchanged between Micaela Bastidas and rebel leaders in late March 1781 reveal that they knew the enemy was closing in on them from all sides. Micaela continued to direct operations from Tinta, receiving intelligence from the field and sending provisions where possible. Little escaped her notice.

On April 7, 1781, a week after the battle at Pucacasa, Tupac Amaru arrived in Langui, a village south of Cusco. There disaster struck. He was captured by erstwhile supporters and handed over to royalist Commander del Valle. Dozens of rebels were seized with him, and sixty of them were executed on the spot. When word of Tupac's capture reached Micaela, she and sons Hipólito and Fernando loaded the family's valuables on pack mules and were planning to escape southward to La Paz. But they were too late. Micaela and her party were captured on April 8, 1781. Less than a week later, Tupac Amaru, Micaela, their two sons, and many rebel leaders were sent to Cusco for trial. Still, even though the rebellion had lost its top leaders, Tupac and Micaela's middle son, Mariano, and cousin Diego Cristóbal remained at large and continued the rebellion until 1782.

A witness to the arrival of the prisoners in Cusco described the scene. Tupac rode sidesaddle, his ankles shackled. He was dressed in his accustomed finery of white silk shirt and black velvet coat. Micaela rode just behind him on a mule. Both were under heavy guard. Their sons Hipólito and Fernando, Tomasa Tito Condemayta, Antonio Bastidas, and other leaders of the rebellion were paraded into the city as well. Residents lined streets and balconies to witness the spectacle. Neither Tupac nor Micaela wore hats so all could recognize them. *Visitador* Areche ordered them to bid each other farewell; they would not be permitted to see each other again.

The captives did not have long to await their fates. While Tupac's earlier experience with the legal system was characterized by delay and inaction, the trials of the rebels were almost instantaneous. The Spanish knew that the rebellion was far from over. In fact, Diego Cristóbal and Mariano Tupac Amaru tried and failed to free the prisoners on April 18, just days after their capture. By the time Micaela was interrogated on April 22, many of her scribes and former supporters had already testified, their words transcribed and presented in court. Voices of these witnesses come through court records showing they desperately sought to save themselves by convincing the court that they participated in the rebellion against their will and in fear of their lives. Among those most at risk were the scribes and armaments makers who were so important to the rebellion. They became hostile witnesses against Micaela Bastidas, describing the full range of her actions in the rebellion, even describing her as at times more terrifying and fiercer than her husband.

By the time Micaela Bastidas appeared in court, no one doubted her guilt or her pivotal role in the uprising. Still, Spanish officials wanted more information about the revolt. How could these minor figures from the rural highlands have organized and carried out such a rebellion? When did they start planning it? Did Tupac Amaru intend to become the ruler of highland Peru, a new Inca, thereby supplanting the king himself? Who had encouraged and supported the rebellion? And they wanted to hear from the woman Micaela, what she knew and what her role had been in the uprising.

The transcription of Micaela's interrogation is called her confession. It is, rather, a series of questions posed by the court, followed by her careful answers. From the earliest days of the uprising, she had few illusions about the fate awaiting rebel leaders should they be captured. Still, she intended to cause as little damage to her family and supporters as possible while at the same time defending herself. There was a chance that royalist authorities might show mercy to a woman. After all, they did not believe a woman capable of planning a rebellion, much less committing treason against the crown. They might have been persuaded that her husband had forced her to join the rebellion. Spanish law, in fact, did not contain provisions for the prosecution of women for the crime of *lesa majestad* (disloyalty to the crown), or treason. So Micaela's only hope to save herself was to answer questions in such way as to conform to male preconceptions of feminine passivity.

Micaela's interrogation began on April 22, barely two weeks after her capture. In summary, the interrogation, from Francisco Loayza, ran as follows:

Why are you being held prisoner? Because my husband killed *Corregidor* Arriaga.

What other cause? No other.

Why did you take up arms with your husband? It wasn't against the king or the crown.

What did your husband tell you about the uprising? Only that he would abolish the *repartimiento*, the office of *corregidor*, sales taxes, customs duties, and other abuses. But it was never against the king, nor did he think of such a thing.

When did your husband communicate his plans? I didn't know or hear anything until after the *corregidor* was imprisoned—my husband said he had an order from the king to seize the *corregidores*, and he always treated me sternly.

If you were afraid of him, why didn't you run away? Why didn't you escape when you were at Picchu outside Cusco? I was deathly afraid that I would be recognized and killed.

How could you be afraid if you were often left in charge when your husband was away? It's true I gave orders but they were written by the scribes.

Who were the principal captains of this expedition? Ask my husband, he would know.

Did the captains obey your orders in the absence of your husband? Yes, they obeyed.

Were you aware of the excommunication imposed on your husband and his followers, and if so, why did you not fear it and abandon him? My husband said that excommunication did not apply to us and that God knew his intentions and not to worry.

Do you have any hidden silver, gold, and jewels? I have nothing put away and everything I had I turned over to Inspector del Valle.

Who counseled your husband, who assisted him, who did he write letters to, who sent him letters? I don't know any of this, and my husband told me nothing.[11]

Again and again, Micaela refused to name anyone who had not already testified against her or whose participation was not already known. She was especially careful to protect priests who had supported the rebels. In general priests who had served the rebel cause escaped the severe punishment reserved for Tupac Amaru and his family. Micaela also tried to protect her brother Antonio Bastidas. She claimed that he only became involved in the rebellion because he was afraid of Tupac, who, he claimed, had threatened him with death. Although Micaela tried to protect family members, priests, and members of the rebel inner circle, her efforts did not extend to Tomasa Tito Condemayta. Tomasa had tried to build her own defense by saying that she had been forced by rebel captains to send indigenous fighters to battle and that she had been held prisoner behind bars by Tupac for three months after the siege of Cusco. But Micaela testified that Tomasa had never been held prisoner by Tupac. What's more, she asserted that the *kuraka* had been well taken care of in Tinta and that she had been impatient to attack Cusco because His Majesty's soldiers were threatening everyone with death. Micaela's unhelpful testimony raised questions about the relationship between Tupac and Tomasa. Tomasa had left her husband and joined the rebellion in its earliest days; she was, in fact, present at most of the important battles, often while Micaela was back at headquarters. But whether there was anything between Tomasa and Tupac Amaru is not clear.

On May 3 the prosecuting attorney summarized charges against Micaela Bastidas and called for her execution by the harshest means possible. As documented by Francisco A. Loayza, the court agreed, hoping her suffering would serve as an example to the populace. One day later, on May 4, Micaela was assigned a defense attorney named Gregorio Murillo, a member of the high court in Lima. Murillo weakly defended her by arguing that the "vile traitor" Tupac Amaru had abused her and kept her in fear of her life. Murillo asked the court to sentence Micaela to perpetual exile in one of His Majesty's prisons in Africa and to show mercy to Fernando, Micaela's and Tupac's twelve-year-old son, who, he said, had argued against the rebellion.[12]

A few days later, Micaela's defense attorney followed up with a request to the court that Tupac Amaru be brought in to answer questions about Micaela's participation in the rebellion. As documented by Loayza, the request was granted and Tupac, showing the effects of torture, was brought from his cell on May 9. The questions, and Tupac's answers, as recorded by the court, did little to support Micaela's defense that she was kept ignorant of most details and was deathly afraid of her husband:

Is it true you would beat your wife if she failed to obey you instantly? Yes, it's true I sometimes beat her but not since the uprising began.

Is it true that she begged you with tears and on bended knee not to execute Arriaga? It's not true—I consulted with her and she encouraged me to proceed.

Is it true that she lived in fear of you and blindly obeyed you? Micaela did what I ordered and I did what Micaela ordered, and it is not true that she was afraid of me.

If defense attorney Murillo expected to strengthen Micaela's defense by interrogating Tupac, he was mistaken. The court found her guilty of complicity in the rebellion and sentenced her to death by garrote. The judge believed it would be unseemly to hang a woman.[13]

Ten days later, on May 18, 1781, Micaela, Tupac, their son Hipólito, and fifteen fellow rebels and family members were dragged from prison to Cusco's heavily guarded Plaza de Armas. The crowd watched in silence as the executions were carried out. Even though young Fernando was spared death, he was forced to watch the executions of his parents, his brother, and their chief supporters. Hipólito was among the first to be hanged, with only his mother's admonition "to lose with dignity" to comfort him. Tomasa, then Micaela, were strangled by the garrote, a means of execution never before used in Cusco. As her neck was long and slender, the garrote failed to kill her despite causing her intense suffering. The executioners then tied ropes around her neck. By pulling the ropes back and forth and beating her on the chest and stomach, they at last killed her. Tupac Amaru was the last to die. His tongue was cut out and his arms and legs bound to four horses. Driven in different directions, the horses were expected to dismember him. The attempt failed. Tupac was suspended in the air, "like a spider," according to one witness. Some onlookers wondered whether the rebel leader was made of iron. Finally, *visitador* Areche ordered the executioners to behead the rebel leader. The bodies of those executed were dismembered, and their arms, legs, and heads were displayed in surrounding towns to serve as a warning against rebellion. The remains of Tupac Amaru and Micaela Bastidas were taken to the outskirts of Cusco and incinerated. Their ashes were scattered across hills above the city.[14]

EPILOGUE

Surviving members of the Tupac Amaru family and other supporters of the revolt were relentlessly pursued by Spanish authorities. Son Mariano was at last captured and died on shipboard while being transported to Spain. Young Fernando was sent to a Spanish prison, where he died almost two decades later. Following the Tupac Amaru rebellion, *visitador* José Antonio Areche ordered the suppression of Inca culture and traditional dress, the Quechua language, and even the works of the Inca Garcilaso de la Vega, which had supposedly inspired the original Tupac Amaru revolt more than two hundred years before. But Areche failed to stamp out indigenous culture in highland Peru. In part as a result of this, he was recalled to Madrid in 1783.

The correspondence between Micaela Bastidas and Tupac Amaru more than reflected their affection and friendship; they reveal a strategic alliance in a revolt that endured beyond their deaths. Together, the two began a movement that tapped into and drew from Inca tradition in their rebellion against oppressive colonial measures. This included Micaela's own role in advising her husband, organizing and overseeing provisioning, and other important aspects that helped fuel the rebellion. In the next century, the efforts of Tupac Amaru and Micaela Bastidas came to be seen in a favorable light by many Peruvians. Then, and today as well, they are seen as precursors of Peru's fast-approaching struggle for national independence.

NOTES

1. Salomón Bolo Hidalgo, *Micaela Bastidas Puiucagua, la mujer más grande de América* (Lima: 1976), 347.

2. For more on the *obrajes*, see James Lockhart and Stuart Schwartz, *Early Latin America: A History of Colonial Spanish America and Brazil* (New York: Cambridge University Press, 1983), 142–46.

3. Charles F. Walker, *The Tupac Amaru Rebellion* (Cambridge, MA: Belknap Press of Harvard University Press, 2014), 99.

4. Francisco A. Loayza, *Mártires y heroínas: documentos inéditos del año de 1780 a 1782* (Lima: D. Miranda, 1945), 102–103. See also Ward Stavig and Ella Schmidt, *The Tupac Amaru and Catarist Rebellions: An Anthology of Sources* (Indianapolis/Cambridge: Hackett Publishing Company, 2008), 110–11.

5. Loayza, *Mártires y heroínas*, 103 fn.
6. Loayza, *Mártires y heroínas*, 63.
7. Loayza, *Mártires y heroínas*, 48–49.
8. Loayza, *Mártires y heroínas*, 51–52.
9. Loayza, *Mártires y heroínas*, 53.
10. Loayza, *Mártires y heroínas*, 39, 40.
11. Loayza, *Mártires y heroínas*, 108–18. See also Ward Stavig and Ella Schmidt, "Confession of Micaela Bastidas," *The Tupac Amaru and Catarist Rebellions: An Anthology of Sources* (Indianapolis/Cambridge: Hackett Publishing Company, 2008), 122–27.
12. Loayza, *Mártires y heroínas*, 135–38.
13. Loayza, *Mártires y heroínas*, 143–45.
14. Loayza, *Mártires y heroínas*, 147–48.

REFERENCES

Bolo Hidalgo, Salomón. *Micaela Bastidas Puiucagua, la mujer más grande de América*. Lima: 1976.

Campbell, Leon G. "Women and the Great Rebellion in Peru." *The Americas* (Cambridge University Press) 42, no. 2 (October 1985): 163–96.

Garrett, David T. "'His Majesty's Most Loyal Vassals': The Indian Nobility and Tupac Amaru." *Hispanic American Historical Review* (Duke University Press) 84, no. 4 (November 2004): 575–617.

Loayza, Francisco A. *Mártires y heroínas: documentos inéditos del año de 1780 a 1782*. Lima: D. Miranda, 1945.

Lockhart, James, and Stuart Schwartz. *Early Latin America: A History of Colonial Spanish America and Brazil*. New York: Cambridge University Press, 1983.

O'Phelan Godoy, Scarlett. "*La rebelión de Tupac Amaru: organización interna, dirigencia y alianzas*." *Histórica* III, no. 2 (December 1979): 89–121.

Stavig, Ward, and Ella Schmidt. *The Tupac Amaru and Catarist Rebellions: An Anthology of Sources*. Indianapolis/Cambridge: Hackett Publishing Company, 2008.

Walker, Charles F. *The Tupac Amaru Rebellion*. Cambridge, MA: Belknap Press of Harvard University Press, 2014.

Chapter 9

La Pola, 1795–1817

INTRODUCTION

The eighteenth and early nineteenth centuries were times of ferment throughout the Western world. Ideas given form by Newton and Descartes culminated in the radical individualism of Voltaire, Rousseau, and Benjamin Franklin—great iconoclasts of an iconoclastic age. Men and women began speaking out against ancient social evils and political institutions that ran counter to the new philosophies. Such activity welled up in centers of European thought, threatening age-old absolutist traditions and disrupting order.

An ocean away, Spanish America was hardly insulated from these trends. A dynastic marriage early in the eighteenth century had linked Spain and the French house of Bourbon. With Bourbon influence came a long series of imperial reforms that disturbed patterns of thought and action grown ossified during some two centuries. Then came the phenomenon of revolution in Anglo-America and France and in the breakaway French colony of Haiti. Suddenly Spain's hegemony over her American colonies had grown tenuous. Final impetus to the Spanish American wars of independence came in 1808, when Napoleon Bonaparte imprisoned the Spanish royal family and occupied Spain. Into the void created by absence of legitimate authority in Spain stepped American-born elites known as creoles. So, when it appeared that French arms had stripped Spain of its authority, creoles seized control nearly simultaneously at points as distant as Mexico City, Santafé de Bogotá, Buenos Aires, and Santiago de Chile. While they declared independence from French-dominated Spain, they were careful to insist that they were doing so in the name of imprisoned King Ferdinand VII.

The early euphoria of independence soon faded as grave political afflictions beset Spanish America. The region's new native-born creole leaders fell to squabbling among themselves over several critical issues: Should the new government be centralist or federalist? Should power be vested in the hands of one person or in an elected assembly? What should be the territorial boundaries of the new states? What role should the church play within the new scheme of things? In the Viceroyalty of New Granada, for example, creole leaders of the new independent state of Cundinamarca, the location of New Granada's capital,, favored a strong central government. Bogotá would serve as its capital. Other regions opposed this arrangement, demanding a federal form of government. Strife engulfed the fledgling nation, laying it open to reconquest by imperial Spain, a fate not long in coming. Citizens of New Granada, later to be renamed Colombia, called the years 1808–1814 those of the *Patria Boba*, or "Foolish Fatherland."

In the midst of these and other thorny problems came Napoleon's defeat in 1814 and the return to Spain of Ferdinand VII, an absolute monarch who believed that those who had rebelled, even though in his name, must be severely punished. If the issue prior to 1814 had been the proper political structure of a new government, afterward it became who would escape execution, incarceration, or exile in the face of the king's armies. Only a few were not intimidated. They chose to fight a guerrilla war for independence against Spanish might. They included both male and female patriots. As it was quickly proved, the rebels were initially no match for Spanish arms. During the period 1815–1817, the nadir of Colombia's early revolutionary period, hundreds of creole leaders were captured and summarily executed. Among them were some fifty women. One of them was a heroic, defiant, young woman age twenty-two, nicknamed La Pola. She became the preeminent female figure of Colombia's early revolutionary period.

REVOLUTIONARY RUMBLINGS

The heat of June on one evening in 1805, and the promise of a clear night ahead, drew Policarpa out of doors to sleep in the hammock on the patio. She lay there quietly, listening to the distant noises that drifted over the roof—voices in the street outside, snatches of melody from a *tiple* next door, the steps of an occasional passerby. Just as she dozed off, little Bibiano, her three-year-old brother, left his bed inside to join her in the relative coolness of the hammock. Both were asleep in a moment, and quiet descended on the village of Guaduas, nestled among mountains in the landlocked heart of New Granada.

It was the gentle swaying of her hammock that awakened Policarpa—that, and the frenzied crowing of roosters behind the house. She thought at first that someone had bumped into her in the dark. But instead of slowing, the swaying became more pronounced, almost violent, and a rumbling welled up from deep within the earth. Earthquake! She scrambled from the hammock, lifted her still sleeping brother, and dashed into the street. There she found her father and brothers already on their knees praying aloud as screams and shouts rose from all sides. Policarpa knelt with her family and in the midst of the panic comforted little Bibiano, who sobbed with fright.

Several hours later, when the sun rose above Andean peaks, the villagers assessed their losses. The houses of adobe and bamboo had sustained some damage; several had collapsed; and the hostel built to accommodate travelers between Santafé de Bogotá and the Magdalena River port of Honda required considerable repair. It was not until late in the afternoon that they learned how close they had come to disaster. Messengers en route to Bogotá, the viceregal capital high on the *sabana* of Bogotá, a fertile, intermountain plateau, told of terrible damage suffered at Honda. The earthquake had shaken that key river port with such violence that few structures were left standing. Its two major churches and the convent of San Francisco were reduced to rubble, and many people were dead or injured.

In the days following the earthquake, as the people of Guaduas worked to repair its damaged buildings, Policarpa and her sister, Catarina, shadowed as always by little Bibiano, sought out their friends to ask where each had been and what each had felt when the earthquake struck. In the evenings small groups of girls gathered in the plaza, linked arms, and promenaded slowly around and around, chattering about that major intrusion in their otherwise tranquil lives. For three days special Masses were said, and religious processions wound through the dusty streets to reaffirm the bonds between the Catholic deity and frightened mortals who had been emphatically reminded of their own fragility.

Gradually, as cracked walls were patched and the injured healed, Guaduas resumed its usual rhythm of life. Early every morning, breakfast of hot chocolate and bland *arepas*, patties made of ground white corn, was followed by Mass. Shops opened; the men rode out to work on fincas, or farms; and women swept the dirt floors of their two-and three-room homes, collected eggs in the long grass out back, and spread wet laundry to bleach in the sun. Policarpa and her sister added some elementary schooling to that domestic regimen, and as they grew older, they spent their afternoons learning to cut and sew clothing, first for themselves and their brothers, later for paying customers. After dinner the family said the rosary and then, weather permitting, went to the plaza to see and be seen by their neighbors. Later, as dusk deepened and candles flickered under the eaves of the houses, they gathered to sing the rhythmic songs of the region, accompanied by guitar and *tiple*, and to spin unending threads of talk that bound each person to his fellows and all to events beyond the borders of family and village.

Policarpa had moved to Guaduas from Bogotá in 1802, at age seven, the year her mother, a sister, and a brother had died during an outbreak of smallpox in the viceregal capital. Joaquín Salavarrieta, Policarpa's widowed father, settled his children in a small house two blocks from the town's central plaza. There, Policarpa soon discovered, she could observe the movement of major personages of the Viceroyalty of New Granada. This was because Guaduas was located a day's journey east of Honda, head of navigation on the Magdalena River, between Cartagena, on the Caribbean coast, and the viceregal capital. It had been founded as a way station for travelers ascending from the river up through the Andes to Bogotá. Archbishops, viceroys, royal couriers, and other such travelers rested in Guaduas for a day or two, some for as much as a week, before ascending into the cordillera on horse or muleback. Policarpa thus had ample time to find out where each traveler was going and why. Mail from the coast also passed through regularly, and the people of Guaduas learned of great events before those in the capital itself. In Policarpa's own home, as in others, evening conversations often encompassed matters of local interest, affairs of the viceroyalty, and even events taking place in faraway Spain.

A bond of genuine loyalty and affection seemed to link the people of Guaduas to the crown of Spain. When word came on June 10, 1808, that Ferdinand VII had been crowned king in March of that year, the Salavarrieta family, the residents of Guaduas, and those living throughout New Granada rejoiced. Bells pealed, a special Mass of thanksgiving was said, and for three nights the village was illuminated by candles at every window and door. Scarcely two months later news of Napoleon's Peninsular War and the king's imprisonment by Bonaparte reached Guaduas and, by August 19, Bogotá. The younger Salavarrietas talked excitedly about Napoleon and his brother Joseph Bonaparte, the usurper who now ruled Spain. They abhorred the French and the occupation of Spain by Napoleon's troops. In September, Spanish captain Sanllorente passed through Guaduas on his way to the viceregal capital to raise money for the captive king. Locals despised his haughtiness, but loyalty to the crown outweighed their dislike. Two weeks later he passed through town again bearing coffers loaded with half a million pesos in donations and carrying pledges of loyalty to Ferdinand VII, the "beloved captive."

The creoles of Bogotá, like those of Guaduas and other villages in Cundinamarca province, reacted much as their Spanish cousins, rising up in defense of the captured king and refusing Joseph Bonaparte's seductive promise of increased political freedom and local autonomy. Policarpa and her brothers shared the sense of loyalty to Ferdinand VII but were neither blind nor deaf to local tensions. They could see the effects of inferior government imposed on New Granada by Spain, and they could also hear the words of a small creole minority who knew of the experiments in representative government in North America, and who had read the egalitarian treatises of French political philosophers. Their doubts about Spain's ability to rule were intensified by the behavior of certain *peninsulares*, snobbish Spaniards who routinely belittled creoles. Gossip from the capital classed the viceroy, Don Antonio Amar y Borbón, with those self-aggrandizing Spaniards. The unfortunate man was bereft of administrative talent and deaf besides, and his popularity suffered from his wife's exaggerated conceit. Bogotá's better-off creoles saw little basis for their claim to social superiority and, like the Salavarrietas, suffered from an odd double standard in their attitude toward Spain. They tended to expect the worst of the Spaniards sent to govern them even while they continued to think the best of their imprisoned king.

Policarpa's barely developed ideas, at first nourished only on bits of news and gossip, soon received a far more solid diet of radical thought. Her older brothers José and José María left Guaduas for Bogotá, where they became monks of the Augustinian order. There they came under the influence of Fray Diego Padilla, twice named provincial of the order in New Granada and a fearless proponent of freedom from Spain. By 1809 Padilla had published some fifty pamphlets and preached innumerable sermons on the subject. José and José María became willing converts to the cause, and through them Policarpa received copies of the monk's tracts. She knew as well of the radical proposals of Antonio Nariño and other leading patriots.

Still, Policarpa and others who were gradually withdrawing their sympathies from Spain were startled when news of revolution in Quito reached Cundinamarca in September 1809. That news threw Spanish officials into a panic. Their position could hardly have been more precarious. The king, the true source of their authority, remained in prison, leaving them ever-diminishing support in the restive colonies. And now the worst had happened. Revolution had broken out in New Granada itself. Hoping to contain it, royalist priests and government officials in every town and village preached loyalty to Spanish officialdom and extolled the virtues of peace and tranquility.

Although nothing untoward happened in the key province of Cundinamarca, representatives of the Spanish crown and the population of *peninsulares* experienced well-founded anxiety. In every town, creoles watched the course of Quito's short-lived revolution against Spanish rule and, when it was stamped out a few months later, many a secret patriot, Policarpa among them, mourned its failure. The impulse toward revolution did not diminish after the Quito revolt. Instead, it built quietly toward the day it would burst forth full-grown in New Granada.

On January 26, 1810, Policarpa, by then a skilled seamstress, celebrated her fifteenth birthday. Matured by the responsibilities that she had assumed at an early age, intelligent and forthright, La Pola, as she was nicknamed, moved easily between the houses of her customers throughout Guaduas. In her daily routine and work, she had ample opportunity to study all levels of society. The social differences between racial groups in New Granada were clearly visible, for they corresponded to their skin color. Those of indigenous, African, and mixed descent were confined to menial jobs and generally denied education. Marriage between people of different races was outlawed; thus, their place in the social order was rigidly fixed. Given their Spanish blood, creoles were much more fortunate than the lower castes. Policarpa knew that her brothers could never have become friars had her parents not been legally wed and generally believed to be of pure Spanish descent. After all, a person of mixed blood could not aspire to study law or enter the church. The new races formed by mingling the Old World and the New were relegated to the "low and mechanical occupations" of farm laborer, artisan, domestic worker, primary school teacher, and barber/surgeon, among others.

This state of affairs did not particularly bother Policarpa. She accepted the privileges of her own class and bridled at being seen as inferior by the Spanish-born. Instinctively she rejected the idea that any Spaniard, no matter how ineffectual, was superior to all creoles simply by virtue of place of birth. It seemed unreasonable that an old, indecisive man like Viceroy Amar y Borbón should be sent to govern New Granada when there were far more capable men than he among the creole elite. Yet intelligent and ambitious creoles had to be content with positions in the local *cabildo* or with lower offices in the church. Only a few ascended to high positions, for these were reserved for the Spanish-born. The deep sense of injustice felt by creoles like Policarpa destroyed whatever affinity might have existed between New Granada's two most privileged classes. The consequences of these resentments were soon manifest.

On July 21, 1810, two horsemen rode down out of the eastern cordillera and dismounted in the plaza of Guaduas. They brought sensational news from Bogotá. The day before, a quarrel between creoles and *peninsular* Spaniards had led to riots. Within a matter of hours, the existing royal government was overthrown. A Supreme Junta made up of prominent creoles supplanted the previous regime. This news flew from person to person, down the side streets and out to the fringes of town. Women sent children to the fields for their fathers and brothers, and by evening the entire population of Guaduas knew of the events taking place in the capital. The message the horsemen brought had an impact as powerful in its way as the great earthquake of five years earlier.

The principal actors in that drama called the events a revolution. But in truth the mass uprising proved to be far less than that. While the junta called for a constitution incorporating principles of liberty and independence, its president was Viceroy Amar, and its supreme source of authority remained Ferdinand VII. The oath of office, sworn on the New Testament by junta members, underscored continued loyalty to both king and church. The shackles thrown off on July 20 were not those binding them to Spain, but rather those of creole willingness to honor the Spaniard's belief that they were better than the locals.

HEADY FIRST FREEDOMS AND THE "PATRIA BOBA"

While the creole population of Cundinamarca province rejoiced in the events of July 20, 1810, attending Mass, ringing church bells, setting off fireworks, and organizing balls and other celebrations, events pressed the enthusiastic new government closer and closer to complete independence from Spain. The first tie to be severed was the position of viceroy. So unpopular were Viceroy Amar y Borbón and his wife, Doña Francisca Villanova, that mobs demanded their imprisonment. Doña Francisca, who embodied all the negative qualities of the *peninsular* Spaniard, was attacked by a mob of women who scratched, spit, and screamed at her as she was escorted to jail. By the second week of August, the junta understood that the viceroy and his wife must follow other royal officials back to Spain.

Policarpa pushed to the front of the crowd when the heavily guarded viceroy and his wife reached Guaduas. Their drawn faces peered fearfully through the windows of the coach as if they expected Guaduas to be as dangerous a place as Bogotá had suddenly become. La Pola gazed back from the silent crowd and watched as those symbols of arrogant political legitimacy climbed down unsteadily from the carriage and disappeared into their lodgings. In a few days they were gone, retracing the route they had followed in 1803 when, with great pomp and ostentation, they had arrived from Spain fully invested with royal authority.

Meanwhile, back in Spain, Ferdinand VII's ongoing captivity by the French continued to erode New Granada's allegiance to the crown. As the months and years passed, more and more creoles doubted whether Ferdinand VII would ever be restored to the Spanish throne. Napoleon seemed invincible. News of the heroic Spanish resistance to French rule, and the extent to which it sapped Napoleon's military strength, rarely reached Spanish America. Slowly all hope of a prompt restoration of royal authority faded. By July 1813 Cartagena, Antioquia, and Cundinamarca declared full independence from Spain, a country they now saw as little more than a colony of France.

Residents of Guaduas obeyed the Bogotá junta's command that militias be formed in towns and villages throughout New Granada. La Pola's father, Joaquín Salavarrieta, was active in that undertaking, and Policarpa was unhappy that she could not join the enthusiastic young men who paraded through the streets, brandishing weapons and shouting "viva" to the new regime. Honda, too, organized a militia, counting among its most vociferous members young Alejo Sabaraín, son of the commissioner of the royal mines of Mariquita and an acquaintance of the Salavarrieta family.

After independence was declared, the weightiest question facing the new political regime involved its institutional form. Bitter disagreement developed almost immediately. Santafé de Bogotá, long accustomed to its special position as the viceregal capital, supported the centralist system, hoping to retain preeminence over the other provinces. Rival cities, notably Cartagena, felt that Bogotá was a poor excuse for a capital, landlocked, perched more than a mile and a half above sea level, and almost inaccessible. Under Cartagena's leadership, the United Provinces of New Granada supported a federalist system similar to that of the United States. Bogotá did not give up without a fight, and under Antonio Nariño's leadership, it campaigned for the centralist cause. Thus it was that Alejo Sabaraín's first battle was a local one pitting Ambalema against Honda. The former town had initially allied itself with the federalist provinces that encircled Cundinamarca. Soon after independence was declared, Honda's militia invaded and defeated the forces of Ambalema, on orders from Bogotá. Alejo, who would be later known as La Pola's boyfriend, found the victory satisfying. The brief glories of battle obscured for him the underlying tragedy of internal dissension. He was oblivious to the fact that no blood had been spilled when New Granada broke its ties with Spain and that the first deaths in battle were inflicted by one group of patriots upon another. The significance of such discord was apparent only to older, more objective patriots. They were filled with alarm and foreboding.

For four years, New Granada squandered its energies and wealth on internecine squabbles. This was the case up to 1814, when Ferdinand VII was restored to the throne of Spain. Royalists in New Granada rejoiced, confident that creoles would rally to their rightful king. Others, those who had wearied of the constant bloodshed of the *Patria Boba*—the Foolish Fatherland—welcomed the news as well. Even ardent supporters of independence in 1810 were quietly hopeful that a strong, legitimate government might be reestablished. Members of such groups believed that the experiment in local government had failed, and they complained that constant conflict had disrupted both public tranquility and commerce. In short, much of the steam had gone out of the revolution. The few committed patriots were exhausted by factional strife, and New Granada was in no condition to defend its new freedom against fast-approaching retaliation from Spain.

A SPANISH "RESTORATION"

King Ferdinand VII acted quickly to restore absolute rule over his American colonies. By October 1814 news of his army's landing in Venezuela reached

Cundinamarca and its capital, Bogotá. In a last desperate attempt to unify New Granada, the foremost patriot general, Venezuelan Simón Bolívar, and his federalist army marched into Bogotá and sent troops to Honda and other centralist towns lying along the Magdalena River. Bolívar's action came too late. Spanish commander Pablo Morillo and his troops marched into the heartland of New Granada in early 1815. Even as Bolívar tried to hold regions in Cundinamarca, Morillo, the "pacifier," encircled New Granada with a noose of steel. Cartagena on the coast, Popayán in the south, and Socorro in the north fell with scarcely a shot being fired in their defense. Bogotá fell to Morillo's forces shortly thereafter. By May 1816 all of New Granada was in Spanish hands, and Morillo's reign of terror had begun.

Fear filled the darkened houses of Santafé de Bogotá, the sunlit patios of Guaduas, and other towns and villages throughout New Granada. As Bogotá patriot and eyewitness José María Caballero wrote in his diary: "There is no family that has not cause for tears, there is no man who has not suffered, even those who were loyal to them [the Spanish] and who thought of themselves as faithful royalists. I cannot say more, because pain presses in on me and fills me with a kind of desperation, and thus I am silent, and tell not what I have suffered."[1]

But some patriots refused to withdraw into silence and paralyzing fear; their spirits could not accept the finality of Morillo's punitive outrages. Even as patriot leaders were shot or hanged in plazas all over the viceroyalty, an underground resistance sprang up under the very noses of the Spanish. In Cúcuta, Socorro, Bogotá, Guaduas, and Honda, patriots plotted against Spain and its army of occupation.

La Pola had watched with anguish as the excitement of early independence was overcome by dread of Spanish retribution. Hers, though, was not a fragile spirit, and she did all she could to oppose the Spanish. While most patriots chose the course of judicious silence, Policarpa encouraged vacillating creoles and offered consolation to families whose sons were lost in battle and whose fathers faced the possibility of death or imprisonment. When long lines of patriots, their hands chained and their faces landscapes of despair, began arriving from Bogotá en route to Spanish prisons, La Pola took them food and water and whispered words of sympathy. Among them were twenty priests, many of them highly placed in the church hierarchy. One of them was Fray Diego Padilla, the fiery Augustinian friar whose writings had reached the Salavarrietas six years earlier.

La Pola's most important contribution to the patriot cause was the support she gave creole guerrillas, the vanguard of the resistance. Late at night she would answer a knock at the door, often finding José Antonio Olaya, José Ignacio Rodríguez, or some other patriot leader seeking rest and news. La Pola passed on information on royalist troop movements between Honda and

Guaduas and reported the latest news from Spain. So reliable was her intelligence and so fearless did she seem that those late-night visitors promised to find a way for her to make a greater contribution to the resistance.

Their promise was a timely one. By late 1816 La Pola had exhausted her possibilities for action in Guaduas. Moreover, it was known around town that her sympathies were antiroyalist. Suddenly it became dangerous to be seen with her. Through her own connections in Guaduas, through her brothers in Santafé, and most importantly, thanks to Olaya and Rodríguez's links to the Bogotá underground, La Pola arranged to leave Guaduas for the capital. There she could continue her work with a degree of anonymity.

Her trip arranged, La Pola and her youngest brother, Bibiano, rode out of Guaduas. They started early, and long before the village awoke, they were climbing the verdant foothills of the Eastern Cordillera of the Andes. The first night they lodged with a patriot family in Villeta, and then they continued on the stone-paved trail that wound up through valleys, along cliffs covered with rich vegetation, and over ever higher ridges. At last they saw, spread below them, the *sabana* of Bogotá, almost seven hundred square miles of flat, fertile plain stretching north and south along a wall of mountains rising along its eastern edge. Chilled by the thin air, they pushed on until dark, spending the night in a farmer's hut, one of the whitewashed thick-walled dwellings dotting the *sabana*. After a half day's journey through villages and along fence lines, Policarpa and Bibiano at last neared Santafé de Bogotá, the unpretentious capital whose red tile roofs and more than a dozen church towers stood out against the dark green mountains.

Policarpa and Bibiano entered the city by way of the San Victorino bridge. As they rode through the streets, they saw troops everywhere. On the facades of public buildings, where exuberant patriots had plastered over the king's emblem a few years before, crude representations of the king's coat of arms were now painted. The Academy of San Bartolomé had been turned into headquarters of the Battalion of El Tambo, and Policarpa guessed from the long lines of women waiting in the street outside that it was used as a prison as well. In the central plaza, newly paved by the forced labor of patriots, she saw gallows and a number of low benches used by those condemned to death by firing squad. And off to one side, mounted on a pole, was a cage containing a patriot's head.

Bogotá, a town of a little more than twenty thousand people, showed signs of strain under the rule of Juan Sámano, second-in-command to General Pablo Morillo. Sixty years old, commander of the crown's Third Division, Sámano had recently defeated patriot forces in southern New Granada. He was better known for his cruelty and intransigence than for sensitivity to human concerns.

Other somber sights accompanied them to their destination, a house near the cathedral where Policarpa's friends had arranged for her to stay. During the journey she carried two sets of papers: one for the Spanish guards at checkpoints on the highway, the other to identify her to patriot collaborators. It was for the latter that she reached as the wooden door opened and a young, pleasant-faced woman led her down a narrow corridor to a small living room. She was Andrea Ricaurte, wife of a patriot and close friend of José Ignacio Rodríguez, who had helped her with arrangements to receive Policarpa. Andrea Ricaurte later remembered the young woman from Guaduas as intelligent, young, and beautiful—and that Bibiano looked much like her. She welcomed the travelers warmly, offered them hot chocolate, and urged them to rest while they became accustomed to the altitude and the cool, thin air of Bogotá.

It was easy for Policarpa to sense that under the surface of Bogotá's sullen tranquility there existed enclaves of fierce resistance to Spanish military rule. Pablo Morillo bragged that he had broken patriot resistance through force of arms. Juan Sámano, who arrived in Santafé de Bogotá a few weeks after Morillo, followed his commander's example by dealing harshly with suspected rebels. Both men were lulled into a feeling of confidence by the docility of most *bogotanos*. The patriots, though, were far from cowed. The firm ground upon which Morillo and Sámano believed their reconquest stood was in reality undermined by tunnels of resistance. Not even the king's army was as loyal as its commanders chose to believe. Following the major patriot defeats of 1816, prisoners of war were drafted directly into the ranks of the victorious royalist forces. By 1817 the battalions active on the *sabana* were composed of a high percentage of such draftees. Almost a third of the soldiers in the Battalion of Numancia were former patriots, and the Battalion of El Tambo had many whose loyalty to the Spanish was doubtful.

LA POLA, SEAMSTRESS SPY OF BOGOTÁ

In the first weeks after reaching Bogotá, La Pola established a cover that allowed her to come and go as she pleased. Gradually, she had come to know all the principal figures in the Bogotá underground, among them José María Arcos, clerk of the Battalion of El Tambo. Her skill as a seamstress provided the perfect way to remain above suspicion as she moved freely through the streets, a sewing basket swinging on her arm. Each morning she went to the home of one or another creole family and spent hours sewing and listening to gossip about Sámano's cruelty and about patriot victories in the llanos, the vast lowland plain lying beyond the Eastern Cordillera of the Andes. After long hours of sewing in the cool, high-ceilinged houses of middle-and upper-class creoles, she would take a circuitous route back to Andrea Ricaurte's home, often passing an out-of-the-way corner where a young man stood idly tossing an orange into the air. Dressed sometimes in a gray *ruana*, or poncho-like cloak, sometimes in the long robes of a friar, the youth would exchange his orange for the one hidden in La Pola's sewing basket. In that prosaic way messages from Santafé began their long journey to patriot forces in the eastern llanos.

Many of the messages were reports of Spanish troop movements written by José María Arcos. La Pola learned, too, of the principal meeting places of patriot sympathizers, the sidewalk shops and eating places where young recruits gathered, safe for a while from the watchful eyes of Spanish loyalists. During the hours of gossip in creole homes, she discovered which families were patriots, which had divided loyalties, and which were resolutely royalist. And she learned that the cloth merchants whose stores lined Royal Street were, almost to a man, enemies of the crown. They who sold the fine hand-woven fabrics of Socorro and other textile centers had ample reason to hate the Spanish and their cheap imported cloth. Little by little Policarpa learned who among Santafé's population sided with the patriots.

Central figures of the resistance, landowners and brothers Ambrosio and Vicente Almeyda, devoted their time, money, and lands to the cause of independence. The Almeyda family owned an estate on the *sabana* as well as extensive holdings in Cúcuta, near the border with Venezuela. Their *sabana* hacienda, "Tibabuyes," covered more than twenty square miles of rich land lying northwest of Bogotá. Although they could easily have weathered the Spanish reconquest, they chose instead to enter actively into various plans of resistance. Their home in Bogotá, a few blocks above the cathedral, quietly became a center of insurgency.

At first, diffuse and even impractical plans, as well as a loose network of spies and messengers, were all that emerged from the gatherings in the Almeydas' sprawling Bogotá residence. Then in March and April 1817 events crystallized the Bogotá resistance: A small, poorly equipped rebel force in the llanos won a series of victories. The rebels managed to take several towns from the Spanish, in the process capturing and executing royalist colonel Julián Bayer. To the patriots in Bogotá this news was more encouraging than it perhaps should have been. Ambrosio Almeyda became convinced that the llanos forces would soon march on Bogotá itself.

From that hope emerged a two-part plot. First, arms and men must be sent to buoy up the army in the llanos. The early, rather desultory attempts to encourage desertions from the Spanish ranks must be stepped up and a safe escape route from Santafé to the llanos agreed upon. Policarpa, energetic, still virtually unknown in the capital, would coordinate those efforts. Second, the Almeyda brothers would use every means at their disposal—persuasion and bribery—to ensure that when the patriot army attacked Bogotá, it would find the Spanish battalions full of patriots ready to join in the fight for independence.

Late in March 1817, the underground bolstered its strength in Bogotá and in key towns on the *sabana*. At the same time, Spanish officialdom celebrated the installation of the royal *audiencia*, the judicial branch of viceregal government in New Granada. The royal seal, symbol of Spanish rule by law, was mounted on a silver escutcheon and strapped to the back of a horse whose reins and other trappings were of silk, silver, and gold. Government officials, astride richly adorned horses, accompanied the seal through the streets while Bogotá's citizens looked on. In a sense, the royal seal represented the best that Spain could offer: moderate government that could heal the wounds of the patriot uprising of 1810. But the seat of the *audiencia* could do nothing while new viceroy Francisco Montalvo languished in Cartagena and Santafé de Bogotá suffered under Juan Sámano, who ruled by decree and liberal use of court-martial. The executions continued, eliminating first the leaders of the revolution of 1810, then simple soldiers, deserters, and spies, and finally those merely suspected of giving aid to revolutionary forces.

Fear and mistrust grew within the climate created by Sámano's ruthlessness. Although wiser representatives of the crown lamented his acts, Sámano rarely modified his methods. And when he did, residents of Bogotá reacted with hesitancy and suspicion. Such was the response to a general pardon Sámano announced on July 1, 1817. Amid fanfare, with music and parades, Sámano's aides rode through the streets announcing amnesty for all who had fled the city in fear of their lives. Many who heard the news doubted that Sámano was capable of pardon. "Nothing but a fishhook," José María Caballero noted in his diary. "Thus it has been in the past . . . All those who turned themselves in ended against the stake; that is, shot by a firing squad. An infernal kind of pardon!"[2]

A few did benefit from Sámano's clemency. A number of war prisoners were released that day, among them Alejo Sabaraín, La Pola's boyfriend from her time in Guaduas. She listened intently to his narrative of events dating from the time he left Honda to fight in Antonio Nariño's doomed southern campaign. Sabaraín's experiences, even for those who lived under Sámano's rule, seemed incredible. Alejo's career as a patriot soldier had lasted until the Battle of Tambo Ridge, slightly more than a year earlier, when remnants of the patriot army had flung themselves against El Tambo Fort. Sámano was in command of the victorious Spanish troops, and his handling of captured republican soldiers was typical. Some were absorbed into royalist ranks while others were executed. Alejo had found himself in the latter group and faced a firing squad, when Sámano suddenly ordered the condemned to their quarters. If Sámano had intended that last-minute reprieve as a warning to young patriots, he was sorely disappointed. For Alejo Sabaraín dedicated himself even more firmly to the rebel cause and, on his release, sought ways to combat the Spanish forces.

About the time Alejo Sabaraín joined the guerrillas, a new feeling of urgency started spreading through Bogotá's underground, even as Ambrosio Almeyda proceeded with his plans to subvert Sámano's army. Still convinced that llanos forces would soon liberate the capital, he arranged for three hundred horses to be brought up from the grazing lands of Tolima, the province west of Cundinamarca, in the valley of the Magdalena River. The horses were pastured on land west of the San Victorino bridge. Almeyda's agents worked their way through the barracks, talking to potential insurgents and promising them money, rank, and freedom should they turn on Spanish officials when the invasion began. Meanwhile, Policarpa extended her network of spies and laid out safe routes across the *sabana* and along mountain trails leading down to the llanos. She had contacts in every town along the escape route; some among them were women, and others were priests or family men whose concerns seemed far removed from the political turmoil. With Alejo eager to join the army in the llanos, she made arrangements for able-bodied men to escape Bogotá.

Disaster struck before La Pola's plans could be put into effect. Late one night, after listening to an impassioned royalist harangue in battalion headquarters, one of Ambrosio Almeyda's contacts suffered a change of heart and confessed that he had been approached by patriots within the battalion itself. Questions were asked and names given. Spanish officer Pérez Delgado, whose royalist rhetoric had loosened tongues throughout the ranks, came to learn that Ambrosio and Vicente Almeyda stood at the heart of the conspiracy. Pérez Delgado dispatched guards, and soon the brothers were under arrest.

The possibility of a revolt within their battalions unnerved the Spanish military command. The guard was doubled; persons of doubtful allegiance were closely watched, and in several cases imprisoned. Because of the Spaniards' renewed vigilance, Andrea Ricaurte moved from her house near the central plaza to a smaller place up on the skirts of the cordillera, at the edge of the neighborhood called Egipto. Even though the Almeydas sat in jail, Policarpa decided to forge ahead with the plan she and Alejo had worked out.

On September 9, scarcely three weeks after the arrests, Sabaraín and Miguel Arellano, a friend who had also been pardoned two months before, met with José María Arcos and a handful of conscript soldiers to plot their escape. All were veterans of the doomed southern campaign against the Spanish expeditionary force led by Juan Sámano. All were confirmed patriots, even after a year of imprisonment and forced military service. When they departed Bogotá, Sabaraín carried a series of documents prepared by Policarpa, listing names of patriot supporters in the capital and inside the Spanish battalions. Arcos, too, carried information for the republican commanders in the llanos. In his own writing he described Sámano's plans and troop movements on the *sabana*, this based on intelligence he had gathered as clerk of El Tambo Battalion. Carrying that invaluable information, plus their arms and ammunition, they began the journey northward from Bogotá.

Eleven days passed. Back in Bogotá, Policarpa, Andrea, and Bibiano waited anxiously for word of Alejo's progress. On market day, they searched out their contacts from neighboring towns—women dressed in long black skirts, broad-brimmed hats, and wool *ruanas*, who brought fresh produce from their towns to the capital. Yes, they nodded, the men had passed through four, six, seven days ago; yes, they had left safely.

On September 20, word came that Alejo and his companions had been captured deep in the mountains between Bogotá and the llanos. La Pola understood she was in grave danger. Had Alejo not destroyed the papers he carried, she would be directly implicated in the plot. But before going into hiding, she had one last escape to arrange. Late on the evening of September 23, in the heart of El Tambo Battalion, a corporal named Torneros approached the guard outside Ambrosio and Vicente Almeyda's cell and ordered him off on an errand. When the guard returned, Torneros and the Almeyda brothers were gone. Every effort to find them failed. Well-placed bribes and Policarpa's network of sympathizers carried them safely north of Bogotá, to the village of Machetá, where they stayed with Gertrudis Vanegas, one of La Pola's contacts. There they set to work organizing a new guerrilla group. By the third week in September, Policarpa was in hiding in the new home of Andrea Ricaurte. Bibiano was her only direct contact with the outside, the only source of food and news.

Sámano began searching for La Pola soon after Alejo and his companions were brought back to the capital. The search was not easy. Few of his men remembered what she looked like, and fewer still knew where or with whom she lived and worked. After all, there were more than eleven thousand women in Bogotá, far more women than men, and many were young, dark-haired creoles. Days passed and Sámano's soldiers found no trace of the young woman. Angered, he assigned the search to Sergeant Anselmo Iglesias, an especially effective minion of the king. Iglesias knew that life in Santafé de Bogotá revolved around the small shops that stood on every corner, and he believed that La Pola, if she were still in the city, would eventually be traced from one of them.

Methodically, Iglesias interrogated shopkeepers in central Bogotá, first those north of the cathedral, then those east and south of the plaza. Sometime in the second week of October, he found a shopkeeper not far from El Tambo Battalion who, for a price, admitted knowing La Pola. Her brother came there every day or two, she told him. "Wait here long enough and you'll see him."

Iglesias waited. For several days he stood across the street, watching for the prearranged signal of identification. Late on the afternoon of October 13 or 14, he looked up and saw a boy about fifteen years old leaving the shop and heading down the street. Iglesias followed him at a distance until the youth, unaware that he was being watched, disappeared into a low doorway on a narrow side street.

Not long after Bibiano returned from his errands, the door of Andrea's house burst open and, before either woman could move, Sergeant Iglesias and an escort of soldiers stood in the small living room. All either woman could think of was the sheaf of papers lying on the kitchen table—papers implicating dozens of creole patriots and including letters from commanders in the llanos. Policarpa leapt to her feet and began a tirade against Iglesias and the Spanish army. Using the coarse language of the marketplace, she cursed them and heaped abuse on the names of Sámano, Morillo, the viceroy, and even Ferdinand VII. The men were thrown off balance by the verbal attack. While La Pola held their attention, Andrea slipped into the back room, stuffed the pile of papers into the fire, and returned with her nursing babe in her arms.

Iglesias and his men quickly regained their composure and placed Policarpa and Bibiano under arrest. Andrea Ricaurte escaped arrest because she was nursing a child and because careful search of her house revealed no telltale evidence of her involvement. Bibiano remained in jail for three days; repeated beatings failed to make him say anything that might involve his sister and, incidentally, himself in espionage.

Policarpa was not so lucky. Clearly implicated by the papers Alejo had carried at the time of his capture, she and fifteen others were held in the battalion prison. This time Sámano moved quickly. Deprived of the chance to try the Almeydas, he assigned a prosecutor to Policarpa's case, and evidence was prepared and presented to the court-martial on November 10 and 11. Of the fifteen defendants, nine were sentenced to death, Policarpa and Alejo among them. Two days later, the condemned men and La Pola were moved to the chapel of the Academy of El Rosario, where they awaited their fate.

FINAL DEFIANCE

Prior to her execution, Policarpa continued to conduct clandestine patriot activities—this even from prison—as a certain patriot colonel García told traveling Englishman John Hamilton a few years after the fact. When she learned García was imprisoned in a nearby cell, she had an orange delivered to him containing a note advising him to disavow any knowledge of her. When they were brought to trial, La Pola's assertion that she did not know Colonel García nor had ever been in communication with him matched his own testimony. Thus, as La Pola had planned, García's life was spared.

Among the soldiers assigned to guard the condemned prisoners that day was one who had fought with Alejo and the others in the south. José Hilario López, then age nineteen, was destined to become president of independent New Granada. He wrote an eyewitness account of the eve of Policarpa's execution. The sight of his comrades in arms and their words of farewell so moved López that he wept—strange behavior, to say the least, for a soldier in His Majesty's army. Making an excuse, López moved to a post outside the chapel door. La Pola saw him pass and noticed his tears. "Don't cry for me, little López," she said. "It will be a relief to get away from these tyrants, these wild beasts, these monsters."[3]

From his post López could see La Pola arguing with the priests who had come to advise her on her soul's salvation. Forgive your captors, they said; accept your fate with resignation or you will be forever damned. La Pola reacted to these exhortations with scorn. Let my soul be lost, she shouted. I cannot forgive those monsters of iniquity. My only consolation is the certainty that my death will be avenged. The horrified priests begged her to remain calm, suspecting perhaps that she had lost her sanity under the pressure of approaching death. But the torrent of angry words never ceased until the dark of night. Only sleep calmed her fury.

On the morning of the executions, set for nine o'clock, La Pola resumed her diatribe against the Spanish, against Juan Sámano, against citizens of New Granada who blindly obeyed the Spanish. Three blocks separated the chapel of El Rosario from the central plaza where La Pola and the condemned male patriots were to meet the firing squad. A multitude of citizens was gathered in the square, patriots and royalists alike. Sámano hoped they would derive a moral lesson from the spectacle of death. Since La Pola was the first woman to be executed in Santafé de Bogotá, there were many whose curiosity brought them to witness so unique and macabre a drama. It was upon them she heaped her bitterest words. Policarpa walked through the crowd with firm step and, ignoring her priestly escort, cried out to the crowd, "Indolent people! How different would be our fate today if you knew the price of liberty! But it is not too late. Although I am a woman and young, I have more than enough courage to suffer this death and a thousand more. Remember my example!"[4]

Sámano, watching from a balcony, signaled the drum corps to drown out her words. Soldiers led her to the execution bench, but she refused to stand on it, claiming that such a position was not proper for a woman. So saying, she halfway knelt on the bench, carefully smoothing her skirts as the soldiers blindfolded her and bound her hands. Almost as a single shot, six musket balls pierced her back. Policarpa Salavarrieta was silenced at last.

EPILOGUE

La Pola's body was interred in the Church of San Agustín. But the fact of her execution refused to lie buried. Try as he would, Sámano could not put the ignominy of Policarpa Salavarrieta's execution behind him. Nor was the vengeance she had foreseen long in coming. Within two years Spain's army fell in defeat to patriot forces led by Simón Bolívar. Juan Sámano, dressed in peasant clothing, fled Bogotá in cowardly retreat, jostling aside frightened royalists who crowded the road to Guaduas, and on down to the Magdalena River.

Years later, when chroniclers of the *Patria Boba* looked back on the foolish and heroic acts of that period, Policarpa Salavarrieta stood out among the martyrs of the Spanish Reign of Terror conducted in northern South America. The patriotic bravado of La Pola's last hours came to obscure details of her life up to that moment. Much of her final harangue was preserved in common memory; the statue erected in her honor in Bogotá shows her seated, blindfolded, the moment before Sámano's guns cut her down. Today her face is etched on Colombian currency, as seen in figure 9. Yet the particulars of her life and her flamboyant individuality faded from popular memory until relatively recent times.

In a sense, the historical La Pola was transformed into a symbol of all the female patriots of the resistance. She is revered not so much for her own qualities and dramatic bravery, but because she alone, among women who supported the underground with their deeds and sometimes their lives, had possessed a national audience at the moment of death. The humbly born creole girl of Guaduas, Colombia, whose sharp tongue and nearly irrational fearlessness made her Spanish guards cringe and priests blush, lives on as a national heroine who transcends the fiery young woman she was in life.

Figure 9.1 Policarpa Salavarrieta. José María Espinosa (1855), Wikimedia Commons. The original painting is housed in the National Museum of Colombia, Bogotá, D.F., Colombia.

NOTES

1. José María Caballero, "En la Independencia," in Eduardo Posada et al., *La Patria Boba* (Bogotá: Imprenta Nacional, 1902), 261.

2. José María Caballero, *Particularidades de Santa Fe* (Bogotá: Biblioteca Nacional, 1946), 183.

3. José Hilario López's account of La Pola's imprisonment is found in Ignacio Arizmende Posada, *Gobernantes colombianos*, second edition (Bogotá: Italgraf, 1983), 74–75.

4. José Hilario López, *Memorias del general José Hilario López* (Paris: Imprenta D'Aubusson y Kugelmann, 1857), 87.

REFERENCES

Arizmendi Posada, Ignacio. *Gobernantes colombianos*, second edition. Bogotá: Italgraf, 1983.

Caballero, José María. *Particularidades de Santa Fe*. Bogotá: Biblioteca Nacional, 1946.

Caballero, José María. "En la Independencia." In *La Patria Boba*, Eduardo Posada et al. Bogotá: Imprenta Nacional, 1902.

Chicangana-Bayona, Yobenj Aucardo. "*Imagens, Conceitos e Cultura Política: A pintura sobre a Independência da Colômbia na primeira metade do século XIX.*" *Revista Tempo* 16, no. 31 (2011): 145–76.

Cordovez Moure, José María. *Reminiscencias de Santafé de Bogotá*. Madrid: Aguilar, 1957.

Davies, Catherine, Claire Brewster, and Hilary Owen. *South American Independence: Gender, Politics, Text*. Liverpool: Liverpool University Press, 2006.

Hamilton, John. *Travels Through the Interior Provinces of Colombia*. London: John Murray, 1827. Accessible online.

López, José Hilario. *Memorias del general José Hilario López*. Paris: Imprenta D'Aubusson y Kugelmann, 1857.

Monsalve, José Dolores. *Mujeres de la Independencia*. Bogotá: Imprenta Nacional, 1926.

Montoya de Umaña, Enriqueta. *La criolla Policarpa Salavarrieta*. Bogotá: Tercer Mundo, 1969.

Chapter 10

Manuela Sáenz, 1797–1856

INTRODUCTION

Ideas of political freedom gained motive force throughout Spanish America late in the eighteenth century. This was especially the case among those of the region's most influential social class, native-born whites, called creoles. Two key events of that time turned the creoles' thoughts increasingly to shaking off the heavy hand of Spanish colonial rule. The first of them was Great Britain's defeat at the hands of its colonists in North America. The second, having an even more profound impact, was the French Revolution. Its ideological touchstone was a philosophic statement titled *Declaration of Man and Citizen*, published in 1789. That stirring affirmation of Enlightenment political ideals moved one well-to-do young creole of New Granada to action. Antonio Nariño (1763–1823) committed the illegal and dangerous crime of translating the French human rights declaration into Spanish in 1794, printing copies of it, and distributing them late at night in the streets of Bogotá. His punishment? Spanish officials arrested Nariño, charged him with subversion, and sentenced him to life in prison in a North African dungeon. The time was clearly ripe for revolution in colonial Spanish America.

That moment came twelve years later, when Napoleon Bonaparte arrested Spain's king and imprisoned him in southern France along with his family. Creoles throughout Spanish America seized on the removal of their king as a pretext for rising up against officials sent by Napoleon to govern in colonial America. They overthrew them and set to governing their homelands on their own. That set into motion the Spanish American wars of independence. Twenty years of bloody warfare followed, ending in political independence for the region.

As the revolution unfolded, one leader rose above all others: Simón Bolívar (1783–1830). Born in Caracas to a wealthy creole family and radicalized while studying in Europe, Bolívar vowed never to rest until Latin America was free of Spanish domination. Following initial setbacks, he led his army in driving Spanish armies from Venezuela, Colombia, Ecuador, Peru, and Bolivia. This feat earned him the title "The Liberator."

Women distinguished themselves in the struggle for independence. One of the more notable among them was Quito-born Manuela Sáenz, Simón Bolívar's intrepid companion from 1822 until his death in 1830. Initially Bolívar's mistress, Manuela Sáenz quickly became his trusted adviser, chief of security, archivist, and even protector. Her most notable act came one cold and rainy night in Bogotá when, unarmed and wearing a nightdress, she stood down six heavily armed would-be assassins just outside the Liberator's

Figure 10.1 Manuela Sáenz wearing the Order of the Sun medal. Copy of a painting; Tecla Walker, copyist. Wikimedia Commons. The original painting by Marco Salas is housed in the Casa Museo Quinta de Bolívar.

bedroom door. Her delaying tactic permitted Bolívar time to escape through his bedroom window. For her heroism Manuela Sáenz is honored today as "The Liberator of the Liberator."

MANUELA SÁENZ AND ECUADORIAN SOCIETY

Manuela Sáenz was born in 1797 in the picturesque Andean town of Quito, Ecuador, capital of the southernmost province of the Viceroyalty of New Granada. Having white parents, Spanish immigrant Simón Sáenz and *quiteña* Joaquina Aizpuru, meant that Manuela was born into Quito's highest social class. Yet there was a crucial problem involving her birth: Her parents were not married. Simón Sáenz was a married man with six children. Joaquina Aizpuru was a single woman of age thirty. That made Manuela Sáenz an *hija natural* (illegitimate). In street terms, she was "*mal nacida*" (badly born), a bastard. That meant she was not permitted to grow up in the household of either of her parents.

Details of the affair between the parents of Manuela Sáenz are not known, though her father and Joaquina Aizpuru's father, Mateo Aizpuru, knew each other through work. Simón Sáenz held an appointed seat on the city council (*cabildo*) of Quito, while Aizpuru was an attorney for the high court, or *Audiencia* of Quito. Their office buildings were near each other on Quito's central plaza. The two men were thus members of a relatively small elite class of fewer than three hundred families. Quito's remaining twenty-eight thousand residents were mixed-blood mestizos, indigenous people, and slaves of African origin. The whites were major landowners and bureaucrats. Mestizos were merchants, shopkeepers, and small landholders. Indigenous peoples served as manual labor. Slaves, making up the smallest ethnic group, were servants of elite and upper-middle-class families. Creoles lived closest to city center, mostly in houses of two stories. Mestizos lived just beyond, in one-story houses. Indians and others of the lowest social stratum lived in huts on Quito's outskirts.

The scandal surrounding Manuela Sáenz's birth was short-lived and handled expeditiously. Upper-class women who gave birth out of wedlock were far from unusual in the Quito of that time. The male partner invariably got off lightly, in keeping with the prevailing sexual double standard of the time. The female in question bore both the shame of lost virtue and that of bearing a natural child. Joaquina Aizpuru and her family first tried to place the infant with another family. Failing that they followed the familiar route of placing her in a convent to be raised by nuns. Joaquina Aizpuru had little further contact with her daughter and died some years after giving birth to her. Luckily, Manuela's Spanish father, a leading citizen of Quito, acted responsibly. He could hardly do otherwise, as everyone in town knew he was her father—and he had to protect his reputation. Therefore, Simón Sáenz recognized Manuela as his daughter, meaning she would go through life bearing his name. Also important was the considerable dowry Sáenz paid La Concepción convent for receiving Manuela. Throughout subsequent years he faithfully paid for her maintenance and schooling. Most importantly, Simón Sáenz visited with her often in the convent's reception parlor. He loved his daughter, who was exceptionally attractive and intelligent. And, as the nuns often told him, "*Manuela tiene gracia*" (Manuela has personality).

The convent of La Concepción offered Manuela Sáenz the best education available to young women of the monied class. There she was taught practical skills that served her well in later life. La Concepción was a small city of women, largely free of the patriarchal constraints prevailing outside convent walls. About fifteen hundred women, girls, and children lived in a sprawling complex of buildings occupying a large city block just off Quito's central plaza. It was a warren of living areas, workshops, classrooms, dormitories, and patios, where activity went on throughout the day. Only periodic chapel services brought spells of quiet. The hundred nuns living in La Concepción operated it as a profit-making commercial concern. Among its most important revenue producers were enameled wood, sweets and pastries, fancy needlework, and premium candles made from the oil of sperm whales, known as "*espermas*."

The women who supplied labor for the convent's diverse enterprises were neither nuns nor of elite society. Most were either meztisas or of indigenous descent. Along with producing salable goods, they prepared the convent's meals, did its laundry, shopped for its food, and performed the myriad other tasks required to maintain well more than a thousand women living in close quarters. And more than a few were slaves. Such was the setting in which Manuela Sáenz spent her formative years.

The comfortable if hectic pace of convent life changed dramatically late in 1808. Shocking news reached Quito that French troops had occupied Madrid. The king and his family now lived in France as prisoners of Napoleon Bonaparte. With the disappearance of Spanish political legitimacy in the Americas, the creoles of Quito struck against *peninsular* rule. In August 1809 they seized control of the *audiencia* and arrested its Spanish-born president, proclaiming that he, along with his French-dominated puppet government, had usurped their natural right of self-government. Their uprising, however, was short-lived, and royal troops soon arrived from Lima and jailed the ringleaders. Twelve months passed, and in August 1810, *quiteño* patriots attacked the town's prison to free their colleagues. They failed in the attempt. A fearful slaughter of more than sixty patriots followed. Their leaders were spared only long enough to be hanged, cut down, and drawn and quartered, some while still alive. Their severed heads were displayed in iron cages mounted on poles placed along roads leading into Quito.

Just one patriot leader escaped execution. She was Manuela Cañizares, a creole dissident who had long hosted an anti-Spanish salon in her home. The manifesto leading to Quito's "Men of August" revolt, as it was known, was drafted in her drawing room. Manuela Cañizares fled the city in 1810 and hid from Spanish authorities until 1814. Ultimately, she died of injuries suffered from an accident at a remote finca north of Quito. Her dramatic story made a significant impression on Manuela Sáenz and other students at La Concepción.

During her sixteen years at La Concepción convent, Manuela Sáenz matured into a beautiful, educated, and mature young woman. At length, she decided it was time to depart the convent. The historical record is vague on how she managed to do this. According to one version, she wrote her father, asking to join him in Panama, where he was running a trading company. According to a more romantic account of her departure, Manuela had a clandestine affair with a handsome young officer of the king's guard named Fausto D'Elhuyar that earned her summary expulsion from La Concepción. Regardless of the truth of either version, Manuela Sáenz departed Quito in mid-1815. Servants of the Sáenz family escorted her down through the mountains to the Pacific Ocean port of Guayaquil, where she boarded a ship bound for Panama City.

When Manuela arrived at her father's office, Simón Sáenz saw an abrupt spike in his business. His lovely daughter instantly became a source of excitement among the unattached male population of the city. Bachelor men of business began filing through his office hoping to catch a glimpse of the lovely Manuela. Meanwhile, the subject of attention reveled in her newfound freedom, adopting the custom of smoking cigarillos and enjoying wine with dinner. As Manuela savored joys of life outside the convent, she appraised the eligible bachelors besieging her father's place of work. Marriage was uppermost in her mind, because through marriage she would reach another significant level of independence. Under Spanish law married women shared in half the husband's wealth earned after marriage. So, Manuela and her father watched for a good match, an unattached, well-to-do, and serious male in need of a wife. He promptly appeared in the person of James Thorne, an English merchant and Roman Catholic who enjoyed the favor of Spanish officials. Better yet, Thorne was a close associate of Simón Sáenz, having helped him financially when Manuela's father hastily departed Quito during the "Men of August" uprising six years before. For these reasons Thorne had a clear advantage when it came to courting Manuela Sáenz. Also, he fell in love with her at first sight. Their relationship progressed rapidly and in 1816 Thorne asked Simón Sáenz for his daughter's hand in marriage. Simón

Sáenz and his daughter accepted, and the wedding was set for mid-1817 in Lima. Manuela was ecstatic. Seemingly overnight she had transitioned from unwanted child consigned to life in a convent, to fiancée of a wealthy foreign businessman. Mid-1817 found her living with friends of her fiancé in Lima and awaiting her wedding day. As for James Thorne, he was doubly delighted at the prospect of wedding Manuela Sáenz. Not only was he to be the husband of a delightful young wife, but her father had settled on him a handsome dowry of eight thousand gold pesos.[1]

At first Manuela was happy as the wife of James Thorne. She was mistress of a large house on the outskirts of Lima and for the first time possessed her own money. Prior to departing Panama for Peru, she used some of these monies to purchase two female slaves of her own age, Jonatás and Natán. From that time onward they would be her constant companions. James Thorne also gave Manuela his power of attorney so she could manage his affairs in Lima when he was away on business. Manuela was welcomed by members of the city's elite. She was not only the daughter and wife of successful businessmen but also vivacious and intelligent and one of the most stunning women in the city. Over the first years of her marriage, Manuela carried out an affectionate correspondence with her husband when he was away on business trips. She kept him informed about local events and sent him disarming and humorous vignettes about herself. He responded warmly, filling his own letters with terms of endearment.

Unfortunately, within three years relations between the two had begun to cool. Manuela was barely into her twenties, witty, and outgoing. Her husband was twice her age, short and stocky, and rather dull. Thorne was irritated by his wife's stylish slaves, Jonatás and Natán, who were never far from her side. Even worse, both slaves wore turbans and dressed like men, especially Jonatás, who also behaved like a man. At one point, officials in Lima took Jonatás into custody and accused her of being a hermaphrodite.

Politics was another source of strife between husband and wife. At the time of their marriage, South America was aflame with revolution. Thorne was a royalist who owed his fortune to favorable treatment by crown officials. His wife was a creole who had hated the Spanish from the moment she witnessed their barbaric execution of *quiteño* patriots in 1810. By the time Manuela Sáenz and James Thorne entered their fourth year of marriage, in 1821, it was clear that South America's two great revolutionaries were closing in on the royalist bastion of Peru. General José de San Martín had liberated Chile from the Spanish and was readying his army for a full-scale invasion of Peru. Meanwhile, to the north, General Simón Bolívar had driven the Spanish from the heartland of New Granada and was doing the same in his home country of Venezuela, in the northeast. Next, he would march his army southward to Spanish-controlled Quito. James Thorne grew frightened and irritable. Not only was his livelihood threatened but he had apparently lost control of his wife—as if he had ever been able to control her in the first place. Manuela's enthusiasm for the revolution only grew as reports of patriot victories poured into Peru. She ignored her husband's pleas to curb her involvement with the patriots.

A "WORTHY FEMALE PATRIOT"

Lima's patriots, among them Manuela Sáenz, were thrilled when San Martín at last marched his troops into the city. Months earlier she had joined a secret society of elite women working to turn the Peruvian capital's seven-hundred-man Numancia Regiment to the patriot cause. She influenced at least one soldier, her half brother José María Sáenz. An officer in the regiment, José María went over to the patriot side and began helping his sister prepare Lima for San Martín's arrival. In June 1821 the Spanish withdrew token forces from the city and took up positions in mountains to the east. A month after that San Martín marched into Lima at the head of an army of twenty-three thousand men. Then Manuela and her women's group started raising money to supply the patriot force. At the same time, she was thrilled by a series of liberal decrees of San Martín, one of which was the "law of free birth," an abolitionist measure requiring the freeing of children born to slaves. Manuela Sáenz happily complied with the new law, freeing the newborn child of one of her slaves. Her patriotic acts did not go unnoticed. In late 1821 San Martín created the Order of the Sun, a society recognizing "the patriotism of the most delicate." Manuela Sáenz was one of 112 "worthy female patriots" of Lima who received the honor in a ceremony presided over by San Martín himself.

The break between Manuela Sáenz and James Thorne came suddenly, during a business trip in 1822. Thorne was on his way to Panama, and Manuela to Quito, where she wanted to say farewell to her father, who was returning to Spain. She also planned to file a legal claim to her share of the estate of her maternal grandfather, Mateo Aizpuru. Manuela and her slaves attracted attention as they made their way up the highway toward Quito. All three rode astride, dressed in green wool uniforms styled after those of Peruvian republican soldiers. They were clearly not to be trifled with. Manuela, Jonatás, and Natán were protected by a squadron of soldiers and Manuela carried pistols in saddle holsters.

As they approached Quito the highway became clogged with bedraggled Spanish soldiers on their way out of the province, escorted by soldiers of Gran Colombia, the name of the new nation created by Simón Bolívar. The new confederation consisted of Colombia and Venezuela—and now the province of Quito. Just days earlier, on May 24, Bolívar's army had liberated Quito at the Battle of Pichincha. Manuela was filled with happiness as she gazed at the passing soldiers, dressed in blue uniforms, trimmed in red and gold, and carrying tricolor banners of the same gold, blue, and red colors. That was now her flag, something she had dreamed of her entire life.

When Manuela rode into her hometown in late May 1822, she found everyone in a state of high excitement. On the twenty-fourth of that month, Simón Bolívar's army had routed Spanish forces on the slopes of Mount Pichincha, the snowcapped Andean peak rising above Quito. The city and province were now free. The great man would soon march into the city at the head of his army—at least as soon as he had recovered from a combination of illness and exhaustion. Bolívar had not commanded his forces in the Battle of Pichincha, but rather had been carried away from the battlefield on a stretcher, leaving the victory to his top subordinate, General Antonio José Sucre. In truth Bolívar was growing old before his time. Only forty, he had been a commander in the field for more than a decade, battling Spanish forces in the mountains and the plains, riding through fair weather and foul. His soldiers had marveled at his endurance in the saddle, affectionately nicknaming him "old iron ass." But the Liberator was tired and showing early signs of the tuberculosis that would claim his life eight years later.

On June 16, 1822, Quito's thirty-five thousand residents crowded the narrow streets through which Simón Bolívar would pass. Gold, blue, and red bunting decorated houses along the town's central streets. Three hundred officers of the liberation army, accompanied by provincial leaders, escorted the Liberator toward the central plaza. Seven hundred soldiers and town officials awaited him there, flanking a colorfully decorated speaker's platform. As Bolívar approached the plaza, elegantly dressed women showered him with roses from second-floor balconies. One of them, Manuela Sáenz de Thorne, tossed a garland to the hero. According to a witness it struck Bolívar on the head, earning an angry glance from the great man. His face softened, however, when he noticed the beauty of his attacker.

Simón Bolívar loved women, though when his young wife had died of yellow fever a few months after their marriage, he vowed never to marry again. Only twenty when they married, Bolívar remained faithful to that promise. But he went on to have many liaisons. The Liberator's casual affairs suited the lifestyle of a military commander in the field. Those who knew him said Simón Bolívar planned his affairs as he did his military campaigns, with precision and attention to detail, and with an ultimate goal of conquest followed by passionate enjoyment of the fruit of victory. That matter likely played on Bolívar's mind the day he rode into Quito, resplendent in his dress uniform and mounted on his war horse, Pastor.

Manuela Sáenz met Simón Bolívar at the gala ball given in his honor at Quito's theater. She arrived on the arm of her half brother, José María, now an officer in the liberation army and aide-de-camp to Bolívar. When Sáenz introduced his sister to the guest of honor, the two fell into deep conversation and later danced together many times. By early hours of the morning, it was clear to all whom Bolívar had chosen to warm his bed during the two weeks he planned to stay in the capital of Gran Colombia's southernmost nation. That evening Manuela made the same decision regarding Bolívar. She would happily become his lover.[2]

After very few days, during which Bolívar bombarded Manuela Sáenz with love notes, bouquets of flowers, and gifts, Manuela entered into a passionate affair with the supreme commander of patriot forces. Late each evening, after the Liberator had finished his day's work, Manuela was escorted to his rooms, slipping away before dawn. All Quito knew of the affair. Those of her social class disapproved. But Manuela Sáenz did not care: She knew they always scorned her illegitimate birth, and she had tired of her husband and wanted to be rid of him. In a land where divorce was illegal, what better way to achieve separation from an unwanted spouse than through a flagrant affair? And what an affair! Simón Bolívar was everything James Thorne was not. He was dashing, lithe, and charming. Thorne was the opposite, and also a foreigner. It was important for Manuela Sáenz that Simón Bolívar was a native-born American, just like her.

The idyllic interlude between Manuela Sáenz and Simón Bolívar came to an end two weeks after it began. For Bolívar his affair with the lovely Manuela had been all he hoped it would be. Still, he knew it would end as all the others had, abruptly and without further consequence. They would part amid pledges of undying love and with copious shedding of tears. He would promise to write as soon as he reached his destination, in that case the port city of Guayaquil. But such promises were meaningless to Bolívar. What he did not know, as he rode away from Quito on the fourth day of July 1822, was that Manuela Sáenz would not permit the Liberator to treat her as he had all the others.

Bolívar's trip to Guayaquil was pivotal to his plans. There he would meet with José de San Martín, who had arrived seeking his colleague's help in liberating Peru. Bolívar, however, wanted much more than a partnership with the patriot from la Plata. His intention was, first, that Guayaquil and the province of Quito should remain part of Gran Colombia. Second, and more importantly, he wanted for himself the glory of liberating Peru. Ill and tired of battle, San Martín yielded to Bolívar on both counts. He hastily departed Guayaquil and returned to Lima, where he resigned his position as Protector of Peru. He next returned to Buenos Aires, visited his wife's grave, collected his daughter, and traveled to Europe, where he lived out the remainder of his life. Back in Guayaquil, Simón Bolívar set to work readying his army for sea transport to Lima's Pacific Ocean port of Callao. Then fate intervened.

Early in November word came that the royalist town of Pasto, in southern Colombia, had risen up against the new republic of which it was now part. The Liberator, General Sucre, and several thousand troops hurried north to crush the rebellion. Their route took them through Quito. Simón Bolívar would again see Manuela Sáenz.

When Bolívar reached Quito and called on her, Manuela railed at him. How dare he show his face when he had not written her in four months? How dare he call her "my love" after sleeping with half the women in Guayaquil? How dare he tell her that pack of lies at their tearful parting in July? Her anger quickly subsided and the two made up—as each knew they would. The next day Bolívar and his forces traveled on to Pasto and easily reunited it with Gran Colombia. Heading southward again the Liberator and his men paused to regroup at the cold Andean village of Yacuanquer. There the man who never wrote to his former lovers penned his first letter to Manuela Sáenz. In it he apologized for not writing sooner and complained of the cold and boredom of the place: "Here we conjugate the verb *ennuyer* (to bore)." Four days later, his letter in hand, Manuela Sáenz sent Bolívar a rather sober response signed "The most fervent of your friends, who is Manuela."[3]

The fact that Bolívar had kept his promise to write informed Manuela Sáenz that she could move forward with her plan to keep the man she now loved. She understood that Bolívar was bound by his youthful vow to drive the Spanish from their American colonies and that every personal consideration was secondary to that task. She decided to become his most loyal confidante and adviser, the guardian of his health, and to do everything else in her power to help him realize his vision of an independent Spanish America. When Bolívar reached Quito in early 1823, exhausted and ill following his punishing four-hundred-mile round trip to Pasto, Manuela took charge of his household. She nursed him back to health, oversaw his daily agenda, and shielded him from the unending flow of visitors looking for favors and jobs. In short, by sheer force of will she turned their relationship into something akin to a marriage, lending youthful vigor to a man worn down by constant hardship. At first Bolívar resisted Manuela's intrusion into his life. He held traditional views on women and frowned on their participation in public life. During the weeks he spent in Quito, Bolívar complained about Manuela's bossiness, but in the end, he accepted the fact that she would be useful to him when he traveled to Lima to undertake the liberation of Peru.

On September 3, 1823, Bolívar and his army landed at Callao. He established his headquarters on the road between Callao and Lima. Not long afterward Manuela Sáenz arrived there from Quito offering—demanding—to join in the war effort. Bolívar's personal secretary, Colonel Daniel O'Leary, suggested that she could best help by becoming the Liberator's archivist. When Bolívar agreed, a delighted Manuela threw herself into the task. She had a

Gran Colombian cavalry uniform designed for herself and proudly wore it as she rode back and forth to work. It was a striking uniform consisting of blue pants and jacket, both trimmed in red. The tunic had golden epaulets with a silver laurel wreath on each shoulder, a colonel's insignia.

Simón Bolívar remained in Peru for three years. During that span he completed the liberation of South America through crushing victories over Spanish armies at the Battles of Junín in August 1824 and Ayacucho in December 1824. That same year he was elected to a second four-year term as president of Gran Colombia, and he published a call for all Latin American republics to assemble in Panama to create a United States of Latin America. The following year, again back in Lima, Bolívar wrote a constitution for the new nation of Bolivia, previously known as Alto Peru. Its grateful citizens had named their country in his honor.

In 1826 Simón Bolívar stood at the height of his power and prestige. His exploits were celebrated throughout Europe and America. Honors and emoluments poured in. A grandson of George Washington sent Bolívar a lock of the great Virginian's hair. The Marquis de Lafayette wrote to him, addressing his letter "To the Second Washington." In Paris fashionable women wore hats *à la Bolívar*. Through it all Manuela Sáenz stood at the Liberator's side, resplendent at social functions in fashionable gowns decorated with her sash and Order of the Sun insignia. But at last, the celebrations ended. Bolívar was called back to Gran Colombia. Trouble had broken out in Venezuela, where General José Antonio Páez, commander in chief of that country, had rebelled against membership in the three-nation confederation. Meanwhile the political situation in Bogotá had become toxic. Vice president of Gran Colombia, Francisco de Paula Santander, sent Bolívar a gloomy assessment of politics in the capital. Bolívar quickly departed Lima on September 3, 1826. He left behind Gran Colombian troops to maintain order and to protect citizens of Gran Colombia residing in Peru. Foremost among them was Manuela Sáenz.

With Bolívar gone, the security of Manuela Sáenz and other Gran Colombians deteriorated rapidly. Troops were homesick and wanted to leave Peru. Meanwhile Peruvian officials wanted all of the foreigners out of their country. By early 1827 Gran Colombian troops were in a mutinous mood. Even Manuela Sáenz, wearing her cavalry uniform and speaking passionately to them on behalf of their commander in chief, found it hard to control them. On January 26, 1827, the mutineers struck. They seized their barracks and imprisoned their officers. This action opened the floodgates to anti-Bolivarian sentiment throughout Peru. When Manuela, operating from her villa La Magdalena, tried to intervene, Peruvian officials placed her under house arrest. When she persisted and contacted imprisoned Gran Colombian officers, she was then sent packing to a women's prison. She sent a sizzling letter to her country's consul protesting his failure to protect the rights of a citizen of Gran Colombia. She drew on Enlightenment legal theory, demanding "the privileges which the Rights of Man extend to persons imprisoned."[4] Her protests were useless. She and her compatriots were deported from Peru in April 1827. Manuela found herself disembarking once more at Guayaquil and preparing to make her way up through the mountains to Quito. This time, though, no horses or mules could be found. Manuela was forced to walk. Her party consisted of a four-man military escort, Jonatás and Natán, and numerous porters carrying their baggage, which included the archive of Simón Bolívar.

Manuela undertook the nearly two-week climb in good spirits. After all, each step took her that much closer to the man she loved. By then she was sure Bolívar loved her too. On his way along the same route several months earlier, he had paused long enough to write her a passionate letter reading in part, "I want to see you again, and touch you and smell you and taste you and unite with you through all the senses." Earlier, Bolívar had taken to introducing his letters with phrases like "Darling," "My adored one," and "My love."[5]

When Manuela reached Quito, she was distressed to learn that no letter from Bolívar awaited her. Nor did one arrive during the six months that followed. She grew increasingly angry. It was true that at that time the Liberator was eight hundred miles away ending the Páez revolt in Venezuela. But surely, she fumed, he could have found time to write. When the long-awaited letter from Bolívar, now in Bogotá, at last reached her, in November 1827, Manuela Sáenz was only slightly mollified by its passage reading "Manuela, the memory of your enchantments dissolves the frost of my years.... Come. Come to me. Come now."[6] In her response she agreed to depart Quito as soon as possible. But her letter carried an angry accusation and a command: "You had a little love for me, but our long separation has killed it.... Never order me away from you again. I will never leave your side."[7] She soon departed Quito for the capital of Gran Colombia.

CONVENTION AND CONFLICT IN BOGOTÁ

Bogotá was not an impressive place in 1828. With less than forty thousand in population, it consisted of one-and two-story houses hugging the foothills of mountains extending along its eastern edge. The city lay on an intermontane plateau 8,600 feet in elevation, making it a chilly place often bathed by glacial rains. Bogotá's saving feature was its central plaza, an ample space at the center of city life. Government buildings lined its northern and southern sides, while its cathedral and church offices stood to the east. Stores and shops were arranged along its western side. Weekly market was held in the plaza on Sundays, as were holiday festivals and religious events.

In late January, Manuela Sáenz and her party made a dramatic entrance into the southwestern corner of Bogotá's central plaza. People stopped and gaped at the travelers. For more than forty days they had trekked over mountains and plains and had crossed dozens of rivers and streams. A squadron of lancers escorted the party, commanded by Colonel Charles Demarquet, aide-de-camp of general and president of Gran Colombia, Simón Bolívar. At the front of the procession rode three women, one a beautiful young creole and the other two colorfully dressed black women. Trailing behind were dozens of horses and mules, half of them heavily laden and tended by sturdy *arrieros* (muleteers). It was clear that the creole woman was someone important. Word quickly spread through Bogotá: The Liberator's controversial mistress Manuela Sáenz had arrived.

Despite its sleepy appearance Bogotá was rife with drama and political intrigue: Two factions had emerged there while Bolívar was away liberating Quito, Peru, and Bolivia. That factionalism was founded in the same liberal and conservative principles at the time giving rise to modern politics in both Europe and the United States. Philosophic beliefs, and mundane considerations as well, had given rise to continental Europe's first political parties, the Liberal and the Conservative. The same development took place in Latin America. In Gran Colombia Vice President Francisco de Paula Santander became point man for the country's liberal faction. President Simón Bolívar was undisputed leader of those starting to call themselves conservatives.

At the moment Manuela Sáenz led her cavalcade up through the streets of Bogotá to Bolívar's *quinta* (country house) on the northeastern outskirts of the city, members of Colombia's two political factions—liberals and conservatives—were locked in a battle that each believed would decide the fate of the republic. Elected delegates were being convened to rewrite the liberal Constitution of Cúcuta. Simón Bolívar believed the document's failure to provide a powerful executive branch of government would be Gran Colombia's undoing. Liberals were convinced that Bolivarian delegates to the convention intended to turn the country into an outright dictatorship with Simón Bolívar at its head. As proof they cited the constitution Bolívar had written for Bolivia three years earlier, mandating a lifetime presidency. The notion sent cold chills through liberals of Gran Colombia. They girded for political war at the mountain village of Ocaña, nearly four hundred miles north of Bogotá. Manuela Sáenz had arrived in the midst of a political firestorm.

When in Bogotá, Bolívar preferred to live at his *quinta* rather than at the presidential residence, the Palace of San Carlos, in downtown Bogotá. The *Quinta de Bolívar*, as it became known, possessed a spacious villa located on an ample piece of ground covered with cedars, pines, and guava trees and having lawns lined with flower beds crowded with hydrangeas, roses, and calendula. It also boasted a frigid pool where the Liberator took therapeutic baths early most mornings. Bolívar's *quinta* was the gathering place of his leading supporters, most of whom were also friends and admirers of Manuela Sáenz. Thus, when Manuela arrived there in early 1828, she immediately joined in the heated conversations about the upcoming constitutional convention. Two months after she reached Bogotá, delegates to the convention began departing the city for Ocaña. Bolívar was not a delegate, nor did he attend the convention for fear of being a disruptive presence there. He followed deliberations from the town of Bucaramanga, located a hundred miles south of Ocaña.

All Gran Colombia followed events unfolding at the constitutional convention. Manuela Sáenz kept up steady correspondence with Bolívar. When it became clear that Santander's delegates were in the majority and therefore in a position to write the new constitution without input from Bolívar or his followers, she offered her lover one solution to handling the troublesome Santander: "We shall kill him." Manuela was fond of saying, "I love my friends and hate my enemies."[8]

The Congress of Ocaña ended in failure. Bolivarian delegates walked out when it became clear they were not in the majority. Lacking a quorum, the congress adjourned. Failure at Ocaña drove political tensions to unprecedented heights. Simón Bolívar governed under siege-like conditions as liberals filled their newspapers with invective against his regime. Extremist liberals, known as *exaltados*, began plotting to assassinate Bolívar. Bolívar attempted to defuse tensions by appointing Santander minister to the United States. But the liberal leader dragged his feet and never left Bogotá. He suspected something important might happen and wanted to be in town when it did.

On July 28, Bolívar's most fervent supporters gathered at the *quinta* to celebrate his forty-fifth birthday. Though the Liberator was out of town, Manuela hosted the event. The celebration was marked by partygoers' high spirits, which were driven ever higher by steady consumption of alcoholic beverages. Late in the afternoon someone suggested a mock execution of Santander. Manuela, Jonatás, and Natán found a discarded uniform, stuffed it with rags, and propped it against a wall. The celebrants, most of them military officers, then riddled the effigy with bullets. The incident created outrage in Bogotá, and most blamed it on Manuela Sáenz. Bolívar's friend and colleague General José María Córdoba, who did not like Manuela and who had witnessed the incident, sent an irate letter to Bolívar placing full blame on her. Bolívar sent Córdoba a letter promising that he would banish Manuela from the *quinta*. In it he referred to her as "a lovable madwoman."[9]

Manuela's banishment from the *quinta* served her purposes. She rented an apartment in the center of Bogotá, across the street from the presidential palace. From there she could monitor the comings and goings of visitors to the building. Meanwhile, she studied intelligence brought to her by Jonatás and Natán, who collected it at public venues throughout the city. The three women thus became an unofficial security arm of the Gran Colombian government. During those tense days Manuela held ongoing *tertulias* (gatherings) at her apartment in the Plazuela de San Carlos. There the Liberator's unconditional supporters talked, often far into the night, about the state of national politics and of the need to keep alive the man they believed vital to national security. Manuela was central to those conversations. The young French scientist, and admirer of Manuela, Dr. Jean-Baptiste Boussingault cogently stated her position at that moment: "Beyond the gaudy display of her baroque personality she demonstrated her ability and skill at political intrigue in a hundred ways."[10]

The first attempt on Bolívar's life by liberal *exaltados* took place at a masked ball at the city's theater, located across the street from the Palace of San Carlos. The occasion was the seventh anniversary of Bolívar's decisive victory over Spanish forces at the Battle of Boyacá. Luckily Manuela had learned details of the plot. She appeared at the door of the theater dressed in her cavalry officer's uniform, along with Jonatás. Manuela warned Bolívar of the plot as he was entering the building and then accompanied him back across the street to the presidential residence. The plotters redoubled their efforts and bided their time.

The *exaltados* struck seven weeks later, on September 28, 1828. Twenty of them stormed the lightly guarded presidential residence one minute before midnight. That evening Manuela Sáenz had joined an ailing Bolívar in his quarters and had read to him until he fell asleep. Hearing the commotion outside she confronted the attackers dressed only in a nightgown, delaying them until Bolívar could throw on his clothes and escape through his bedroom window. She was beaten to the floor with the flats of sabers and kicked in the head for good measure. The crisis passed quickly. Troops loyal to the president retrieved him from his hiding place under a nearby bridge and escorted him to their barracks. There he bathed and put on a fresh uniform. When dawn broke there was a brief ceremony in the central plaza during which Bolívar assured the citizenry all was well. Later in the morning he visited Manuela at her apartment, where she was recovering from her injuries. Bolívar embraced her and acknowledged her as "The Liberator of the Liberator."

Fourteen executions followed. Among those condemned was the man who had shot and killed Bolívar's friend and longtime adviser General William Ferguson on the stairway of the presidential palace. Others executed included those who had cut the throats of sentries standing guard outside the building. Bolívar wanted Santander executed but was persuaded to spare his rival and to exile him instead. Manuela Sáenz intervened on behalf of several conspirators, among them Florentino González and Ezequiel Rojas, who later became leaders of Colombia's Liberal Party. Travel restrictions were imposed on liberals and others. Manuela returned to live at the *quinta*, where she took care of a distraught Bolívar. "My heart is broken," he said.[11] The experience of his near assassination and its immediate aftermath worsened his tuberculosis.

Early in 1829 Bolívar traveled south once again, this time to put down an uprising in southern Colombia and turn back a Peruvian invasion of Ecuador. For some the trip had the aspect of a death wish. The Liberator's physical condition was such that he could remain in the saddle only two hours per day—this for a man once renowned for his ability to ride for days on end in any sort of weather. His tasks in the south kept Bolívar away from the capital for more than a year. In his absence his followers explored the idea of making Gran Colombia a constitutional monarchy with either France or Great Britain serving as its protector. This sent liberal fears to new heights. Meanwhile, some of the Liberator's oldest allies deserted him, among them General José María Córdoba. When Córdoba died in an uprising, Bolívar wrote "My grief knows no bounds. I cannot bear more."[12] In his desperation to preserve Gran Colombia, Bolívar moved rightward, offering concessions to the church and to plantation owners. Nevertheless, he held firm to his conviction that slavery must be abolished, a conviction Manuela Sáenz shared. For some years she had been manumitting children born to her slaves.

When Bolívar returned to Bogotá in January 1830, it was clear to all that his time had passed. Pale and emaciated, with less than a year left to live, he saw that his dream of a great nation embracing all of northern South America was dead. His home country, Venezuela, was effectively out of the union. It was time for him to give up power. In early May Simón Bolívar resigned the presidency of Gran Colombia. Before departing Bogotá, he gave his *quinta* to a friend. In a tearful farewell to Manuela Sáenz he explained his plan to leave Colombia and establish a home for them in Jamaica or in Europe. Then he would send for her. With that he and a military escort traveled west from Bogotá and down to Honda, where he boarded a riverboat and descended the Magdalena River, ultimately reaching Cartagena. From there he wrote Manuela, warning her to be more cautious than ever before.

Caution did not come naturally to Manuela Sáenz. Fully expecting Bolívar to return to power, she became his loudest and most ardent defender. When she learned that liberals planned to burn effigies of the Liberator and herself in the central plaza, she donned her cavalry uniform and, along with Jonatás, galloped into the plaza and tried to destroy the effigies. Militia quickly arrested both women and took them away to jail. Manuela and Jonatás were charged with scandalous behavior and subversion, and of dressing like men. Bolivarians defended Manuela in their newspapers. Even liberal women came to her defense. Manuela finally agreed to depart Bogotá before either she or a member of her household suffered physical violence. She rented a house in the village of Guaduas and awaited word from her lover. In November Bolívar wrote asking her to remain in Guaduas a while longer. In hopeful preparation for his arrival, she had dinnerware and home furnishings sent down from Bogotá.

Simón Bolívar never saw or wrote to Manuela Sáenz again. His health declined rapidly and on December 1 he was sent ashore from a Jamaica-bound brig and transported by stretcher to the sugar hacienda San Pedro Alejandrino, just north of Santa Marta. He remained there until his death on December 17, 1830. The next day an aide sent a letter of condolence to Manuela, which reached her in Honda, just as she was preparing to travel to the coast to join Bolívar. A hysterical Manuela Sáenz returned to Guaduas and attempted suicide by allowing herself to be bitten by a venomous fer-de-lance viper.[13] But the snake proved no match for her, and she lived another twenty-six years after the loss of her greatest love.

Manuela Sáenz lived in Colombia for another three years following Bolívar's death, in a small rented farmhouse outside Bogotá. There she gathered Bolivarians around her and continued in her role as a leading spokesperson of their political faction. Unfortunately for them, their fortunes were in decline. From that moment, and during the five decades that followed, there was an upwelling of ideological liberalism in Colombia that abated only in the decade of the 1870s. That was the case elsewhere in Latin America as well, where liberalism grew dominant in part thanks to its defense of free trade and with it, a growing economy. As it rolled through the region, liberalism also embraced virulent anti-clericalism. By the 1850s every country in Latin America had its liberal and conservative parties. Conservatism, however, eventually triumphed in Colombia, in the 1880s, remaining dominant there until the year 1930. By then Conservatives claimed Simón Bolívar as their party's founder, while Liberals looked to Francisco de Paula Santander, once a commander in Bolívar's army.

During 1831–1832 Colombian liberals took control of both houses of congress, going on to invite their leader, Santander, back from exile to help draw up a new national constitution. In September 1831 *exaltados* celebrated the third anniversary of their attempt on Simón Bolívar's life. A month later, in another posthumous slap at the Liberator, they changed the country's name to New Granada. The following year they elected Santander president.

No sooner than Santander was inaugurated, Bolivarian radicals, along with a Spaniard named José María Sardá, conspired to assassinate him. This had consequences for Manuela Sáenz. During mid-1832 police and military hunted down Sardá and the other conspirators. All of them were promptly executed in Bogotá's central plaza, shot while resisting arrest, or handed long prison sentences. Though she insisted she played no part, government officials implicated Manuela in the conspiracy. She was ordered to leave New Granada. Santander feared her political influence and disliked her personally because of her unconventional behavior. Simón Bolívar had also exiled Santander's mistress Nicolasa Ibáñez de Caro. Santander thus felt justified in doing the same to the mistress of Bolívar.

Manuela Sáenz refused to leave the country, arguing that Santander had no legal right to deport her. The new president lost patience. On January 1, 1834, he decreed her immediate expulsion. On that day twenty soldiers appeared at her doorstep and dragged Manuela, fighting all the way, from her house and hustled her away under heavy guard. The US minister to New Granada pronounced her "as brave as Caesar."[14]

Manuela Sáenz was escorted to the town of Honda, and then on to Barranquilla, and then to Cartagena, where she was imprisoned until such time a departing ship could take her to Jamaica. As soon as she arrived in Jamaica, Manuela began planning her return to Quito.

MANUELA IN EXILE

Much had changed in Ecuador over the six years since Manuela Sáenz had last visited her hometown. The southernmost nation of Gran Colombia had broken from the confederation in 1830, declaring itself the Republic of Ecuador. It went on to elect General Juan José Flores its supreme military commander and president. A Venezuelan, Flores had risen through the ranks during the wars of independence, eventually becoming one of the Liberator's most trusted generals. Manuela asked her old friend for help during her Jamaica exile. Flores responded as she knew he would, sending her a letter of safe conduct and agreeing to help her sell a hacienda she owned not far from Quito. Four years passed while Manuela Sáenz dealt with the paperwork granting her the right to return home.

Her arrival in Ecuador could not have come at a worse time. When Manuela disembarked at Guayaquil in October 1834, she learned the country had a new president, Vicente Rocafuerte, a liberal and friend of Francisco de Paula Santander. Santander had told Rocafuerte of Manuela Sáenz's travel plans and had warned him about her. Even worse, Manuela's half brother, General José María Sáenz, had recently died in an attempt to overthrow Rocafuerte. For these reasons, and others, Vicente Rocafuerte resolved to bar Manuela Sáenz from returning home. He had soldiers stop her at the village of Guaranda, a few miles south of Ecuador's capital. There they handed her a letter from the chief executive's Minister of the Interior, ordering her to immediately remove herself from Ecuador. With no evidence to support his charge, Rocafuerte had accused her of spreading sedition on behalf of her late half brother and his revolutionary group, the Society for a Free Quito.

As well as fearing Manuela Sáenz as a political rabble-rouser, Rocafuerte disliked her because of her unconventionality. Despite his virtues as an international diplomat, scholar, and liberal theorist, Vicente Rocafuerte was much the patriarchal male of his day. For him, women had no place in public life. In an exchange of letters with Juan José Flores, Rocafuerte defended his shabby treatment of Simón Bolívar's mistress. He accused her of acting "in a way alien to her sex" and of being in violation of "the rules of [feminine] modesty and morality." He informed Flores that he, Rocafuerte, was well aware of her "character, talents, vices, and prostitution." He compared Manuela Sáenz to notorious women of the past, women of "loose morality" who used their beauty to destabilize politics. Rocafuerte ended one such letter noting: "Women are the ones who do the most to stir up the spirit of anarchy in these countries." Therefore, he concluded, his government was justified in expelling Manuela Sáenz from Ecuador.[15]

For the first time in her life, Manuela Sáenz was forced to admit defeat. She made her way back down through the mountains to Guayaquil, boarded a ship, and left Ecuador for the last time. But she did not travel far. When her southbound schooner put in at Paita, Peru, some three hundred miles down the coast from Guayaquil, she disembarked. Her traveling companions were her maid Juana Rosa and Juana Rosa's children Domingue and Mendoza. Jonatás and Natán were no longer with Manuela, having been effectively manumitted when she was expelled from New Granada.

Paita was an uninviting town of four thousand residents, most of whom earned their living from fishing. Behind the town was a desert. Rain almost never fell there because of what became known as the Humboldt Current, which kept ocean waters so cold that rain rarely formed. Despite its desolation, Paita had its redeeming features. When Manuela arrived there, it was a main provisioning port for US whaling vessels, many of them out of New Bedford, Massachusetts. That gave it a rough-and-tumble cosmopolitan character, with foreign sailors wandering the streets looking for strong drink, tobacco, and female companionship. Sometimes they bought souvenirs to pack away in their seabags. Ecuadorian tourists also visited Paita on their way forty miles inland to the town of Piura, where they bathed in the sarsaparilla-rich water of the Piura River. That medicinal shrub grew abundantly along the riverbanks and was thought to cure syphilis.

From the moment Manuela Sáenz set foot in Paita, she became both the town's leading celebrity as well as a focus of admiration and sympathy. Many in the port village had followed her career and knew of her recent troubles. Her fame and warm personality quickly put Manuela on intimate terms with the town's leading citizens. She became their honored guest at parties, baptisms, weddings, and other social events. Sadly, though, she reached Paita in a state of near poverty. Driven unceremoniously from both Santander's New Granada and Rocafuerte's Ecuador, she had been unable to liquidate her assets in either place. That meant she could rent only a small, two-story, termite-infested house with living quarters upstairs and a storefront downstairs. There she sold tobacco, pastries, and crochet-work. She and Juana Rosa made the latter two items themselves.

Manuela earned small sums through her translations for the US consul in Paita. An early commission, as interesting as it was lucrative, involved the New England whaler *Acushnet*. In late 1841 sailors on the vessel rose up against their abusive ship's master, charging that he "treated them like slaves" and beat them with marlinspikes at the slightest provocation. Charges were filed with local authorities both by the ship's officers and its crew. Manuela translated their testimony into Spanish for Paita's judicial officials. One of the sailors interviewed was twenty-two-year-old Herman Melville, who at the time was planning to write a novel on whale-hunting. Years later, when Melville had become a famous novelist, he wrote of Manuela Sáenz with poetic apostrophe: "Humanity, thou strong thing, I worship thee not in the laurelled victor but in the vanquished one."[16]

Manuela remained politically active during her first years in Paita, always in pursuit of Bolivarian ideals. She did this chiefly by helping two of her friends, Ecuador's Juan José Flores and Bolivian Andrés Santa Cruz. The two men figured among Bolívar's generals who shared his vision of strengthening South America through international union. When he became president of Peru in 1836, Santa Cruz created a Peru-Bolivia Confederation. His colleague Flores then suggested that Ecuador join his country's two sister republics. To achieve that all he needed to do was drive Vicente Rocafuerte from power. Manuela Sáenz was delighted to help with the scheme, which Flores termed "The Great Project." It was not unlike Bolívar's proposal to create an Andean Confederation uniting the five states he had liberated.

In the end, the proposed federation of Peru, Bolivia, and Ecuador came to nothing. By 1845 both Santa Cruz and Flores were living in European exile. It was at that time that Manuela wrote to a friend "I no longer dabble in politics."[17] That was not entirely true. Over the 1840s she befriended a young Ecuadorian exile named Gabriel García Moreno. García Moreno later became conservative president of Ecuador, mocked by liberals for dedicating his country to the Sacred Heart of Jesus. Manuela's helpfulness to García Moreno suggests she was something of a transitional figure in Latin American politics. Once suffused with enlightened liberal ideals, she ended her years befriending a noted figure in the conservative resurgence seen throughout late-nineteenth- to early twentieth-century Spanish America.

The first years of the 1850s found Manuela Sáenz living in repose in Paita. An accident suffered sometime earlier had rendered her an invalid. By one report she either broke or dislocated her hip when the termite-weakened stairway in her home collapsed beneath her. From then until her death, she was confined to her bed, to her hammock, or to a large leather-upholstered wheelchair. All the while she remained Paita's leading celebrity. In 1851 Giuseppe Garibaldi, a founding father of modern Italy, sought out the woman he called "the Andean revolutionary heroine."[18] Garibaldi later wrote of spending several afternoons in delightful conversation with Manuela Sáenz at her modest home. Three years after Garibaldi's visit, Peruvian folklorist Ricardo Palma traveled to Paita to see her. Palma wrote that Manuela Sáenz received him "majestically" in her large leather wheelchair.[19]

The end came quickly and tragically for Manuela Sáenz. Her inability to walk left her both obese and subject to respiratory infections. In early 1856 she contracted bronchitis that she could not shake. Then, in November of that year, disaster struck Paita. An ailing sailor was put ashore and within days the town was engulfed in a raging diphtheria epidemic. Those who could flee did so. Many who could not perished. Among them were Manuela and Juana Rosa. Juana Rosa succumbed to the disease on November 21, 1865. Manuela died two days later, just a month short of her fifty-eighth birthday. Both bodies were buried in a mass grave at the edge of Paita. The exact location is not known.

EPILOGUE

Manuela Sáenz was willfully forgotten by historians of Gran Colombia in years following her death. Not so Simón Bolívar. By the 1850s the Liberator was fully rehabilitated by his people. Bogotá's central plaza was formally designated the Plaza de Bolívar. That was the case, too, in Caracas and Quito. Residents of Bogotá later named a plaza in honor of Francisco de Paula Santander, though it was smaller and located two blocks north of city center. During the 1860s Colombia returned to the name given it by the Liberator. No longer was it called New Granada.

The counterpart of Simón Bolívar's rehabilitation was expunging all mention of Manuela Sáenz and her relationship with him. By mutual agreement among Colombian historians, all of them males, Manuela's "scandalous history" had no place alongside that of Bolívar. As well as not mentioning their relationship, historians took permanent action of a sort, purging libraries and archives of documents relating to the couple. This explains the fate of volume 56 of Daniel O'Leary's magisterial study of Bolívar, titled *Memorias*. Volume 56, titled *Correspondence and Documents relating to Señora Manuela Sáenz,*

Which Demonstrate the Esteem in Which Various People of Note Held Her and the Part She Played in Political Affairs, was stolen from Colombia's national archive and presumably destroyed.

Latter-day scholars have restored Manuela Sáenz to her rightful place in history. During the 1970s Marxists praised Manuela for her sensitivity to issues of class struggle. In the 1980s, feminists held Manuela up as a case study of woman's struggle against patriarchy and misogyny. American feminists traveled to Paita in 1989 and there held a congress celebrating Manuela's life and work. Ecuadorians also celebrate Manuela Sáenz. On May 24, 2007, at the 185th anniversary of the Battle of Pichincha, her fellow citizens awarded her the rank of General Officer in the Army of Ecuador. Of all her posthumous awards, that is the one she would have liked best.

NOTES

1. Victor W. Von Hagen, *The Four Seasons of Manuela. A Biography* (New York: Duell, Sloan and Pearce, 1952), 126.

2. Manuela Sáenz was not the only *quiteña* swept off her feet by the Liberator. Bolívar's chief aide, General Daniel O'Leary, who also attended the ball, noted that "Bolívar's captivating charm endeared him to all the inhabitants of Quito." Robert F. McNerny Jr., ed., *Bolívar and the War of Independence*, abridged version of General Daniel Floriano O'Leary, *Narración* (Austin: University of Texas Press, 1970), 70.

3. Von Hagen, *The Four Seasons*, 64–65.

4. Von Hagen, *The Four Seasons*, 163.

5. Pamela S. Murray, *For Glory and Bolívar: The Remarkable Life of Manuela Sáenz* (Austin: University of Texas Press, 2008), 44.

6. Murray, *For Glory and Bolívar*, 51.

7. Murray, *For Glory and Bolívar*, 51; Von Hagen, *The Four Seasons*, 173.

8. Von Hagen, *The Four Seasons*, 193.

9. David Bushnell, *Simón Bolívar: Liberation and Disappointment* (New York: Pearson, 2004), 187.

10. Von Hagen, *The Four Seasons*, 205.

11. Von Hagen, *The Four Seasons*, 227.

12. Von Hagen, *The Four Seasons*, 250.

13. Richard W. Slatta and Jane De Grummond, *Simón Bolívar's Quest for Glory* (College Station: Texas A&M University Press, 2003), 293.

14. Murray, *For Glory and Bolívar*, 95.

15. Murray, *For Glory and Bolívar*, 100–102.

16. Von Hagen, *The Four Seasons*, 287.

17. Murray, *For Glory and Bolívar*, 132.

18. Von Hagen, *The Four Seasons*, 296.

19. Murray, *For Glory and Bolívar*, 132.

REFERENCES

Bushnell, David. *Simón Bolívar. Liberation and Disappointment*. New York: Pearson, 2004.

Hennes, H. "Gender, Sexual Desire and Manuela Sáenz in the Writings of Jean-Baptiste Boussingault and Ricardo Palma." *Bulletin of Hispanic Studies* 87 (2010): 347–64.

McNerny, Robert F. Jr., ed. *Bolívar and the War of Independence*, abridged version of General Daniel Floriano O'Leary, *Narración*. Austin: University of Texas Press, 1970.

Murray, Pamela S. *For Glory and Bolívar: The Remarkable Life of Manuela Sáenz*. Austin: University of Texas Press, 2008.

Rumazo González, Alfonso. *Manuela Sáenz, la libertadora del Libertador*. Buenos Aires: Almendros y Nieto, 1945 [first edition 1944].

Slatta, Richard W., and Jane De Grummond. *Simón Bolívar's Quest for Glory*. College Station: Texas A&M University Press, 2003.

Vilalta, María José. "Historia de las mujeres y memoria histórica: Manuela Saénz interpela a Simón Bolívar (1822–1830)." *European Review of Latin American and Caribbean Studies/Revista Europea de Estudios Latinoamericanos y del Caribe* 93 (October 2012): 61–78.

Von Hagen, Victor W., with Christine von Hagen. *The Four Seasons of Manuela. A Biography. The Love Story of Manuela Sáenz and Simón Bolívar*. New York: Duell, Sloan and Pearce, 1952.

Glossary

aguardiente	sugarcane-based alcoholic beverage
alcabala	sales tax
alumbrismo	heresy promoting personal prayer and absolution
arepas	toasted patties of ground white corn
arriero	muleteer
audiencia	highest court in colonial Spanish America
auto-de-fe	public penance imposed by the Holy Office, or Inquisition
ayllu	Inca kinship group
beata	pious woman
bozales	newly arrived enslaved Africans
cabildo	municipal or town council in colonial Spanish America
cacique	indigenous chieftain
camino real	primitive highway system of Spanish America
campesino/a	country person; farmer; agricultural worker
chapetón	"spurred one"; pejorative term for Spaniards in Spanish America
ch'arki	jerky
cilicio	spiked belt used in penitential religious practice
cimarrón	runaway slave (Spanish America)
cordillera	mountain range
corregidor	district administrator in colonial Peru, and in some other parts of Spanish America
Cortes	Portuguese assembly with parliamentary function
costumbrista	one who writes on local or regional customs of Spanish America
criado/a	servant
criollo/s	Spanish American of European descent; English version: "creole"

cruzado	Portuguese coin
despedida	farewell celebration
disciplina	chain or whip used in penitential religious practice
doctorcito	little doctor
don/doña	*Spanish term* of respect added to first names
donadas	nuns who worked as servants in convents
encomendero	holder of an *encomienda*
encomienda	grant of indigenous labor awarded by the crown to early settlers in Spanish America
engenhos	plantations in Brazil usually producing sugar cane or manioc (cassava)
escala	stairs
espiritual	spiritual
fazenda	farm (Brazil)
finca	farm (Spanish America)
gente decente	persons of good birth
hidalgo	aristocrat of Spain or Spanish America
hijo, hija	son, daughter
inspector	high-ranking military official
junta	assembly or council
kuraka	used in the Viceroyalty of Peru to designate a local chief of either indigenous or mixed-blood descent
kurakazgo	the region administered by a *kuraka*
La Compañía	church and buildings on the central plaza of Cusco, first owned by Jesuits
ladrón	thief
les majesté	act of treason against the crown
liceo	high school
limeño/a	male or female of Lima, Peru
llama	Peruvian beast of burden related to the camel
llanos	flat, grassy plains found in various parts of Latin America
machismo	accentuation of masculine characteristics
machista	one who practices machismo to excess
maestra/o	teacher
marianismo	femininity; cult of Maria, cult of the virgin, counterpart to machismo
marqués; marquesa	marquis; marquise or marchioness
mazombo	white person born in Brazil

Glossary

mercedes	mercies
mestizo/a	offspring of European and indigenous parents; literally: a "mixed-blood"
mineiro/a	person from the Brazilian state of Minas Gerais
mita	Spanish forced-labor system imposed on indigenous peoples
monja	nun
obraje	colonial-period workshops, frequently using conscripted indigenous labor
pachamanca	roasted meat and potato dish of highland Peru
palenque	community of runway slaves in Spanish America (mocambo or quilombo in Portuguese America)
pardo/a	"brown-skinned"; in pre-emancipation Brazil, term used to designate a mixed-blood slave
párvulo	unlettered child
patiloca	footloose
Patria Boba	period of division in Colombia 1810–1816; literally, "Foolish Fatherland"
patrón	patron, boss, chief (Spanish America)
Patronato Real	power granted by the Catholic Church to the Spanish crown to wield power over clerical appointments in its overseas colonies
paulista	person from the city or state of São Paulo
peninsular	colonial synonym for a Spaniard living in America
peso	unit of currency used widely in Spanish America
preto/a	"black"; in pre-emancipation Brazil, designation of a slave of unmixed African descent
proceso apostólico	church process leading to beatification and canonization
proceso ordinario	church process leading to beatification and canonization
quiquiriquí	cock-a-doodle-doo
quiteño/a	a person born in Quito, Ecuador
reparto	forced sale of goods to indigenous peoples, especially practiced in highland Peru
ruana	a square woolen overcoat with a split in the middle, worn in Andean Colombia
sabana	Andean plain where Bogotá and smaller Colombian towns are located
santa rositas	small roses and birds named after Saint Rose of Lima

saya y manto	shirt and veil used by *limeñas* in colonial times
tertulia	gathering, a salon
toca	wimple; a cloth headdress, generally worn by nuns
tributo	head tax imposed on indigenous peoples
visitador	literally, "visitor"; an official sent by the Spanish crown to overseas colonies to deal authoritatively with emergency matters

Index

Academy of San Bartolomé, 202, 209
Aconcagua Valley, 72
Adelantado of Hispaniola, Columbus, B., as, 20, 22, 25–26
Admiral of the Ocean Sea, Columbus, C., as, 17–22
Africa, 8; African slaves in Brazil, 147–48; African slaves in Quito, 215
aguardiente (alcoholic beverages), 177–78, 182
Aguilar, Jerónimo, Mayan language and, 46
Aguirre, Francisco de, 69, 72
Aguirre, Ordoño de, 111
Aizpuru, Joaquina, 215–16
alcabala (sales tax), 177
Alcántara, Order of, 32, 35, 36
alcoholic beverages *(aguardiente)*, 177–78, 182
Alderete, Jerónimo de, 77–78
Almagro, Diego de, 64, 66–67
Almeida, Pedro de, 163
Almeyda, Ambrosio, 204, 206
Almeyda, Vicente, 204, 206
altepetl (local political entity), 43, 57
Altolaguirre, Lope de, 110
alumbrista (heresy), 96
Alvarado, Pedro de (Captain), 53
Álvares Cabral, Pedro, 147

Amazons, 1–2
America: Catholicism installed in early Spanish, 62; First Americans, 13; Lima in early colonial Spanish America, 83–84; Portuguese, 3, 7; Spanish, 3, 7, 8, 193
Anacaona of Xaraguá (Queen), 8; challenges for, 22–31; high-ranking status of, 26; likeness on Cuban stamp, *24*; marriage of, 15–16; Ovando invasion of Xaraguá and death of, 35–37; rule of Taíno chiefdoms, 14–15
anarchy, in Hispaniola, 27–28
Andes Mountain range, 116–17, 172, 195, 196, 202, 219–20
Andrade, Gomes Freire de, 157
Annals of Potosí, 105
Annunciation, 138
Antilles islands, 14
apostolic process *(proceso apostólico)*, 100
Araucanians, 81n1. *See also* Reche-Mapuche people
Araucanian Wars: Erauso, C., in, 112; Valdivia as casualty of, 79–80
Arawak people, 13–14
Arcos, José María, 203
Areche, José Antonio de, 185, 186, 190

Arellano, Carlos de, 109
Arellano, Miguel, 207
areyto (song-poem), 24–25, 28, 36
Aristotle, 135
Arraial do Tejuco, 148–49, 152
Arriaga, Antonio de, 184; *corregidor* and, 176–79
Asbaje, Juana Inés de. *See* Cruz, Juana Inés de la
Asbaje, Juana Inés de, *loa* of, 127
Atacama Desert, 61, 69–70
Atlantic crossing, Suárez in, 62–63
Audiencia of Lima, 176–77
Augustine, Saint (Augustinian), 85, 94, 197, 201
Ayacucho, Battle of, 223
Ayala, Bartolomé de, 94
ayllu (kinship group), 174
Aztecs, 6, 41–42; Alvarado attack of, 53; conquest of, 57–58; Cortés as ruler of, 55; empire, 8–9; gold gifts of, 49; religion, 44–45; sacrifices of, 44–45; Tenochtitlán destroyed, 1

bandeirantes (explorers, fortune-seekers, slave-hunters), 147–48
baptism, 46, 152, 154; of Carib and Taíno people, 34; of da Costa, 151
Barreto, Tomás Robi de Barros, 157
Basque, region of, 7, 106
Basques, 105, 113, 119
batey, 14, 24, 28, 35, 36
Batista, Lourença, 160
Batista, Teodósio, 160
Battalion of El Tambo, 202, 206–7
Bayer, Julián, 204
beatas (piety), 86–91, 93–94, 95–96, 98, 99
beatification, of Rose of Lima, 99–100
Bemberg, María Luisa, 144
Bilbao, Luis de, 96
Bilbao, Spain, 108–9
birds *(santa rositas),* 89–90
black *(preta),* 152
Black Death, 86

Bobadilla, Francisco: Bobadilla replacement of Columbus, C., 28, 31; transported back to Spain, 32
Bogotá, Colombia, 10, 194, 195, 200–201; insurgency in, 204–5; Salavarrieta, P., and Salavarrieta, B., arrival in, 202–3; Spaniards relationship to creoles of, 196–97, 198
Bohechío (Chief), 15, 23–24, 25, 27, 28
Bolívar, Simón, 213–14, 233; affair with Sáenz, M., 220–21; death, 229; Gran Colombia and, 225; invasion of centralist towns, 200–201; relationship with Sáenz, M., 10; Sáenz, M., as advisor to, 222; trip to Guayaquil, 221–22; with tuberculosis, 227–28
Bonaparte, Napoleon, 193, 194, 196, 199, 213, 216–17
Book of Prayer and Mediation (de Granada), 97
Borbón, Antonio Amar y, 197, 198, 199
Bourbon, House of, 171–72, 183
Bourbon Reforms, 171–72
Boussingault, Jean-Baptiste, 227
Boyacá, Battle of, 227
Brazil: African slaves in, 147–48; diamond contracts under state control, 166; *engenhos* of, 5; patriarchal society of, 165; as world's greatest sugar producer, 147–48
Buenos Aires, Argentina, 193
Buriti farmhouse, 164

Caballero, José María, 201, 205
cabildo (town council), 56, 64–65, 198; of Quito, 215; of Santiago de Chile, 71, 75
Cabrera, Miguel, *137, 161*
cachaça (white rum), 151
caciques, 43, 45, 46, 76; Cacique Huenchullán, 113; capturing of, 72–73; Castilians *vs.* warriors and, 52; Cortés summoning of, 51; the

"fat cacique," 48; Quispiguancha, Francisco, 115; of Totonac tribe, 48
Cádiz, Spain, 31, 63
Callao port, 78, 94–95
Calleja, S. J. Diego de, 143
camino real (royal highway), 175
Campo Grande, Battle of, 3
canay, 14, 25, 36
Candelaria, María, 2, 3
Cañizares, Manuela, 217
Cano, Gerónimo, 176
canonization, 94, 99–100
Caonabó (Chief), 15, 16, 18, 20, 21–22
Caracas, Venezuela, 213–14
Cárdenas, Beatriz de, 110
Carib people, 14, 15, 18, 21; baptism of, 34; improved relations of Taíno people and, 27; raids of, 19
Carlos V (Charles V), 41, 47, 67, 68, 84; *cédula real* of, 63; Cortés gifts for, 49; struggle against Montezuma, 48–49; treason against, 51
Carmelite Order, 130
Carreto, Leonor, 127, 132
Cartagena, Colombia, 200, 205, 228
Carvajal, Agustín de, 119, 120–21
Carvajal, Gaspar de, 1–2
Casas, Bartolomé de las, 8, 25, 26, 32, 33; cassava plantation of, 37; *The Destruction of the Indies*, 38
cassava, 14, 17, 22, 23–25, 33, 37
The Castalian Flood (Cruz), 141
Casta painting, *161*
Castelo, Andrés, 184
Castilians, 20, 105; allyship with Totonac, 49; caciques and warriors *vs.*, 52; Catholicism and, 46; Cempoala departure of, 50; departure from Tenochtitlán, 54; hostage over Montezuma, 52–53; Tabascans fighting, 45; Tendile negotiating with, 47
Castillo, Juan del, 94, 96
Catalans, 105

Catherine of Siena (saint), 100–101; and Dominican order, 92–93; Rose of Lima influenced by, 9, 85–88
Catholicism, 3–4, 123, 126, 151, 174; Castilians and, 46; Catholic Counter-Reformation in Lima, 83–84, 85; in Guaduas, 195; installed in early Spanish America, 62; in life of Suárez, 80; Rose of Lima and, 90–91
cédula (decree), 34–35, 63
Cempoala, Mexico, 48, 50
centralism, political: Bolívar invasion of centralist towns, 200–201; federalism *vs.*, 193–94; Santafé de Bogotá support of, 200
Cerda, Gaspar de la, 141
Cerralta, Francisco de, 108
Cerro Blanco Hill, 79
Cervantes, Miguel de, 126, 129
Chapel of the Rosary, 98
Charles III, 171, 177
Charles IV, 216
chiefs *(kurakas)*, 172, 173, 175–79, 182, 188
Chile, 61, 62; Suárez and Valdivia conquest of, 9, 68; Valdivia trade of Peru and, 77–78
Cholula, Cholulan, 50
Christ, Order of, 167
Church of San Agustín, 210
Church of San Francisco, 80–81
Cibao, 26, 36
Cingapacinga, 51
civil war, in Potosí, 117–18
clemency, of Sámano, 205–6
Coatzacoalcos province, 43
Codex Azcatitlan, 41
Colegio de San Francisco de Borja, 173
Colombia (New Granada): conservatism in, 229; Eastern Llanos, 203–4; federalism in, 193–94, 199–200; guerrilla warfare in, 194, 201, 206, 207; *Patria boba* period, 194,

199–200, 210; Viceroyalty of New Granada, 10
colonization, 7, 17–18, 27, 61; indigenous labor within, 35–38; Lima in early colonial Spanish America, 83–84; Ovando colonization of New World, 32–37
Columbus, Bartolomè, 31; as Adelanto of Hispaniola, 20, 22, 25–26; Roldán, F., rebellion against, 26–27; Taíno people greeted by, 23–25; unsuccessful gold fields of Columbus brothers, 27
Columbus, Christopher, 8, 13–14, 15, 147; as Admiral of the Ocean Sea, 17–22; allyship with Roldán, F., 28, 29; charged by king and queen of Spain, 28; enslavement of Taíno people, 20, 28; execution of Guevara and Mújica, 30–31; fourth expedition to New World, 32–33; impact on Vega Real, 21–22; in New World, 17–21, 31; replacement by Bobadilla, 28, 31; return to Hispaniola, 27; search for gold of Taíno people, 17–19; travel to Hispaniola, 16–17; unsuccessful gold fields of Columbus brothers, 27
Concepción, Chile, 112–13, 115
La Concepción convent, 216–17
Concepcíon de la Vega, 26
concubinage, 6, 153–55, 157, 159–60
Condemayta, Tomasa Tito, 182–83, 188
Condorcanqui, José Gabriel (Tupac Amaru II), 172; captured by Valle, 186; death, 189–90; in Jesuit school, 173; as *kuraka*, 175–79; marriage to Puyucahua, Michaela, 10; rebellion and recruitment of soldiers, 179–84; in trail of Puyucahua, M. B., 187–90; victory in Battle of Sangarará, 181
confession, 90–91, 186–90
Congress of Ocaña, 226
Coñori (queen), 1
conservatism, in Colombia, 229

Constitution of Cúcuta, 225
convent, 91–93; La Concepción, 216–17; Cruz, J., at, 130–32, 136, 139, 142; of San Sebastián, 110
Convent of the Discalced (Barefoot) Carmelites, 130
Copiapó River valley, 67
Córdoba, José Maria de, 226–27, 228
corregidores (local district administrator), 174–75, 176–79, 180, 182
Cortés, Hernán, 8–9, 41, 42, 43, *58*; caciques summoned by, 51; defeat of, 54; gifts for Carlos V, 49; Honduras expedition and, 56; Marina as interpreter of, 49–50, 52; Marina loyalty to, 51; move to Cempoala, 48; as ruler of Aztecs, 55; in Tenochtilán, 52–53; victory of, 46–47
"cosmic race," 6. *See also mestizo*
Costa, Domingos da, 149, 153, 164
Costa, Maria da: baptism of, 151; birth of daughter, 152–53
Cotubanamá, 37
country house *(quinta),* 225, 226–27, 228
Couto, Manuel Vieira, 154
creoles, 6, 193, 225; creole families as patriots, 204; creoles in New Granada, 197–98; Flores, G., status as, 85; Spaniards relationship to creoles of Bogotá, 196–97, 198; Supreme Junta of, 198–99; women in Lima, 88–89
creole women *(criollas),* 5
criada (domestic servant and nurse), 67
criollas (creole women), 5
Cristobál, Diego, 184, 185, 186
Cruz, Juana Inés de la, *137*; Aristotle and, 135; at convent, 130–32, 136, 139, 142; in court of Marqués of Mancera, 129; death, 125, 144; dowry of, 131; poetry of, 126,

128–29, 131, 132–34, 136, 138–40, 142–44; study of music, 136
Cuauhtémoc, 54–55
Cuba, 16; Anacaona likeness on Cuban stamp, *24*; Columbus, C., exploration of, 18–19
Cundinmarca, Colombia, 194, 197, 206
Cusco, Peru, 172–73, 177, 186, 188; Erauso, C., departure from Potosí to, 118–19; Suárez in, 64–65

Declaration of Man and Citizen (1789), 213
decree *(cédula)*, 34–35, 63
De la Gasca, Pedro, 84
Delgado, Pérez, 206
D'Elhuyar, Fausto, 217
Demarquet, Charles, 225
Descartes, René, 126, 135–36, 190
The Destruction of the Indies (de la Casas), 38
Diamantina, 148–49, *150,* 152; diamond contracts in, 155–63; Francisca *parda* in, 153–55, 168; Silva, C., and Oliveira as part of Diamantina society, 163–68
diamonds, 152, 155–63, 166
Díaz del Castillo, Bernal, 43, 46, 57
diphtheria epidemic, 233
disloyalty to the crown *(lesa majestad),* 187
distribution *(reparto),* 176
domestic servant and nurse *(criada),* 67
Dominic, Saint (Dominican), 85, 86, 94; Catherine of Siena and, 92–93; Erauso, C., raised in Dominican convent, 107, 110; Rose of Lima seeking help from, 91
Don Quixote (Cervantes), 126
dowry, 131, 218
dugouts, of Taíno people, 16–17, 26

Ecuador, 230, 234
education, of children of Silva, C., and Oliveira, 165–66

elite, families of Lima, 92
Encarnación, Doña, 117
encomiendas; encomenderos (indigenous labor), 35–38, 57, 62, 66, 68; Flores, G., awarded, 84; of Santiago de Chile, 75–77
engenhos (sugar estates), of Brazil, 5
Enlightenment, 223–24
Erauso, Catalina de (Nun Ensign), 7, 9, 106, 113, *122*; in Araucanian Wars, 112; armed combat of, 110–11; attacks on Mapuche people, 114; in battle at Concepción, 112–14; capture of, 115; departure from Potosí to Cusco, 118–19; disguise of, 107–9; in Dominican convent, 107, 110; escape to Tucumán, 116; as Guzmán, 108; imprisoned at Huamanga convent, 120; jailing of, 119; in Mexico, 121–23; petition for pension, 121; religious rites of, 118–21; return to New World, 121–23; return to Spain, 121; transfer to Trujillo, 111; transporting of food to Potosí, 118; travel to Paita, 109–10; travel to Vitoria, 107–8
Erauso, Miguel de, 109–10, 113, 115
La escala mística (Rose of Lima), 93
Escobar (member of Valdivia's expedition), 68
escravas de tabueiro (food tray slaves), 151, 153
escudos de monja (nun's medallions), 136, *137, 138,* 144
Esquivel, Juan de, 33–34, 35
Estella de Navarra, Spain, 109
exaltados (extremist liberals), 226, 227
explorers, fortune seekers, slave-hunters *(bandeirantes),* 147–48
Extremadura, Spain, 32, 61, 84, 105

famine, on La Isabela, 21
"the fat cacique," 48
federalism, 193–94
Felipe IV, 126–27

Ferdinand II of Aragon, 17–18, 21, 28
Ferdinand VII, 193, 194, 196, 198, 199
Ferguson, William, 227
Fernández de Santa Cruz, Manuel, 141
1500s, expeditions of Spaniards in, 42
Flores, Gaspar: *encomiendas* awarded to, 84; status as creole, 85; travel to Panama, 84
Flores, Isabel. *See* Rose of Lima
Flores, Juan José, 230, 232
Florida, Narváez expedition to settle, 3
food tray slaves *(escravas de tabueiro)*, 151, 153
Fort Sano Tomás, 19
France, occupation of Madrid, 216
Francis, Saint (Franciscan), 85, 92, 94
Francisca *(parda)*, 153–55, 159, 168
Francisca *(preta)*, 154, 157
Francisca de Paula, birth of, 160
Franklin, Benjamin, 193
French Revolution, 213
Fundo Creek, 149, 151

Gaete, Doña Marina Ortiz, 43, 66, 79, 80; death, 56; as interpreter of Cortés, 49–50, 52; *la lengua* nickname of, 49–53; loyalty to Cortés, 51; La Malinche as, 46–56; marriage to Jaramillo, J., 56. *See also* La Malinche
Galve, Luis, 141
Galvez, José de, 177
Gamboa, Pedro de, 71
Ganabara, 25–26
García de Ramó, Alonso, 113, 114
García Moreno, Gabriel, 232
Garibaldi, Giuseppe, 233
garrote, 189–90
Garvajal, Gaspar de, 1–2
gatherings *(tertúlias)*, of Sáenz, M., 227
General and Natural History of the Indies (Gómara), 2
"*gente decente*" (people of good birth), 85
gods *(teules)*, 45, 47, 50, 52, 53

gold, 32, 149, 153; gifts of Aztec, 49; gold rush in Vega Real, 33; Marga-Marga gold mines, 71–72; in Rio de Janiero, 147–48; of Spain, 125; of Taíno people, 17–19; unsuccessful gold fields of Columbus brothers, 27
Golden Flower. *See* Anacaona of Xaraguá (Queen)
Gómara, Francisco Lopez, 2
Gómez, Pero, 68
Góngora, Luis de, 126, 129, 133, 135
González, Florentino, 227–28
González, Rodrigo, 75–76
Granada, Luis de, 97
Gran Colombia, 221, 222–23; Bolívar and, 225; as Republic of Ecuador, 230; Sáenz travel to, 224
Greater Antilles, 14
Grijó, João Fernandes de Oliveira, 167
Guacanagarí of Marien (Chief), 16–17, 18
Guacar (Juracán), 16
Guadalquivir River, 110
Guaduas, Colombia, 210, 228–29; Catholicism in, 195; connection to Spain, 196; earthquake in, 194–95; Salavarrieta, P., departure from, 202
Guarionex (Chief), 15, 32
Guarocuya, 31
Guatiguaná (Chief), 19–20
Guayaquil, Ecuador, 221–22, 224, 230
Guerrero, Lobo, 120–21
Guevara, Hernando de: arrival of, 29–30; Columbus, C., execution of, 30–31; conflict with Roldán over Higuamota, 29–30
Gulf of Paria, 63
Gúzman, Juan, 69

Habsburg, House of, 171
Haiti, 14, 37–38, 193
Haley's Comet, 139
Hamilton, John, 209
head tax *(tributo)*, 175
heresy *(alumbrista)*, 96

Hernández de Puertocarrero, Alonso, 46, 49
Herrera, María de Oliva, 84, 85, 91–92, 95, 96
Higuamota, 15–16, 19, 27; birth of daughter Guarocuya, 31; Roldán conflict with Guevara over, 29–30
Higüey province, 14, 15, 22, 26
hija naturale (illegitimate), 215
Hispaniola, 8, 14, 15; *batey* played on islands of, *24*; Columbus, C., return to, 27; Columbus, C., travel to, 16–17; decline into anarchy, 27–28; Ovando "just war" against indigenous people of, 33–34; resistance and rebellion on, 19–22; settlement and subjugation of, 17–19
Holy Communion, 127
Holy Crusade, 94
Holy Office. *See* Inquisition
Honda, Colombia, 195, 201
Honduras expedition, 56–57
Hoz, Pedro Sancho de la, 67; binding agreement with Pizarro, F., and Valdivia, 68–70; revolt led by, 78
Huamanga, Peru, 120
Huancavélica, Peru, 171
Huanchillán (Cacique), 113
Humboldt Current, 231

Iberian Peninsula, 8, 20, 108
Ice Age, 13
Idiáquez, Juan de, 108
Iglesias, Anselmo, 208
illegitimate *(hija naturale)*, 215
Immaculate Conception, 138
imperialism, 17–18, 31
Inca Empire, 1, 6, 85, 172, 177
Inconfidência Mineira (1788–1789), 168
Independence Period, 6
Indigenous labor. *See encomenderos; encomiendas*
indigenous people, 6, 8; colonization of, 17–18; *encomienda*, 35–38; First Americans, 13; indigenous fighters of Tupac Amaru rebellion, 184; Ovando "just war" against, of Hispaniola, 33–34; of Peru, 190; of Quito, 215; revolt in Andean Peru, 10; of Santo Domingo, 32
Inquisition, 95, 135, 142; of Isabella of Castile, 126; of Rose of Lima, 96–101; of Sardinha, 157
insurgency, in Bogotá, 204–5
Inundación castálida (Cruz), 141
"In Which a Suspicion Is Satisfied with the Rhetoric of Tears" (Cruz, J.), 134
La Isabela, 18; famine on, 21; Guatiguaná attack on hospital of, 19–20
Isabella of Castile, 17–18, 21–22, 34, 37; charging of Columbus, C., 28; Inquisition of, 126
Islam, 3
"The Island of Vera Cruz," 147

Jacmel port, 36
Jagüey Inés (Inés's Pool), 70
Jaramillo, Beatriz, 57
Jaramillo, Juan, 56
Jaramillo, María, 56
Jesuits, 83, 130, 139, 141, 152, 156; Condorcanqui, J., in Jesuit school, 173; expulsion of Jesuits from Spain, 177; Rose of Lima and, 91, 94, 96
Jonatás (enslaved companion of Sáenz, M.), 218, 219, 224, 226, 227, 228, 231
Junín, Battle of, 223
"just war doctrine," 20; Ovando and "just war" against indigenous people of Hispaniola, 33–34

Kino, Eusebio, 139
kinship group *(ayllu)*, 174
kurakas (chiefs), 172, 173, 175–79, 182, 188
kurakazgo (kinship-based group), 173, 174–75, 178

Lafayette, Marquis de, 223
Lake Titicaca, 172, 175, 180–81, 185
Langui village, 186
"law of free birth," 219
la lengua (nickname of Gaete, M.), 49–53
lesa majestad (disloyalty to the crown), 187
Liberal Party (Colombia), 227–28, 229
"the Liberator." *See* Bolívar, Simón
"Liberator of the Liberator." *See* Sáenz, Manuela
Lienzo de Tlacala, 58, *58*
Lima, Peru, 5, 72, 222; Audiencia of Lima, 176–77; Catholic Counter-Reformation in, 83–84, 85; creole women in, 88–89; in early colonial Spanish America, 83–84; elite families of, 92; founding of Pizarro, F., 83; *limeños*, 9, 83; patriots of, 219; silver in, 84–85; Suárez arrival in, 64
limeños (people of Lima), 9, 83, 87, 90, 92, 94–95
Lisbon, Portugal, 156, 167
llanos region, 203, 204, 206, 208
loa (short play), of Asbaje, J., 127
Loayza, Francisco, 183, 187
Loayza, Pedro de, 92, 97, 99
local district administrator *(corregidores)*, 174–75, 176–79, 180, 182
local political entity *(altepetl)*, 43, 57
long skirt *(saya y manto)*, 89
López, José Hilario, 209
López de Arguijo, Juan, 118
López de Sosa, Antonio, 173
Lorenzana, Juan de, 96, 98
Loyola, Francisco, 108

Macaúbas (religious retreat), 166, 167
machismo, 3–4
machista, 8
Madrid, Spain, 190, 216
maestra (teacher), 87

Magálon, 123
Maguá chiefdom, 15, 18–19, 21
Maguana chiefdom, 15, 26
Malinalli, 41, 43–46. *See also La Malinche*
La Malinche, 8–9, *58*; death, 56; Honduras expedition and, 56–57; as Malinalli, 41, 43–46; as Marina, 46–56; slavery and, 42, 43
Malintzen. *See* La Malinche
Mancera, Marqués of, 126–27; Cruz, J., in court of, 129; departure from Mexico, 132
Manco Inca Yupanqui, 64
Manila, Philippines, 84–85
manumission, 148, 163, 167
Mapocho Valley, 70
Mapuche people, 112, 114
marianismo. *See* Virgin Mary
Marien province, 16–17
marriage: of Anacaona, 15–16; Rose of Lima and, 91–92
Martín, 57
Martínez, Diego, 96
Mártires y heroínas (Loayza, F.), 187
Matos, Miguel de Carvalho Almeida e, 154
Mayan language, 43, 46, 47
Maza, Gonzalo de la, 94, 96, 97
Mediterranean, social theory of, 4
melancholy, of Rose of Lima, 91–95
Melo, Sebastião de Carvalho, 156
Melville, Herman, 232
Men of August Uprising, 217
mercantilism, 125–26
Las mercedes (Rose of Lima), 93
mercury, 84, 171
mestizo, 3, 6, 9, 42, 80, 116–17, 172–73, 177, 215
Mexico, 8, 128; Carmelite Order in, 130; Erauso, C., return to, 121–23; Marqués of Mancera departure to, 132; as New Spain, 3; Valley of, 44
Mexico City, Mexico, 144, 193

Michimalonco, attack on Valdivia, 72–73
Milho Verde, 149–51, 154
militia, 199–200, 228
El Mina Castle, 149
Minas Gerais ("General Mines"), 147–48, 149, 151–52
mineiros, 149, 163
mining boom, 148; mining laws of Portugal, 149; in New World, 105
Miranda, Juan de, 144
mita (forced labor), 175, 179, 181, 182
mixed-blood *(parda),* 152–55
Mogrovejo, Toribio de, 88, 92
Monastery of Saint Clare, 92
la monja alferez. See Erauso, Catalina de (Nun Ensign)
Monroy, Alonso de, 72, 73
Montalvo, Francisco, 205
Monteiro, Isabel Pires, 158
Monte Verde, Chile, 13
Montezuma, 41–42; Carlos V struggle against, 48–49; Castilians hostage over, 52–53; death of, 53–54; defeat of Castilians in Cholula, 50; reign of, 44–49; tax collectors of, 48–49
Morillo, Pablo, 201, 202, 203, 208
mortifications, of Rose of Lima, 87–88, 90, 97–98, 100
Mújica, Adrián, 29, 30–31
Murillo, Gregorio, 188–89
music, Cruz, J., study of, 136
mysticism, 85–86, 88–89, 96–97

Nahua people; Nahuatl language, 43, 44, 45, 47, 57
Nariño, Antonio, 197, 205, 213
Narváez, Pánfilo de, 3
Natán (enslaved companion of Sáenz, M.), 218, 219, 224, 226, 227, 228, 231
La Navidad, 17, 18, 19
New Bedford, Massachusetts, 231
New Granada, 194, 209; creoles in, 197–98; Morillo invasion of, 201; Quito as Viceroyalty of, 215; Viceroyalty of, 10. *See also* Colombia
New Spain, 61, 131, 136; status of women in, 140. *See also* Mexico
Newton, Isaac, 190
New World: Columbus, C., in, 17–21, 31, 32–33; early traditions and Transatlantic encounter, 13–17; Erauso, C., return to, 121–23; mining boom in, 105; Ovando colonization of, 32–37
Nezahuapilli, 43
Nieva, Count of, 5
Noche Triste ("Sad Night"), 54
Nogueira, Luis de Barros, 153
Noguera, Rosa, 173
El Nuevo Cid, bandit, 119
Numancia Regiment, 219
Nun Ensign. *See* Erauso, Catalina de
Núñez, Antonio, 130, 131, 138, 143
Núñez, Fernán, 65
nun's medallions *(escudos de monja),* 136, *137, 138,* 144

obraje (textile factory), 87
obrajes (workshops), 174, 180
Ojeda, Alonso de, 18–19, 20; captivity of Chief Bohechío, 27; invasion of Xaraguá, 28–29
O'Leary, Daniel, 222–23, 233
Oliveira, Fernandes de, 155
Oliveira, João Fernandes de, Jr., 155–56, 157–58; death, 167; in Diamantina society, 163–68; education of children, 165–66; as Knight of the Order of Christ, 156; partnership with Silva, C., 159–63; purchase of Silva, C., 159–60
Olmedo, Bartolomé de, 46, 47–48
Order of Santiago, 56
Orellana, Francisco de, 1–2
Orinoco River, 14
Oropesa, Spain, 177
Our Lady of Carmão, 165

Our Lady of Monserrate, 80
Our Lady of the Conception, 166
Our Lady of the Holy Sacrament, 152
Our Lady of the Pleasures, 150–51
Our Lady of the Rosary, 92
Ovando, Nicolás de, 8, 31; *cédula* for, 34–35; colonization of New World, 32–37; "just war" against indigenous people of Hispaniola, 33–34; Ovando invasion of Xaraguá and death of, 35–37; in Santo Domingo, 33

Pachecho, Francisco, 121
Padilla, Diego, 197, 201
Páez, José Antonio, 223
Páez Revolt (Venzuela), 224
Paita, Peru, 10, 109–10, 231–32
Palace of San Carlos, 225
Palha farmhouse, 163–68
Palma, Ricardo, 89
Palos port, 17
Panama, 84
Paraguay, War of the Triple Alliance in, 3
parda (mixed-blood), 152–55
Paredes, Conde de, 138–39, 141, 143
Patria Boba ("Foolish Fatherland"), 194, 200, 210
patriarchy, 165
patriots: creole families as, 204; of Lima, 210; Sáenz, M., support of, 218–19; Salavarrieta, P., support for, 201–2; in the Spanish battalions, 207
peninsulares, 196–97, 198, 216
Peninsular War, of Bonaparte, N., 196
people of good birth *("gente decente"),* 85
people of Lima *(limeños),* 9, 83, 87, 90, 92, 94–95
Pernambuco, Brazil, 147
Peru, 8; Erauso, C., in, 9; indigenous people of, 190; revolt of indigenous peoples in Andean, 10; Valdivia trade of Chile and, 77–78; Viceroyalty of, 61, 75–76

Peru-Bolivia Confederation, 232
Philip IV, 121
Philippines, 100, 102n1
pícaros (rogues), 109
Pichincha, Battle of, 219–20, 234
Picunche tribe, 70–71
piety *(beatas),* 86–91, 93–94, 95–96, 98, 99
Pinta ship, 42
Piribebuy, Battle of (1868), 3
pirogue, 16
Pizarro, Francisco, 1, 9, 32, 64, 66, 79, 84; binding agreement with Valdivia and de la Hoz, 68–70; founding of Lima, 83
Pizarro, Gonzalo, 84
Pizarro, Hernando, 64, 84
Plaza de Armas, 95, 177, 184, 189
poetry, 126, 128–29, 131, 132–34, 136, 138–40, 142–44
La Pola. *See* Salavarrieta, Policarpa
Pombal, Marquis de, 166–67
Porres, Martín de, 94
Porto de Castro, Mathias, 152
Porto Seguro, 147
Portugal, 147; mining laws of, 149; Portuguese America, 3, 7
Potosí, Bolivia: civil war in, 117–18; Erauso, C., transporting of food to, 118; silver at, 83, 84–85, 105, 111–12, 171; trade route from Tucumán to, 117
Potosí mountain, 175, 177
preta (black), 152
prickly pear, 61, 70
proceso apostólico (apostolic process), 100
proceso ordinario (religious process), 98–99
Protestantism, 126
Pucacasa, battle at, 185–86
Pumacahua, Mateo, 184
Purén, valley of, 114–15
Puyucahua, Manuel Bastidas, 173

Puyucahua, Michaela Bastidas, 9, *180*; confession of, 186–90; death, 189–90; early years, 172–74; resistance activity, 10, 179–90; trial of, 186

Quechua language, 179
Quesada, Luis de, 57
Quetzalcoatl, 44, 47
Quevedo, Francisco de, 129
Quiñones, Baltazar de, 119
quinta (country house), 225, 226–27, 228
Quinta de Bolívar, 225–26
Quiroga, Rodrigo de, 69, 72, 79, 80
Quispiguancha, Francisco, 115
Quitéria, 152
Quito, Ecuador, 10, 222; *cabildo* of, 215; demographics of, 215; revolt in, 197; as Viceroyalty of, 215
Quives, Peru, 87–88

"racial democracy," concept of, 168
Ramírez, Antonio, 117, 119
Ramirez de Guzmán, Antonio. *See* Erauso, Catalina de (Nun Ensign)
Ramón, García, 113, 114
Ramos, Alejo Sabaraín, 199–200, 205–6, 208–9
Reche-Mapuche people, 67, 76–77, 80
Reconquista, 32
religion: Aztec, 44–45; Macaúbus retreat, 166; in Minas Gerais, 152
religious brotherhoods, Silva, C., and, 165
religious orders: Augustinian, 85, 94; Dominican, 85, 86, 91, 92–93, 94, 107, 110; Franciscan, 85, 92, 94
religious process *(proceso ordinario),* 98–99
religious rites, of Erauso, C., 118–21
repartimiento, 28, 75, 77
reparto (distribution), 176
Republic of Ecuador, Gran Colombia as, 230
residencia (judicial inquiry), 28

La Respuesta (Cruz), 141–44
revolt, 78, 197
Ribera, Alonso de, 112–13
Ribera, Payo de, 131, 136
Ricaurte, Andrea, 203, 204, 206
"Riddes Offered to the House of Pleasure" (Cruz), 143
Rio de Janeiro, Brazil, 147–48
Rio de la Plata, 177
River Maule, 112
Rocafuerte, Vicente, 230–31
Rocroi, Battle of, 125
Rodrigues de Fontoura, Alexandre, 153
Rodríguez, Gonzalo, 114–15
Rodríguez, José Ignacio, 201–2, 203
Rodríguez de Montalvo, Garci, 1
rogues *(pícaros),* 109
Rojas, Ezequiel, 227–28
Roldán, Francisco, 22, 32; allyship with Columbus, C., 28, 29; conflict over Higuamota, 29–30; rebellion against Columbus, B., 26–27
Roman Empire, 62
Romano, Angelino Medoro, 94
Rome, Italy, 123
Rosa, Juana, 232, 233
Rose of Holy Mary, 88
Rose of Lima (saint), 4, *101*; canonization of, 83–84, 99–100; Catherine of Siena influence on, 9, 85–88; Catholicism and, 90–91; confession of, 90–91; death of, 98–99; Inquisition of, 96–101; Jesuits and, 91, 94, 96; *La escala mística,* 93; marriage and, 91–92; melancholy of, 91–95; mortifications of, 87–88, 90, 97–98
Rousseau, Jean-Jacques, 193
Royal Commentaries of the Incas (de la Vega), 178–79
royal highway *(camino real),* 175
royal inspectors *(visitadores),* 171–72, 178, 185
Royal Road (Estrada Real), 151, 156

252   Index

Sá, Antônio de, 152–53
Sabana of Bogotá, 202
Sacred Congregation of Holy Rites, 100
sacrifices, of Aztec, 44–45
Sáenz, Manuela, 214, *214*; as advisor to Bolívar, 222; affair with Bolívar, 220–21; arrest of, 223–24; banishment from *quinta* by Córdoba, 226–27; dowry of Thorne and, 218; expulsion and transition from La Concepción, 217–18; gatherings of, 227; as *hija naturale,* 215; Jonatás and Natán enslaved by, 218, 219, 224, 226, 227, 228, 231; as "Liberator of the Liberator," 227–28; permanent exile, 229–33; relationship with Bolívar, 10; support for patriots, 218–19; translation work, 232; travel to Gran Colombia, 224
Sáenz, Simón, 215, 217
Salavarrieta, Bibiano, 194–95, 202–3, 208
Salavarrieta, Joaquín, 195–96, 199–200
Salavarrieta, Policarpa, 10, 194, 195, 210, *211*; arrest of, 208; arrival in Bogotá, 202–3; departure from Guaduas, 202; execution of, 209; as seamstress and spy, 203–9; support for patriots fighting Spaniards, 201–2
sales tax *(alcabala),* 177
Sámano, Juan, 202, 205–6, 207, 209–10
Sangarará, Battle of (1780), 181
San Patricio Seminary, 156
San Pedro Alejandrino (hacienda), 229
San Salvador, 13–14, 16
San Sebastián, Spain, 107, 108, 110
Santa Cruz, Andrés, 232
Santafé de Bogotá, 193, 195, 200, 201, 202, 203
Santa María (ship), 17
Santander, Francisco Paula de, 223, 225, 227, 229, 230, 233
santa rositas (birds), 89–90
Santiago, Battle of, 70–73

Santiago de Chile, 193; Battle of, 70–73; *cabildo* of, 71, 75; *encomiendas* of, 75–77; founding of, 9; rebuilding, 75–78
Santo Domingo, 22–23; construction of, 26; indigenous people of, 32; Ovando in, 33
Sardá, José María, 229–30
Sardinha, Manuel Pires: concubinage of, 153–54, 157; Inquisition of, 157
Sardinha, Simão Pires, 154, 157–58, 161, 165–66, 167–68
saya y manto (long skirt), 89
Serra do Espinhaço (Spiny Mountains), 149, *150*
Serro Frio district, 153, 157
servants *(yanaconas),* 65, 68, 70, 72, 76
Sevilla, Spain, 20, 62, 110
short play, of Asbaje, J. *(loa),* 127
Sigüenza y Góngora, Don Carlos, 134–35, 138, 139, 142
Silva, Chica da, 9, *161*; baptized as da Costa, 151; in Diamantina society, 163–68; education of children, 165–66; fortunes of, 155–63; freedom for, 162–63; partnership with Oliveira, J., 159–63; purchase of, 159–60; religious brotherhoods and, 165; as slave-owner, 163, 164; in "slave trail," 148–53
Silva, Juan de, 115
silver: at Potosí mountain, 83, 84–85, 105, 111–12, 171, 175, 177; of Spain, 125; in Tucumán linked to Spain, 116–18
Sinner's Guide (de Granada), 97
Sisa, Josepha Puyucahua, 173
Sistine Chapel, 100
slavery, 5, 6, 8, 33–34; African slaves in Brazil, 147–48; Columbus, C., enslavement of Taíno people, 20, 28; Isabella of Castile and Ferdinand of Aragon and, 17–18; "law of free birth," 219; La Malinche and, 42;

in Minas Gerais, 151–52; Silva, C., and, 9, 162–63, 168
"slave trail," *150*; renamed as Royal Road, 151; Silva, C., in, 148–53
Society for a Free Quito, 230
Solarte, Diego de, 111–12
song-poem *(areyto),* 24–25, 28, 36
Sor Juana. *See* Cruz, Juana Inés de la
Spain, 10; Alderete voyage to, 77–78; Bobadilla transported back to, 32; Columbus, C., charged by king and queen of, 28; connection to Guaduas, 196; economic decline in, 171; *encomiendas* of, 35–38; Erauso, C., return to, 121; expulsion of Jesuits from, 177; gold and silver of, 125; silver in Tucumán linked to, 116–18; Spanish America, 3, 7, 8, 193
Spaniards, 1–2; conflict with Taíno people, 22, 26; expeditions in 1500s of, 42; patriots in the Spanish battalions, 207; relationship to creoles of Bogotá, 196–97, 198; Salavarrieta, P., support for patriots fighting, 201–2; Xaraguá visited by, 22–25
Straits of Magellan, 66–70
Suárez, Inés de, 61, 67, 69, 71–77, *74,* 81–82; arrival in Lima, 64; in Atlantic crossing, 62–63; Catholicism in life of, 80; conquest of Chile, 9, 68; in Cusco, 64–65; Jagüey Inés, 70; marriage to Quiroga, 79; relationship of Valdivia and, 78–79; Valdivia with, 65–66; in Venezuela, 63–64
Sucre, Antonio José, 220
sugar: Brazil as world's greatest sugar producer, 147–48; production in Pernambuco, 147
sugar estates, of Brazil *(engenhos),* 5
Sun, Order of the, 223
Supreme Junta, 198–200
syphilis, 19–20, 27

Tabascans, 43–44, 45
Taborda, Manuel Ribeiro, 155, 157
Taíno people, 13, 21; Anacaona rule of Taíno chiefdoms, 14–15; baptism of, 34; Columbus, C., and search for gold of, 17–19; dugouts of, 16–17, 26; enslavement of Taíno people, 20, 28; greeting Columbus, B., 23–25; improved relations with Carib people, 27; revolt of, 19–20; Spaniards conflict with, 22, 26
Tambo Ridge, Battle of, 205–6
tapadas, 5
tax collectors, 48–49, 176
teacher *(maestra),* 87
Tendile, 47
Tenochtilán, 44, 47, 49, 51–52; Castilians departure from, 54; Cortés in, 52–53; destroyed, 1; fall of, 53–55
the Tenth Muse. *See* Cruz, Juana Inés de la
tertúlias (gatherings), of Sáenz, M., 227
teules (gods), 45, 47, 50, 52, 53
Texcocans, 43
textile factory *(obraje),* 87
theater, at Palha farmhouse, 164
Thorne, James, 217–18; dowry of Sáenz and, 218
Tinta, Peru, 179, 184–85
tlatoani (emperor), 43
tobacco, 14
toca (wimple), 88
Toledo, Fadrique de, 121
Toledo, Francisco de, 84
town council. *See cabildo*
Tradiciones peruanas (*Peruvian Traditions,* Palma), 89
Transatlantic, early traditions of New World and Transatlantic encounter, 13–17
treason, 51, 187
Treaty of Madrid (1750), 157
tributo (head tax), 175
Trujillo, Peru, 111

tuberculosis, 227–28
Tucumán, Argentina: silver linked to Spain in, 116–18; trade route from Tucumán to Potosí, 117
Tungasuca, Peru, 173–74, 179–80, 181–82, 184
Tupac Amaru II. *See* Condorcanqui, José Gabriel
Tupac Amaru Revolt (1780–1782), 172, 184–90
Tupinambá people, 147

Universal Declaration of Human Rights, 38
University of Coimbra, 151, 156, 167
University of Mexico, 129, 134–35
University of San Marcos, 96
University of the Cloister of Sor Juana, 144
upper class, 4–5, 62, 90, 156, 162, 204, 215
Urban VII, 99–100
Urban VIII, 121
Urquiza, Juan de, 110
Usátegui, María de, 94, 95, 97, 98

Valdivia, Pedro de, 61, 62; Atacama Desert crossed by, 69–70; attack on Michimalanco, 72–73; binding agreement with Pizarro, F., and de la Hoz, 68–70; as casualty of Araucanian Wars, 79–80; conquest of Chile, 9, 68; encounter with Reche-Mapuche people, 76–77; expedition toward Straits of Magellan, 66–70; relationship of Suárez and, 78–79; with Suárez, 65–66; trade of goods from Chile and Peru, 77–78
Valladolid, Spain, 108
Valle, Commander del, 185–86, 188
Valparaiso Bay, 78
Vanegas, Gertrudis, 207
Vargem farm, 155–56, 158–59, 160, 166
Vatican, 99–100
Vaz de Caminha, Pero, 147

Vega, Inca Garcilaso de la, 178, 190
Vega, Lope de, 126
Vega Real, 15, 19; Battle of, 20; Columbus, C., impact on, 21–22; gold rush, 33
Velásquez, Alonso, 96
Velázquez de la Cadena, Pedro, 131
Venegas, Vicente Montes, 91
Venezuela, 63–64, 228
Veracruz, Mexico, 121–23
Vera Paz, 37
Vespucci, Amerigo, 28–29
Vida de Santa Rosa de Lima (de Loayza, P.), 97
Vila do Príncipe, 148, 150, 153, 157, 158
Villagra, Francisco de, 68, 78
Villalobos, Juan de, 96
Villanova, Francisca, 199
Virgin Mary, 4
visitadores (royal inspectors), 171–72, 178, 185
Vitoria, Spain, 107–8
Voltaire, 193

War of the Triple Alliance (1864–1870), 3
Wars for Independence, 181
white rum *(cachaça)*, 151
wimple *(toca)*, 88
women, Latin American: status of, in New Spain, 140; in stratified society, 62
workshops *(obrajes)*, 174, 180

Xaraguá province: Ojeda invasion of, 28–29; Ovando invasion of Xaraguá and death of Anacaona, 35–37; Roldán settling in, 26–27; Spaniards visiting, 22–25
Xavier, Joaquim José da Silva, 168
Xicalangos, 43
Xilotepec, 57

yanaconas (servants), 65, 68, 70, 72, 76

Yanaoca, Peru, 179
Yaque River (River of Gold), 18

Zacatecas, 171
Zocotlán, 51